MORE PRAISE FOR

TRADITIONAL NEW ORLEANS JAZZ

"In an era when critics are pondering the denouement of jazz, there is a tendency to relegate New Orleans's role to first act status and to leave it at that. Thomas Jacobsen's book contradicts that assumption in exploring how New Orleans jazz has thrived in the last half century, continuing to attract and produce exceptional jazz talent. In this compilation of interviews, each with a distinct character, 'new generation' stars such as Irvin Mayfield, Evan Christopher, and Tim Laughlin, British expatriates Trevor Richards, Clive Wilson, and Brian Ogilvie, and such major unsung heroes as Lionel Ferbos, Eddie Bayard, and Jack Maheu talk about their lives in New Orleans music. Any jazz lover who picks up this book will not be able to put it down."

—BRUCE BOYD RAEBURN
curator of the Hogan Jazz Archives

"Jacobsen's knowledge of New Orleans jazz is deep and wide ranging. *Traditional New Orleans Jazz* is skillfully written, researched with a scholarly thoroughness, and is clear, readable, and useful. I am confident this significant book will be welcomed by musicians worldwide."

—JAMES GILLESPIE
editor of *The Clarinet*

"Thomas Jacobsen is not only incredibly knowledgeable about jazz, he is clearly at ease with the community of artists he writes about—authentic to the core. Much has been written about the originators of jazz in New Orleans. Jacobsen's contribution is to show the vitality of many of today's key traditional jazz artists. He has given us an accurate, heartfelt, and downright entertaining picture of many of today's leading traditional jazz artists in New Orleans. Jacobsen, a fine jazz scholar, could have given us yet another book on early New Orleans pioneers. Happily, he chose to profile working artists, each with their own links to the city's rich jazz past."

—CHARLES SUHOR
author of *Jazz in New Orleans: The Postwar Years through 1970*

TRADITIONAL
NEW ORLEANS JAZZ

Guitarist Danny Barker in a jam session on a cruise boat on the Hudson River as part of the "Jazz on the River" series, New York City, 1946. The bassist is New Orleans native George "Pops" Foster. *Photograph from the estate of the late Charles Peterson, courtesy of Don Peterson.*

THOMAS W. JACOBSEN

TRADITIONAL NEW ORLEANS JAZZ

CONVERSATIONS WITH THE MEN WHO MAKE THE MUSIC

LOUISIANA STATE UNIVERSITY PRESS

BATON ROUGE

Published by Louisiana State University Press
Copyright © 2011 by Thomas W. Jacobsen
All rights reserved
Manufactured in the United States of America
LSU Press Paperback Original
First printing

DESIGNER: Michelle A. Neustrom
TYPEFACE: Whitman
PRINTER: McNaughton & Gunn, Inc.
BINDER: Dekker Bookbinding

Except where otherwise noted, all photographs were taken by Thomas W. Jacobsen.

Grateful acknowledgment is made to the owners of *The Mississippi Rag*, in which most of these interviews first appeared, albeit in somewhat different form.

LIBRARY OF CONGRESS CATALOGING-IN-PUBLICATION DATA

Jacobsen, Thomas W., 1935–
Traditional New Orleans jazz : conversations with the men who make the music /
Thomas W. Jacobsen.
    p. cm.
Includes index.
ISBN 978-0-8071-3779-6 (pbk. : alk. paper) 1. Jazz musicians—Louisiana—New Orleans—Interviews. 2. Jazz—Louisiana—New Orleans—History and criticism. I. Title.
ML395.J33 2011
781.65′3—dc22
                                                          2010029105

To Mr. Lionel Ferbos, the oldest active jazz musician in New Orleans
and a truly class act, as he approaches his personal centennial

CONTENTS

CONTENTS

ILLUSTRATIONS

PREFACE

No matter what you play, if you live in New Orleans, you have to
play some jazz. You have to know some traditional jazz.

—DON VAPPIE

I T IS WIDELY ACCEPTED THAT JAZZ MUSIC FIRST APPEARED
and took root in New Orleans and its immediate vicinity around
the turn of the twentieth century, though its precise form and the
exact date remain unsettled. Those issues become somewhat clearer by
the end of World War I with the recordings of the Original Dixieland Jass
Band from New Orleans. These are generally considered to be the earliest extant jazz records. Thereafter, in the early 1920s, jazz had clearly
become established, as is apparent from the recordings of pioneer artists
such as King Oliver, Freddie Keppard, Louis Armstrong, and Jelly Roll
Morton. That era was dubbed the "Jazz Age" by contemporary author
F. Scott Fitzgerald.

The early forms of this music are now generally referred to as "traditional jazz." "Classic jazz" is another term that normally includes early
jazz styles. "Dixieland" sometimes implies the same general meaning but
more often seems to have a slightly different stylistic connotation. In any
case, the term "traditional jazz" (or occasionally the shortened British
"trad") will be used for the most part in this book. It is the music that
has made New Orleans famous and given the city its reputation as "the
birthplace of jazz."

Traditional jazz is normally performed in small groups, the largest
of which are either sextets or septets made up of a standard "front line"
of trumpet/cornet, clarinet, and trombone with a rhythm section composed of piano, bass (brass or string), and drums. Many bands also added
a banjo or guitar. Traditional jazz does not include the larger swing bands

of the later 1930s and '40s, but we must always be careful not to overstress the use of labels to describe jazz styles. As one of the great traditionalists—banjoist, guitarist, and bandleader Eddie Condon—simply put it, "We called it music."

The history of traditional New Orleans jazz has been continuous since its origins, but it has had some ups and downs in terms of popularity. The early apex was reached in the 1920s and early '30s, its popularity being eventually superseded by that of the big dance bands of the Swing Era. But there was a resurgence of trad (and Dixieland) in the 1940s and 1950s (sometimes termed the "Trad Revival"), which seems to have lasted in New Orleans (perhaps more than elsewhere in the States) into the 1960s. Notable forces in this local phenomenon were the formation of the New Orleans Jazz Club in 1948 and the foundation of Preservation Hall in 1961 and its short-lived clone, Dixieland Hall, the following year. Indeed, the NOJC and Preservation Hall have helped to keep traditional jazz alive in the Crescent City to the present day.

Though many of the clubs on Bourbon Street featuring trad jazz or Dixieland began to disappear after the 1960s and 1970s, there exist today a number of venues where that music can still be heard on a regular basis: the Palm Court Jazz Café, Fritzel's European Jazz Pub, the Maison Bourbon, and, of course, Preservation Hall, all located in the French Quarter.

Traditional jazz is, fundamentally, dance music, and there are a number of additional places in town today where it can be heard and danced to, such as the annual (now fall and spring) Nickel-A-Dance series, the spring French Quarter Festival, the Economy Hall tent at the annual New Orleans Jazz and Heritage Festival, and the temporary Visitors' Center of the New Orleans Jazz National Historical Park, as well as several smaller festivals and other occasional venues.

New Orleans jazz had begun to spread to other parts of our country and, indeed, the world by about 1920. A major artery for the dissemination of the music and the musicians within the United States was, of course, the Mississippi River. The excursion boats that plied the river from New Orleans to St. Paul had a long history, and most included bands of one kind or another. One of the riverboat lines, the Streckfus Line, featured a polished orchestra led by one Fate Marable. It was Marable who persuaded Louis Armstrong, along with other jazz pioneers such as Johnny St. Cyr, Baby Dodds, and Pops Foster, to join his band on the riverboats in the late teens. Armstrong learned a great deal while playing with the Marable musical organization before he eventually decided to leave and move on to Chicago in 1922.

The riverboats continue to have a place in traditional New Orleans jazz. The steamboat *Natchez*, for example, features daily jazz cruises (morning, afternoon, and evening) in the city's harbor area. It has been the home of the popular Dukes of Dixieland for many years. In fact, many of our interviewees—cornetist Eddie Bayard in particular—have a history of leading or playing in jazz bands on the Mississippi riverboats.

Nearly every part of Europe, from Scandinavia to the Mediterranean littoral, has a long and distinguished history of jazz performances, first by American bands, then by often very good host-country groups and individuals. (The large number of present-day European jazz bands with "New Orleans" in their names is but one indicator of the city's significant impact on the music.) And annual jazz festivals, often featuring New Orleans music and musicians, have become abundant throughout Europe. Much the same may be said for the Far East, where Japan in particular has been a solid bastion of traditional jazz for decades. In many of these countries, jazz music may well be more popular than even in its homeland.

This book aims to give a picture of the traditional jazz scene in New Orleans *today*, a century or so after the inception of this music, as gleaned from interviews with some of its leading local practitioners. The interviews were conducted by the author over the last fifteen years. Most were first published elsewhere, though one of them appears here for the first time. All have been updated with brief introductions.

The interviewees may be divided, broadly, into three groups: native New Orleanians (Chapters 1–6), "transplants" from elsewhere in the United States (Chapters 7–11), and transplants from abroad (Chapters 12–14). It is important to recognize that, given its important place in the history of jazz, the Crescent City has acted as something of a magnet, drawing talented musicians from many other geographical regions to the city. It is also worth noting that it is not uncommon for local musicians who started out here and moved elsewhere to have been drawn back eventually to their hometown. A classic example of this phenomenon is legendary guitarist/banjoist/vocalist Danny Barker, whose profound influence on younger local musicians is considered in Chapter 6. In short, the city has long had a special gravitational pull for talented musicians. And that pull remains strong to the present day.

As one reads through the narratives that follow, one will encounter a wide variety of personalities, personal backgrounds, and musical tastes among the interviewees. But there are many common denominators as well. All are exceptionally talented musicians, and all are totally dedicated and committed to their music. Most come from homes where music was a significant part of daily life and several from families with long and distinguished musical histories.

The reader will have an opportunity to gain insight into the lives of these musicians and what it takes to become a true professional; some of the issues of the local music business (including race); and a variety of views of what it is like for a musician to live and work in New Orleans today.

New Orleans was voted the number-one city in North America for live music in a 2009 poll of members of the Society of American Travel Writers. This surely is a reflection, at least in part, of the great variety of music that one can hear in the city, jazz obviously being just one aspect of that musical spectrum. A number of the musicians interviewed here—like so many others in the city—are able to perform in various musical idioms. As California-raised clarinetist Evan Christopher has observed, "The thing I like about New Orleans and the music here—no matter what the style is—is it's flavored so much by the culture that surrounds it. There is no other city like it in the United States."

A native New Orleanian, trumpeter Wynton Marsalis, perhaps best known as a "modernist," is outspoken in stressing the fundamental importance of traditional jazz for contemporary jazz musicians. Yet some present-day observers have considered trad a static phenomenon with an essentially unchanged repertoire. That may be true in some individual cases and in some places both in the States and abroad. You will see, however, that most musicians interviewed here do not consider that a valid criticism. They tend to be a restless and creative lot. Indeed, many of the best New Orleans musicians today are also composers, and they have introduced new compositions as well as new ways of playing old tunes into their repertoire. Traditional jazz is, in short, alive and well in New Orleans today, and despite the post-Katrina economic downturn, we must believe that it will continue to be so in the future. It represents the very heart of the city's music scene.

Finally, just a word or two about the devastation created in the wake of Hurricane Katrina in late August 2005. The flooding that resulted from the levee breaks had an enormous effect on the musicians and music business in the city. Every musician, including those interviewed here, was affected by the catastrophe in one way or another. Since all of these interviews were conducted prior to that time, I have made an effort to bring each one up to date and, when possible, indicate the implications of the disaster for each of these musicians. It is not a happy story.

ACKNOWLEDGMENTS

I would like to express my most sincere gratitude to all the talented musicians who gave so freely of their time and knowledge in the interviews that make up this book. Their patience in responding to my insistent questioning was heroic. Obviously, that which follows would not have been possible without them.

Thanks are also due to Jody Hughes, sister of the late Leslie Johnson of Minneapolis, who, for thirty-five years, published and edited *The Mississippi Rag,* long and widely recognized as "the Voice of Traditional Jazz and Ragtime." All but one of the following interviews were first published in "The Rag," and Ms. Hughes has kindly given me permission to reprint them here, with varying degrees of modification.

To my longtime friend and colleague Donald Marquis, author of the seminal study of jazz pioneer Buddy Bolden, I give my most sincere thanks for his generosity in allowing me to reprint the interviews that we conducted jointly with "Danny's Boys." It was, in fact, his idea that led us to undertake that project in the first place.

Another friend, Dr. Charles Suhor, musician and author of *Jazz in New Orleans: The Postwar Years through 1970,* has given me much sound advice and encouragement. I am deeply indebted to him.

Also giving freely of advice and encouragement over our years of friendship, which go back to his days as editor of *Jazz Times*, is Dr. W. Royal Stokes. Author of numerous books and articles on all periods of jazz, he is one of the nation's leaders in American jazz journalism.

I also wish to thank Donald Peterson, son of famed jazz photographer Charles Peterson, for sharing his father's photographs of Danny Barker with me. One of them appears at the front of this volume.

Finally, to my wife Sharyn, who has patiently read through all of these interviews prior to their publication, I offer thanks for her keen eye and thoughtful suggestions about how each could be improved. Obviously, such mistakes and infelicities as still remain are my responsibility alone.

New Orleans
June 2010

TRADITIONAL
NEW ORLEANS JAZZ

1

LIONEL FERBOS
New Orleans Gentleman of Jazz

Trumpeter Lionel Ferbos is an extraordinary human being. In so many ways.

Most notably, at the age of 99, he still plays in bands with which he has been performing for more than thirty years. He continues to appear at the New Orleans Jazz and Heritage Festival every year as well as playing his weekly Saturday night gig at the Palm Court Jazz Café, along with making a variety of other special appearances.

Widely respected as the "oldest active jazz musician" in the city, he has received countless awards in his hometown over the years, not to mention the New Orleans City Council's proclaiming his birthday, July 17, as "Lionel Ferbos Day" in 2004.

When talking about bands he has played with in the past, he notes repeatedly that he's the only member of those groups who is still alive. "I'm a survivor," he asserts modestly.

Indeed. He is a survivor in more ways than one, having been evacuated from his home to reside with family in rural Louisiana for many months after Hurricane Katrina (August 2005) before returning to the city with his wife and moving into an assisted-living facility. Soon thereafter his only son, Lionel Jr., who had been ill for some time, passed away on December 30, 2006. Three years later (January 6, 2009), his dear wife of seventy-five years, Marguerite, died. Those were devastating losses for him. Yet he has managed to survive even these events, and he continues to perform and enjoy the admiration and respect of all who know him and listen to his music. I am honored to have known him and pleased to be able to dedicate this book to him.

The following interview was conducted on February 25, 2002, and appeared, essentially in the same form, in The Mississippi Rag *in July 2002.*

IT WAS A SULTRY SATURDAY EVENING IN MID-MARCH AT the Palm Court Jazz Café in the French Quarter, and the club was jam-packed with an appreciative audience. There wasn't an empty seat in the house, not even a stool at the bar, so clarinetist Brian O'Connell and banjoist Les Muscutt sat chatting between sets on the steps leading up to the building's second floor. A reporter approached, interrupting their conversation and train of thought, to ask what it was like working with 90-year-old trumpeter Lionel Ferbos who fronts the house band every Saturday night. Taken aback a bit, both paused for a moment before speaking.

Then O'Connell said, "It's a rare opportunity to play with a musician whose playing is not derived from jazz records. [Clarinetist] Willie Humphrey was the same way. He had no record collection at all. I feel, when I'm hearing Lionel play, that his trumpet playing must be what one would have heard a hundred years ago. And don't overlook his singing. It's wonderful. It's light, it floats, and it swings."

Muscutt nodded in agreement, adding, "Although he plays pretty close to the melody as written, he has his own way of phrasing that makes every tune uniquely his own. It's Lionel."

O'Connell smiled as he said, "What a wild, far-out concept—to play the melody! I've never met a sideman, clarinetist or whatever, who doesn't love playing with Lionel Ferbos."

Agreeing, Muscutt again added, "Yeah, [pianist] Steve Pistorius will cancel any gig—no matter what it pays or where it is—to play with Lionel Ferbos. And many other musicians feel the same way. When you talk to Lionel, one word comes to mind: professional, 100 percent professional."

They went on, talking about Ferbos's modesty and humility, agreeing that he has no ego problems whatsoever.

This snippet of a dialogue between fellow musicians captures remarkably well the spirit Lionel Ferbos brings to New Orleans music today and the respected position he holds in the New Orleans musical fraternity. He is one of the true gentlemen in the city's music business. He celebrates his 91st birthday this month and recalled some of the highlights of his life for the *Rag* in a recent interview.

Born near Broad and Orleans in the city's Seventh Ward on July 17,

Lionel Ferbos at the Jazz and Heritage Festival, April 2005. Bassist Chuck Badie is in the background.

1911, Lionel Ferbos has lived in the Seventh Ward all his life. As a child, he suffered from asthma. It got so bad, he said, "I couldn't play with the children anymore. So, my dad would buy me all kinds of books, and I learned so much by reading. I only went to one year of high school."

Music has never been a full-time occupation with him, except, he said, when there was no other work. His father, Louis, was a sheet-metal worker who had learned the trade from his father. "My dad was a real good sheet-metal man," Ferbos said. "He had a shop on Governor Nichols, between Royal and Chartres, but he learned from his daddy. When I started learning, I learned from books. It was altogether different."

Ferbos eventually took over his father's business, and he has kept the family tradition alive by passing it on to his son, Lionel Jr.

Young Lionel's parents were Creoles of Color, and, as such, both spoke French. "My mother spoke real French because her family spoke all French, but my dad spoke Creole," he remembered. "And so they would have words sometimes. My mother would say to my dad, 'But you're saying it wrong.' He'd say, 'No, I'm right.' To each his own, but they never taught us children. I don't know why they didn't."

The lad's asthma delayed his start in music. He wanted to play trumpet, but his mother said, "You can't breathe now. How you going to play trumpet?" She encouraged him to try banjo, but pioneer banjoist Charlie Bocage was too busy playing with A. J. Piron's popular band to take Ferbos on as a student. Eventually, Mrs. Ferbos seems to have relented, and Lionel bought a used cornet at a pawn shop.

Where to begin? "There were all these good blues players," he said, "but my mother didn't like blues records in the house. She wouldn't have 'em. So all I heard was a nice type of music all the time."

Under the circumstances, it's no surprise that he started his musical training in 1926—at the age of 15—with "Professor" Paul E. Chaligny, who was a widely respected music teacher in the city. "I don't know whether you've heard of him," Ferbos said, "but all the musicians—Harold Dejan and many others—took lessons from Chaligny."

After Chaligny, Ferbos was taught by Albert Snaer, another Chaligny student who later traveled with big bands and recorded with Sidney Bechet. Ferbos said, "Snaer lived just around the corner from me. He taught me, but then he would leave town. He used to work on the boats."

Later Ferbos met Gene Ware, who was playing with Sidney Desvigne's orchestra. "So," said Ferbos, "he started to teach me. I owe him a whole lot for the simple reason I didn't have any money. It was during or before the Depression, and he taught me. I used to play like this [Ferbos puffs out his cheeks like Dizzy Gillespie], but not as bad as Dizzy, and he eliminated that."

The method Ware used was to tie a necktie around Ferbos's face from top to bottom, like icing a toothache. "I took lessons from him for a good while," said Ferbos. "He was a very nice trumpet player and a very good teacher."

By the time he had begun to work with Ware, Ferbos was playing around town and listening to music. When Ware left town, he approached Manuel Perez for instruction, but it didn't work out. Ferbos recalled, "I went to Mr. Perez and he said, 'Lionel, I understand what you say, but what could I show you? 'Cause you've been playing a long time.' I think he did that because he was ill, just to get out of it. I knew he could have taught me because he was a very good trumpet player."

Ferbos began playing professionally in the late 1920s as a teenager. "When I first started," he said, "we had a little band they called the Starlight Serenaders, and we'd play for house parties, mostly for free. After that, Sidney Cates and Harold Dejan's brother [Leo] had the Moonlight Serenaders. Then the brothers left, and they asked me to play with them. We used to play stock numbers. Then we'd divide the band and play at parties, maybe four or five pieces. I found that reading the number is nice, but it becomes dull.

"So, I would always break it up. I might not add too many notes, but I broke up the division and gave it a different sound. And that's the way I do now. Sometimes I can add a lot of notes, but I'm not much of an improviser, you know. Sometimes I can add notes and sometimes I don't, but I'll never play it just like it's already written. The next time I play it, I'll add some notes or delete some notes and so forth, and it comes out good. They think I'm a jazz player, but I'm not a real jazz player."

In 1932 Ferbos joined Captain John Handy's Louisiana Shakers when their first trumpet player left the band. "Ricard [Alexis] came to me to play," he recalled. "I said, 'I can't play with that band. You play all jazz. I can't play that.' He says, 'Talk to Handy.'

"So, when I talked to Handy, he said, 'Look now, all you do is read them parts.'

"And that's the way it was. I didn't have any problem with him, but he would get very angry sometimes, you know, when people wouldn't act right. But he could play. He could stand there and play twelve, thirteen choruses and no repeat. He never played the clarinet, just the alto [saxophone]. He told me he was a very good clarinet player. He was outstanding.

"But I tell you, I've worked with so many good men. I've been lucky to work with fellows like that because, to me, I didn't play all that good.

"My son says, 'Dad, you're good.' I say, 'You're prejudiced!'"

Ferbos laughed heartily as he recalled those comments, then went on to describe his musical life, saying, "I was playing with John Handy's band, and we played at the Roosevelt Roof. Papa Celestin's [band] was on the other side, and Walter Pichon was the pianist that night. He came to me at intermission and said, 'I'm making up a band. Do you want to play with me?'

"I wasn't making much money anyhow, so I said, 'Well, I guess so.' So, sure enough, I played with him, and he had a good band. He used to play all his own arrangements because he was a very good arranger. We'd play all those big arrangements."

Ferbos did some traveling with Handy during the Depression and he also toured with Pichon, playing the Saenger Theater circuit and backing stars such as Mamie Smith—even after he got a job in a factory. Pichon would pick him up at home on Friday afternoon, then take him directly to work the following Monday morning.

The Great Depression was an especially difficult time for musicians, yet some succor was provided by the federally funded Works Progress Administration. In New Orleans, the WPA put together a large band comprised of some of the city's finest musicians. All had to be good readers. Louis Dumaine was one of the leaders, and band members included Cie Frazier, Manny Gabriel, Albert Glenny, Israel Gorman, Willie Humphrey, "Kid Shots" Madison, Andrew Morgan, and Louis Nelson, among many others.

Ferbos inquired about joining the WPA band, but he was told that there were plenty of trumpet players. A short time later, there was an audition for the band at the musicians' union hall. When he showed up he was handed a sheet of music and was asked if he could play it.

"I said, 'Sure, I can play it.' And when I played it, he said, 'How come you're not in the band?' I said, 'Well, you said you didn't want me.' So, he said, 'You're in it now.'

"When I was in the band, George McCullum—a very fine trumpet player—would sit next to me," Ferbos said, "and we would play all those hard marches, but he could walk through it . . . I'd play 'em, but it would give me sand [a real hard time]."

Consequently, Ferbos decided to approach Angelo Castigliola Sr., a classically trained teacher, for more lessons. "He didn't teach black people, you understand, but he said he would take me. So, I went in, and he said, 'You're advanced.' I said, 'Of course I'm advanced, but there's a lot of things I don't know.'

"So I got 'solfèged' to death. He taught me how to double-tongue, triple-tongue. I saw why George was walking through those numbers, but I had no trouble after that. We used to play pop tunes and plenty of marches. We used to play in the street. We played concerts—in the public schools, at the parish prison or at Charity Hospital, things like that.

"The band was big, some 40-some odd pieces. I have pictures of the WPA band, and everybody is gone but me. I'm the only one left. The last one was Willie Humphrey . . . and another one was Lionel Tapo. I'm the survivor."

The WPA band was terminated during World War II. By then Ferbos was in his thirties, and he began working in his father's sheet-metal business. "I was working in factories for a long time, with all that lint and stuff," he recalled. "Then I started working outside with my dad, and my asthma left."

During the 1940s and '50s his playing was confined largely to weekend gigs with a variety of bands. One of the most popular of them was The Mighty Four—Ferbos, trumpet; Harold Dejan, saxophone; George Guesnon, banjo; and Alex Bigard, drums—clearly a stellar group. They held forth at the old Melody Inn for several years in the early '50s and were recorded on the American Music label in the early '60s. Ferbos even laid out of music for five years for health reasons.

In 1962 he joined Herb Leary's Society Syncopators, which he calls "a really good band." The Syncopators were a black society band that, over the years, included many fine jazz musicians. They played mostly social events, such as Carnival balls. Ferbos worked with Leary until 1970, a year that proved to be something of a watershed in his career. It was at that time, at the age of 59, that he began his long association with pianist and bandleader Lars Edegran and the New Orleans Ragtime Orchestra (NORO).

"They were looking for a trumpet player," he said, "and Dick Allen [of Tulane's Jazz Archive] knew me from the Melody Inn. He told Lars to give me an audition. Really, I wasn't too much interested, but I went to Lars's place and he played some numbers on the phonograph. Those were things that we had played in the WPA band, and I said, 'I can play that.' And that's how I started with them."

He still plays with NORO, more than thirty years later. "I'm the only one left of the original band," he adds. "We had Bill Russell, Paul Crawford, 'Orange' [Orjan] Kellin. We changed drummers, and we changed bass players. Cie Frazier was playing drums first, but he was with the Preservation Hall Band and had to leave to play with them. So, I told Lars, 'My friend, John Robichaux, try him.' [John Robichaux later lost his life, at the age of 90, in the flooding of Hurricane Katrina.]

"Robe could read pretty good, so he fit in pretty nice. He played eight or nine years and quit. The first bass player was James Prevost. He played with us for a while and then left, and we finally got Walter Payton. He played with us for many years. The real band for many years was Payton, Robichaux, and on the front line, Bill, Orange, Paul, and myself." [Walter Payton died October 28, 2010.]

NORO did a great deal of traveling over the years, and that has been one of the highlights of Ferbos's career. "I remember the first trip we made," he recalled enthusiastically. "We were gone six weeks. We did about eleven countries. Started in Finland, Norway, and so forth, and then we came into [the rest of] Europe, but we never did play France. I've never been to France yet. Eight different trips I made to Europe and Scandinavia, but I've never been to France. Isn't that odd?"

That is especially unfortunate since his family has roots in France. Ferbos's granddaughter, Lori, traveled to France a couple of years ago to investigate those roots, but, for lack of time, she came up empty-handed. She was not even able to find a bottle of wine bearing the family name, Chateau Ferbos.

"I enjoyed every trip," Ferbos continues. "I know it was an advantage for the simple reason that I would not have the money to go to those places. We were always treated first-class, probably because Lars and Orange were Europeans [both originally from Sweden]. It was wonderful because I had a camera, and we only worked about an hour and forty-five minutes a day. So, we had the whole time to go, and I just went every place. I would travel with Paul or Payton. I have [collected] so much junk. Some places would have placards, you know, where they put the food on, and I'd take them—they'd only throw them away—and stack the stuff up. It was nice."

Once in Italy, Ferbos met a wealthy man who was a serious record collector and jazz fan. "He owned a hotel and had a beautiful house overlooking the Mediterranean. When we were talking, he said, 'I heard you play with Walter Pichon's band.' Walter didn't make too many records, but he referred to one of Walter's records. He could find any record—just like George Buck, he has millions [of records]—and he goes and gets it right now!"

It was during those years that his singing—so admired by Brian O'Connell and many others—began to evolve. "When I was working at the Melody Inn with Harold Dejan, I used to sing a couple numbers, but just because people wanted to hear the words. I never considered myself a singer at all. But when I was with the Ragtime Band, Lars told me, 'You used to sing with Harold, why can't you sing with us?' So, one day when I was doing a number—we were playing at the Presbytere [on Jackson Square] that day—my son happened to be passing by with his girlfriend. He said, 'Oh, listen, the band has a singer now. That's my dad!'"

Ferbos laughed at the memory, then said, "Later, when I was with the *One Mo' Time* show, which I worked for about three years [1978–1981], Bill Russell said, 'Why don't you sing in the show?' I said, 'Oh, man, to go on the stage like that would be something else.'

"But I've got to go back a bit. I was in Sweden, and I'd done a little number. So, the owner said, 'Lionel, you sound nice. Why don't you go to the front of the stage?' I said I'd forget the words. He told me to write the words on a paper so I could remember them. Then I found that Perry Como didn't do nightclubs because he couldn't remember words. If you remember *The Perry Como Show* on TV, he always had a music stand in front of him.

"I'll be frank with you. Some numbers I can't remember. I have the words written out, so I read the words I can't remember. Others just stick in my mind."

There were several other highlights in the 1970s. "I was in a movie,

Pretty Baby," he said proudly. "You know, the part I did, we played a number. I think it was 'Pretty Baby,' but 'Helios Rag' came out on the record [soundtrack]. Can you imagine?"

Ferbos was in another movie, *French Quarter,* in which Vernel Bagneris played Jelly Roll Morton. Said Ferbos, "It's funny how moving pictures work. Bagneris was playing the piano, and—you know how they show your hands—but his hands weren't working right. So, Lars played the piano, and his hands are in the movie."

Ferbos laughed uproariously, then continued, "But the whole trouble with the movie was that it was on the same basis as *Pretty Baby.* It was a small company. *Pretty Baby* was Paramount, I think. You know, I still get residuals from *Pretty Baby!* Twenty-five, thirty dollars, something like that. I still get it whenever they perform it. It pays my union dues," he chuckles.

Ferbos continued to work with NORO throughout the 1980s, recording two albums (one for GHB and another for Stomp Off) and performing in a television documentary devoted to Armand Piron and his music. He also recorded an album under his own name for the 505 label, and he made one last European tour with the *One Mo' Time* show in 1988.

In 1991 Ferbos took another significant step down his long career path by joining the Saturday night house band at the Palm Court Jazz Café, a gig that he still performs regularly. At that time the band was led by the late Pud Brown, for whom Ferbos continues to have great respect. "I worked with Pud for three years with the *One Mo' Time* show, but we were all reading. Not that Pud would read because Pud knew the program by head—once he learned it, he knew it by head. I told him I'd have to know what keys he's playing in. Pud was so good. He said, 'You call the keys, you call the numbers.' Like I do now. Most people think I'm the bandleader. I'm not the bandleader. I didn't want to be the bandleader. When Pud died [1996], they wanted me to be the band leader. I said no. Les [Muscutt] is the bandleader now because he knows how to handle it, and he's a very nice fellow.

"I call the numbers," he continued, "on account of the keys, because I can't play in any key. I play in several keys, but some keys I can't play in unless I'm reading it. If I'm reading it, I can play in any key. If it's extemporary, I can't do it. So, Les and I work well together because he was there when I came to play with Pud. Since Pud passed, he's been the leader. He's a very good bandleader, and he's a wonderful player. He knows what numbers to play and what numbers not to play, according to the audience. That's the thing that counts. A lot of fellows play what they want, but the audience might not like it at all. And we play requests. I know about a hundred numbers just like that, but then I have three books with numbers that I can't remember so easy. Mostly it's a guide, it's not really reading. I look it up in my book, and there it is."

Ferbos thoroughly enjoys his work with the Palm Court Jazz Band. "I enjoy playing with them," he said, "because Tom [Ebbert, trombonist] is a very fine musician and knows what he's doing. Chuck [Badie, bass] is another fine musician who knows what he's doing, and Ernie Elly is a very good drummer. Brian [O'Connell] is a very nice clarinet player. I told him the other day, 'I been listening at you play and you play the numbers you don't even know when I pick 'em up, but you're in there already.' He said, 'Well, I'm listening at you. The way you play, I can follow.' That's what a lot of guys told me. Other guys they can't follow, they say. And some real good clarinet players that come in and play in Brian's place say the same thing. I'm glad. It's a pleasure to play with somebody that is good and makes it right."

As colleagues O'Connell and Muscutt have said, Lionel Ferbos plays the melody. "I like numbers that you can enjoy the melody," he asserted firmly.

When asked what trumpet players he enjoyed listening to when he was starting out in the business, he responded, "I used to like to hear Maurice Durand. He played nice horn. And Louie Dumaine. And the one who was really my idol was 'Coo Coo' [Elmer Talbert Jr.]. Coo Coo had a beautiful horn. I knew so many players, but it was hard to tell who could play better than the other because they played different. Like Kid Howard, he played different than Shots Madison would play. But they're all good, real good."

A conversation of any length with Lionel Ferbos is laced with references to his wife, the former Marguerite Gilyot. They were neighbors as children and married in 1934 when he was 22 and she was 21. They have two children, Sylvia and Lionel Jr., and they celebrated their 68th wedding anniversary in April.

"You might think I'm lying, but we've never had a real fuss or fight," he said. "A lot of people at the Palm Court ask me what do I attribute my longevity in marriage to, and I say, for one thing, keep your mouth shut. Women argue for foolish things. Very seldom it's serious. Like, you slammed the door, or you didn't take out the garbage. It can become a big thing, but you just do it. . . .

"I never had plenty money," he continued, "but I always had enough. And then my wife was understanding. I've never had problems with my wife and money, never did. If we had it, we had it. If we didn't have it. . . . She was never extravagant.

"My children could tell you right now that they thought we were rich because they never wanted for anything. My children never got everything. I got them what they needed and not what they wanted. And they understood that."

It's pretty clear that the Ferboses are people with solid, traditional values. Referring to his wife, Ferbos said, "She was sharp, I'm telling you. And then she knew so much from working with other people. She worked at Haspel's [a clothing manufacturer no longer in business] for forty-six and a half years—one spot! She was not a supervisor. They asked her to do it many times, but she said, 'If I can't hire and fire, I don't want to be a supervisor.'

"She was a good worker, and other girls would stop by and say, 'You'd think you own the factory the way you work.' She'd say, 'No, I'm being paid so much, I'm doing what I think it's worth.' I believe that too. If you get paid, you work. And if you don't want to work, don't come to work."

Lionel Ferbos is clearly a class act. "Well, I try to be," he says. "I'm not perfect and I know that, but I try to be right. I get angry sometimes, very seldom, but I never curse."

He feels strongly about lying, too, saying that he avoids it because "I remember, years ago, I told a lie and I was so embarrassed when they caught me in the lie."

Gossiping is also something he and his wife avoid. Said Ferbos, "You can be stupid and ugly, but it doesn't pay. It pays more to be nice because you never know who you're going to need. You never know."

When asked how long he would like to continue to play, Ferbos responded, "Well, I'll tell you the truth. I really don't know. To be frank with you, I thought last year when I played the [Jazz and Heritage] Festival it was my last year. But it's so nice, and the band has been nice to play with, so I just keep on playing. But, like I told my daughter, 'Don't worry about it.' I may play a whole year, maybe not. I don't know. It'll come to me all at once when I decide to stop. And another thing, too. If I get so that my playing is bad, then they won't have to tell me." He laughed as he added, "They might fire me. You never know.

"I was only fired from a job once, and, believe it or not, I never remember asking anybody for a job either because I never thought I was good enough. You know, guys jam and all that stuff. I never did that. I didn't think my playing was good enough."

Certainly, that modest self-assessment isn't borne out by the facts—Lionel Ferbos's playing is good enough to have kept him on bandstands for the better part of his 91 years. Despite serious surgery that hospitalized him for nine days in early April, Ferbos was back at Jazzfest with NORO by the end of the month. And, after a brief respite, he's still doing his Saturday night gigs at the Palm Court.

As his friend Les Muscutt says, "That's Lionel."

2

EDDIE BAYARD
Crescent City Cornetist

A native New Orleanian who was introduced to jazz in the musical West Bank neighborhood of Algiers, Eddie Bayard left home as a teenager to join the air force. That ultimately led to a lengthy stay in Ohio working with the government while performing extensively thereabouts and making periodic trips back to his hometown. Like so many émigré local musicians, Bayard was drawn back to his native city in the 1970s. His jazz career took off immediately, but by the late 1990s, he began to cut back on his performance schedule.

Bayard is now retired after more than a half century in the music business. Having endured severe damage to his present home in the Lakeview neighborhood during the Katrina flooding in late August 2005, he suffered a serious heart attack in May 2009. Complications of various kinds have had him in and out of hospitals since that time. But as of this writing, he is well on his way to full recovery.

Most of what follows was gleaned from a conversation with Bayard at his then–New Orleans East home in August 1997, shortly after his 63rd birthday. It was published in the January 1998 issue of The Mississippi Rag.

E DDIE BAYARD HAS EXPERIENCED VIRTUALLY EVERY DImension of the jazz music business. He has been a sideman and leader and can be heard on numerous recordings in both capacities. He has seen much of the world because of his music, but he has also spent some three decades playing riverboats on the Mississippi. And he has been both owner and manager of jazz clubs in New Orleans.

Born and raised in New Orleans, Bayard is one of the few horn players currently working in the city who can claim to be a native. Yet he left the city as a teenager and resided upriver in Ohio for more than twenty years before returning home for good in the mid-1970s.

Eddie Bayard was born on August 1, 1934, in the 800 block of Elysian Fields Avenue, just beyond the French Quarter. "I looked up the address," he now says. "It was a house, but there's some public building there now. I was born there at the house. I wasn't born in a hospital."

Eventually his family moved to Algiers on the "West Bank" across the river, where he spent most of his teen years and first got hooked on jazz. While his father played the mandolin (not professionally) and taught him to play the harmonica, he says, "I'm the only one [in the family] that played music and stuck with it."

It all seems to have begun in the late 1940s. "I can remember hearing Harry James play on the radio, and I guess the sound of the trumpet caught my ear," he recalls. "I decided I wanted to learn to play the trumpet, so I talked my parents into getting me some music lessons. I went to Werlein's [the well-known New Orleans music store, then located on Canal Street]. They had a deal, five weeks of music lessons for a dollar a week, and they furnished the horn. After that you had to buy a horn, but my parents couldn't afford a horn so I didn't play anymore."

That was only a temporary setback, for he was soon playing baritone horn in school bands. "I played in the marching band," he notes. "One day I showed up in school with a trumpet, and [band director] Milton Bush asked, 'Where is your baritone?' He kind of got upset about that, but I played a concert the following week on the school's old beat-up baritone."

It was at that time that he began to take trumpet lessons from jazz pioneer Manuel "Fess" Manetta, a fellow Algerine. The "professor" was a multi-instrumentalist whose professional career went back to playing piano in Lulu White's Mahogany Hall in Storyville and who was a long-time music teacher in Algiers. Bayard studied with Manetta for nearly two years until he joined the air force in 1952.

By that time Bayard and school friends had started a Dixieland band that was playing regularly at the Teenage Center (which he helped to establish in a VFW hall) and elsewhere in Algiers. His lessons with Manetta were valuable. "Every once in a while we'd get him to write out lead sheets for us on Dixieland tunes. He wrote out the lead sheet on 'Milneburg Joys' for us. He wrote out the clarinet solo on 'High Society' in his own handwriting, which I loaned to somebody and never did get back. But he was mainly teaching us how to read music.

"One day I walked in with a Louis Armstrong book of solos. He looked at the book and looked at me and shook his head and said, 'You're not ready for that.'

"Well, I can tell you today, I'm still not ready for that," Bayard laughs. "I still have the book, and there are some solos in there that only Louis can play—or play them right. There are a lot of people who can read the spots, but it doesn't come out the same."

Growing up where he did was a wonderful environment for a lad who had designs on becoming a jazz trumpet player. "Back when I was taking lessons from Manetta," he recalls, "I used to go up Teche Street [in Algiers] where there were little bars. One night I was standing in a doorway—I was 16 or 17 years old—and listening to [trumpeter Henry] "Red" Allen play along with the jukebox. Some other guy had a tray on top of an old wooden beer keg, and he was playing with the drumsticks to a jukebox. [Clarinetist] George Lewis also lived over there on the West Bank. We used to see a lot of jazz funerals over there, too. Those things were common in those days, more common than today."

And he was listening to local trumpet players whenever he could. Among his favorites was Sharkey Bonano. "He always had a great band, always a real swinging band with good players."

And Al Hirt. "He was such an inspiration. He had full command of the instrument. Tony Almerico used to say that he had such power—if he pushed the wrong valve, the right note would come out."

But young George Girard—one of those legendary jazz prodigies who died prematurely—topped his list. "I first heard Girard on a local TV show," Bayard remembers, "but he got to be my idol after hearing him and seeing him in person at Lenfant's on Canal Boulevard. He's the one I really liked. Of course, he died at 26 years old [in 1957]. George Girard played with so much drive and so much feeling . . . I really idolized him. I would go listen to him every chance I could. When I was in the service and came home on a furlough I would go to the Famous Door and listen to him. At that time he was away from the Basin Street Six [with a young Pete Fountain] and had his own band called the New Orleans Five.

"My friend Barry Hildebrand and I were sitting at the bar the night that [trombonist] Bob Havens came and sat in with Girard. Havens was with Ralph Flanagan's band at the Blue Room and sat in and [regular trombonist] Joe Rotis sat down. We wondered what this little guy was going to do, playing with the big boys. When he started playing, we listened! Curly the bartender said to Rotis, 'You're going to work your butt off when you get back there now.' Havens was playing with Girard when he died. He stayed in town and then started playing with Al Hirt's band.

"I listened to George as much as I could and thought I had almost everything that he recorded. But I understand that [drummer] Phil Zito has a lot of recordings with Girard that have never been published. Girard actually played with Phil Zito's band first. Phil keeps telling me to come out to his house and listen to them, and I'd better go because Phil's getting up in age, too." [Zito died just a year later, in 1998, at the age of 83.]

"One of the first bands I put together in Ohio," he goes on, "was called the Bourbon Street Five. [New Orleans trumpeter] Roy Liberto used to come through once in a while, and he had a group called the Bourbon Street Six. That was later on, when he had the house band at the Famous Door, after George Girard passed away. So, I decided to use the name Bourbon Street Five up there. It was Jim Campbell on clarinet, Bob Butters on trombone—he's still around and plays great—, Stan McCauley on piano, a drummer from Xenia, Ohio, called Al Davenport, a great little drummer. Jim Bonecutter played bass, and sometimes Gene Mayl played with us. We made two recordings up there. The first one we did was in 1963. Then I did one in 1968 called *Stomping at the Village Inn*. I was playing a pizza house south, and Gene Mayl was playing the same pizza house north, across town. Some of the personnel changes, of course, on those two records. Jim Campbell was on both of them."

While in Dayton, Bayard not only finished up his high school diploma but he enrolled for two years in music school at the University of Dayton. "I was only interested in taking the music courses," he explains. "I wasn't planning on getting a degree. I just wanted the music courses to make me play better. What made me do that was hearing all those jazz greats who came into Dayton. George Wein would bring groups in: Ruby Braff,

Pee Wee Russell, Marshall Brown, Arvell Shaw, Muggsy Spanier, Bob Scobey—every great band you could think of in those days would come through Dayton at this place called Kenkel's. Once he brought in Duke Ellington and Si Zentner on the same night.

"There was a late-night place in Dayton where everybody would go after hours, and we used to go down there. So, I'm sitting around the table with Ruby Braff and all those people and they're talking music and music theory. It was all Greek to me. I said to myself that I got to understand what these people are talking about. So, I went to the University of Dayton and found out what the "tonic" was and the "sub-dominant" and "chord progressions" and "cadence" and all that stuff. I took two semesters of piano, and I had to play a Bach thing to pass my piano course and I did that. It paid off."

It was in Dayton, about 1960, when Bayard decided to switch from trumpet to cornet. "There was a cornet player in Dayton who could play it very, very well. His name was Jim, but I can't think of his last name. He said, 'If you ever switch, you'll never go back.' I often thought I'd go back, but I never have.

"Gene Mayl put together a band in Kenkel's one time," he continues, "and it included Andy Bartha, who used to play cornet with Pee Wee Hunt's band. I was talking to Andy a lot. I went up to his hotel room one time to get a lesson from him. He was in there brushing his teeth, with a glass of bourbon. He gave me a sheet and said, 'Play this while I brush my teeth.' It was 'Weatherbird Rag.' So, I started playing it, and he came out and looked at me and said, 'That's pretty good for sight-reading.' I said, 'Well, there's a lot of notes there.'

"I told him I wanted to get a cornet, so I went down to the music store and they had a Selmer K modified cornet there. I took it out on loan and brought it in to Kenkel's and asked Andy to try out the horn. He played it and sounded wonderful. He said, 'The thing is beautiful. It plays so much in tune. You don't have to use the trigger or anything.'

"I asked him what size mouthpiece he was using. He said a Bach 10 ½ C. So, I said all right and went out and bought the horn and got a 10 ½ C. And that's how I got started on the cornet."

Reflecting now on those Ohio years, Bayard says firmly, "It was the smartest thing I ever did. I had the opportunity to play music. I got married up there, and all my kids [four boys] still live there. We still see each other. I go up there, and they come down here."

But New Orleans always had a strong gravitational pull on him. "When I lived up there," he goes on, "I came to New Orleans once or twice a year—always. When my parents were living in Chalmette [a suburb], I'd drive to New Orleans and I'd drive straight past Chalmette and go all the way to Canal Street and drive down Bourbon Street. Every time. It was like a ritual. I had to drive down Bourbon Street with the windows down and hear some of the music, and then I would go home. But I always came back. The guys in Ohio used to like me to go back. They said, every time I'd go to New Orleans, I'd play a little different when I came back. I probably started picking up on the New Orleans style more. So, maybe the trips were worthwhile.

"Bourbon Street will probably never be like it used to be," he says. "Back in the days when Hyp Guinle was alive and he had the Famous Door—it was the classiest place on the street. I went down there one time, and Hyp asked me which band I'd like to sit in with. There were two bands playing all the time—on that occasion Santo Pecora's band and Mike Lala's band. I said, 'Let me sit in with Santo's band since he doesn't have a trumpet player.'

"It was just him and a clarinet player at the time. So, I sat in with Santo and, when I got ready to leave, he came outside and asked me if I wanted to join his band. I said I couldn't because I was working for the government in Ohio and was just home on leave.

"But those days are gone. Back then some of the club owners obviously knew about New Orleans jazz. The Dream Room was going—Santo played there, and Jack Teagarden played there. That's when he died— Connie Jones was working with him at that time [1964]. And Sharkey's band was playing around town. They just had a lot of good bands playing at that time—all playing traditional jazz. You would never hear a rock-and-roll or country band on Bourbon Street back then. Nowadays I think the club owners are just looking for the dollar, and they're all hiring non-union musicians . . . and don't care what they get."

Eddie Bayard's long romance with the Mississippi riverboats also began during his Ohio years. "We did the *Delta Queen* starting in 1968," he says. "We were the regular band every weekend, and we did as many trips as I wanted to do and could pull myself away from the day job to do. They gave us carte blanche on how many trips we wanted to do each year. The trips were from Cincinnati. The weekend trips would go from Cincinnati down to Louisville and back. Some longer trips would go from Cincinnati to Kentucky Lakes and back."

The personnel in his band during those years would change from time to time, but it included most of those heard on their 1972 recording, *Steamboat Journey*. Band members included Bob Butters, trombone; Ralph Unterborn, clarinet; Stan McCauley, piano; Gene Mayl, bass; Vic Tooker, banjo; and Kenny Hall, drums.

The *Delta Queen* gig lasted for about eight years. "When [the owners] started talking about building the *Mississippi Queen*," Bayard recalls, "they kept talking to me. They said, 'You guys got to come on the new boat with us.' They liked the way we worked and the way we took care of ourselves on business and the way we handled ourselves. After talking with the band, I said, 'All right, let's do it.'

"So, I retired from the government. The trombone player, Bill Coburn, retired from the state. Everybody left their jobs and jumped in the car and drove down to New Orleans to meet the boat. We did the shakedown trip when they built it, we did the maiden voyage, and we stayed on there for three years. We played the dedication for the first piece of steel that was laid when they first started building the boat. So, we were involved with it from when it was an idea until it was finished. The maiden voyage was in 1976.

"It was a good job—eight weeks on and two weeks off, seven days a week. It wasn't a hard job. We only played three hours a night. Two weeks off with pay, and they'd fly you back and forth to where your home was. It was a good life. The only reason I left was because management kept changing, and they got people on there telling the band what to play and how to play and everything else.

"The job was for twelve months a year, except once a year the boat would go to the shipyard for maintenance. At that time they were sending us out on the road for promotional tours. We went all up and down the coast of California. We played opposite Arthur Fiedler for a dedication of Faneuil Hall Market Square [in Boston]. We played halftime at the Patriots game one time. Everything was to promote the steamboat company and the tours.

"They got us a spot on *The Dinah Shore Show*. And Lawrence Welk was doing his show right across the hall at CBS Television City. We were over there watching Welk's rehearsal. Bob Havens [then playing in the Welk band] and I had been friends for years, and they came over and watched our show. And Lawrence Welk was a guest on our show, and he wanted to know—it was kind of an impromptu thing—if he could direct our band because he loved Dixieland music. We were supposed to do three choruses of 'Muskrat Ramble' or something. So, he got out there with his baton, and it went on and on. The first thing I told the band when he said he was going to direct the band with his baton was, 'Don't look at him. I'll count it off, but don't pay any attention to him.'

"He was all show business with his band—George Cates used to direct the band. He would do it once in a while, but I don't think his band would follow him either. He gave me the baton. There it is, right over there [*pointing to one wall of his study*].

"The band that went on the *Mississippi Queen* from Ohio was Syl La-Fata on clarinet; Bill Coburn, trombone; Ronnie White, an excellent drummer from the air force band who retired and played with us; Stan McCauley, piano; and Dave Jacobs played bass. Later on, Jerry Rousseau from New Orleans played bass for a while. I continued to use the name Bourbon Street Five.

"I got off there in June 1979. We were on a promotional tour in Florida and my trombone player had a heart attack. We had to leave him there in a hospital and go on to California. Bob Havens couldn't work with us because he was still doing the Welk show. So, somebody gave me the name of Bob Enevoldsen. He did some work in California with us, and then Havens did some. Havens couldn't come back to the boat with us until the show was over, so Enevoldsen came with us for two or three months. He could play anything, and he was a great arranger. He played what they called the 'superbone,' the one with either the slide or the valves. He played bass and, from what I heard, tenor sax, and he wrote arrangements for a lot of people. I did not know that until one night when we had the big band cruises and had Count Basie on. Basie's bass player asked if I ever played any of Eno's arrangements. I said no, and he said he's a great arranger. After hearing that, Bob would go downstairs and write a new chart every night and bring it up and we would rehearse it and play it. He's a great arranger, and he stayed on the boat with us for two or three months. Then Bob Havens came on, and he stayed another two or three months with us."

Bayard bought a home in New Orleans while he was working on the *Mississippi Queen*. After leaving the boat in 1979, he settled in the Crescent City for good. He gigged around town at first, then led a band at the Maison Bourbon and made trips to Russia and the Far East and recorded with the new Louisiana Repertory Jazz Ensemble (LRJE) put together by clarinetist Fred Starr.

In 1980 Bayard made his first foray into the risky business of running a jazz club. The club was located at 701 Bourbon Street, at the corner of Bourbon and St. Peter (now known as "The Cat's Meow"). It turned out to be an abortive undertaking, lasting only about a year before folding. He had a partner from Ohio.

"We leased it," Bayard explains, "from two guys who were not really on the up and up with us. They didn't go along with their end of the bargain. So, we gave it up."

Yet a couple of good things came from the experience. In the first place, Bayard learned some of the problems that arise when a musician tries to run a club.

"I started out by having the house band," he says, "but I soon realized you cannot run a club from the bandstand. It's a full-time job. When you own a club, you're married to it. I put a lot of 18-hour days in the place. You can't concentrate on the music when you've got your mind on everything else. So, I just decided not to do it. I'd rather walk around the club and be the host or manager.

This decision, as it turns out, proved to be a big break for one of today's best-known and most popular bands in the city, Banu Gibson and her New Orleans Hot Jazz.

"It was on a Wednesday night," Bayard explains. "What happened was, I was playing there and I had a gig with the Repertory band, so I asked Banu if she could put together a band to sub on that Wednesday night. She said she thought she could, so she got Charlie Fardella [trumpet], Dickie Taylor [drums], and I think it was Steve Pistorius [piano] and a bunch of other people. I don't think she'd fronted a group before. After my gig was over, I went back to the club and listened to her. It sounded good. So, I said to her, 'It sounds so good, why don't you just keep it.' So, that's how the New Orleans Hot Jazz was born."

Bayard gave club management one more shot—in 1984, in the same building as before. But the result was no more successful than the first time around. In little more than a year "Eddie Bayard's Jazz Alley, the Jazz Corner of the World" had been transformed into a club featuring rock-and-roll music—thanks largely to his new partner who owned 100 percent of the lease.

"I learned something that time too," he reflects. "Always pay yourself first. I cut my wages in half to help the club keep going and make things work. I would have to win the Power Ball [lottery] to get back in the club business, and then it would just be to have a place to hang out. I wouldn't want to run one again," he concludes.

Another milestone in Eddie Bayard's career also occurred in 1984. It was then that he started the New Orleans Classic Jazz Orchestra (NOCJO), a group initially dedicated to recapturing the sound and spirit of the old New Orleans Owls. The Owls flourished in the 1920s and numbered among their famous alumni Louis Prima, Eddie Miller, Nappy Lamare, Johnny Wiggs, and Armand Hug—to name but a few.

"The reason I started the group," Bayard now says, "was the Repertory band [LRJE] was doing the right kind of stuff, but I thought they weren't doing it seriously enough. They were all professional people. J. J. [John Joyce] was a professor at Tulane and John Chaffe was in the electronics business—everybody was doing something else. I don't want to say anything derogatory because I enjoyed working with those guys and enjoyed the travel with them. I just thought that I could put together some musicians who could do it a little better."

Bayard admits that the musical approach of the NOCJO was pretty much the same as the LRJE, but there were differences.

"I had Bob Enevoldsen take a lot of the Owls tunes and transcribe them from the records but also adapt it for our seven-piece band—no matter what the Owls used. Sometimes the Owls used three saxes, sometimes they used the trombone, sometimes they didn't. I had Bob do it

Eddie Bayard and the New Orleans Classic Jazz Orchestra at the French Quarter Festival, April 2004. *From left to right:* Bob Havens, Hal Smith, Bayard, Tom Fischer, John Parker, Tom Saunders (obscured), and John Royen.

consistently for my instrumentation and make it for clarinet and so-prano sax, and trumpet, trombone, and banjo. In my arrangements, even though the structure of the tune might be like the record, sometimes the ensemble has some freedom—we had a lot of freedom—and then there would be passages where he would write out the long parts if there were licks for both of the horns or a lick that was something to identify the tune with. That was very important. In 'Meat on the Table,' that trumpet solo is written out. It's a good solo. It makes the tune sound the way they played it back then. It gives it the flavor intended when they played it. But the Classic Jazz Orchestra has more freedom in our arrangements than the Repertory band had. Bob Enevoldsen did all the Owls' charts for me."

The band enjoyed considerable success from the outset. They made two recordings (*The Owls Hoot*, 1986, and *Blowin' Off Steam*, 1990) as well as a series of international tours (mostly sponsored by the State Department) to: Hong Kong and Japan in February, 1987; China in December, 1987; the South Pacific in June and July, 1988; and the Middle East, Pakistan, and India in January and February, 1992.

"They laid out the red carpet for us," Bayard recalls. "They loved the music. We had press conferences all the time, and they asked us about the music. We gave clinics at the music schools. We taught the military band some tunes and had them jamming with us and reading some of our charts one time. We gave a little concert and class with questions and answers to school kids in school another time.

"The band hasn't played as a seven-piece unit in three years," he continues, "not since the last French Quarter Festival that I played in. I'm not really interested in doing anything right now. I may again, sometime, if I get the right people together. If I had the money to bring Havens to town for a week or two . . . and get everybody together and work somewhere for a couple weeks and dig out some of the charts we haven't recorded, I'd probably do it. But it's not on the front burner. I accomplished everything I wanted to do with the Classic Jazz Orchestra."

In the meantime, he's been back on the riverboats for the last several years. "I've got the band on the *Natchez* full time [every afternoon]. I have to be honest with you, I've been cutting back myself. I'm doing three days on the *Natchez* and [trumpeter] Duke Heitger is doing four. Sometimes I give him five, and [cornetist] Chris Tyle works sometimes. This week I'm working every night on the *Creole Queen* for [reedman] Otis Bazoon because he's gone out of town. I'm taking care of his business. On the *Natchez*, it's just three of us—David Boeddinghaus and Steve Pistorius play piano and Tom Fischer—and Jack Maheu plays his off days—and myself or Duke or Chris. But I'm getting a little . . . I don't want to say burned out because I like to play. I get frustrated with the business and with the people. But the riverboats are about the only place now where you can enjoy playing without having any noise coming from the place across the street or next door. It's really a nice little job."

When asked to reflect on his career, which is now approaching a half century, Bayard responded thoughtfully, "If I had it to do over again, I'd probably do a few things differently. I'd probably study a little harder and study with the right people and maybe do things a little bit better. I'd spend more time on the instrument, to learn the instrument better. To be a well-schooled musician, you've got to put the time in. But music has been good to me. I've played professionally for a long time."

Yes, Eddie, and we look forward to listening to your music for a long time to come.

3

DON VAPPIE
New Orleans Music in His Blood

Don Vappie, now 55, continues to be an outspoken advocate for traditional jazz and what has become his favorite musical instrument, the banjo. Nor is he hesitant to make it known to the uninitiated, whether black or white, that the instrument is of African origin.

Though early respected and recorded as a bassist and guitarist (he continues to play those instruments well), Vappie has become known (and featured) internationally as a banjo virtuoso. He recently admitted with a wry smile, "I have been called the Jimi Hendrix of the banjo."

*While Vappie still tours here and abroad with his excellent band, the Creole Jazz Serenaders, he has increasingly appeared far and wide as a single and billed as a world-class banjoist. His recent recordings on the instrument include his own Banjo à la Creole (2005) and a collaboration with the likes of Otis Taylor and Alvin Youngblood Hart, Recapturing the Banjo (2008). A CD featuring his arrangements of the music of legendary banjoist Harry Reser with the Hot Springs Music Festival Orchestra—*Jazz Nocturne: American Concertos of the Jazz Age—*was released on the Naxos label in 2010.*

Vappie was out of town when Hurricane Katrina hit New Orleans. His home on the north shore of Lake Pontchartrain largely escaped destruction, but his boyhood home in the city—inhabited by his mother—was badly damaged. This led him to create an organization to help dispersed New Orleans musicians called "Bring It on Home."

*Vappie's extended family on his mother's side (the Josephs) gathered every couple of years for reunions in New Orleans. A result of their last reunion prior to Katrina was a recording by his musical relatives—*Valsin, Reunion *(2005)—after Valsin Joseph, from whom most are ultimately descended. A subsequent documentary film, American Creole: New Orleans Reunion,* *by noted filmmaker Glen Pitre (who also penned the notes for the CD), was released in September 2006 and is available on DVD. It is a moving account of Vappie's post-Katrina story, including footage of both him and his musical family members.*

The following interview with Don (joined by his wife Milly) was taped October 31, 2000, and published in the June 2001 issue of The Mississippi Rag.

IREALLY THINK I WAS ALWAYS SERIOUS ABOUT MUSIC, EVEN as a small child. My earliest memory is wanting to be a musician. Neither of my parents played music, but I was always around music. There was always music in the house." So recalls Don Vappie, the outspoken leader of the fine New Orleans repertory band the Creole Jazz Serenaders (CJS).

While his parents may not have played, music was certainly in Vappie's genes. It all seems to go back to pioneer jazz bassist "Papa John" Joseph (born 1877), who may be considered his family's musical patriarch.

Both Joseph and his younger brother, clarinetist Willie "Kaiser" Joseph (Vappie's grand-uncles), worked regularly in The District (Storyville) until it closed in 1917. And then there was their nephew, Earl Fouché, who worked with bandleader Sam Morgan and later Don Albert's big band.

Before moving to New Orleans in 1906 from rural St. James Parish, Papa John was a member of the family band that played professionally throughout the countryside.

"It was a string band," Vappie says. "All of the children in the family— Papa John's brothers and sisters—all played an instrument. There must have been eight or nine kids—there were a bunch of them. My grandmother played guitar and banjo. I didn't know that until she was 90 years old or something.

"The story is that when Kaiser Willie wanted to play clarinet, he was the first one to pick up something that wasn't a string instrument. They said when he practiced it sounded so awful that they made him go out in the fields to play."

By today, the number of musicians in Don Vappie's extended family is almost uncountable. "Yeah," he says, "I don't really know them all, but I guess one of the more famous ones is [tenor saxophonist] Plas Johnson. My grandmother's sister or brother or whatever was Plas's whatever. It's all on my mother's side. All are from the Josephs. It all came from Papa John. We're talking now about doing a family project together. You know, Plas, Stanley Joseph [the CJS drummer], Richard Moten [the regular bass player in the CJS], [pianist] Thaddeus Richard, [Thaddeus's father] Reynold [Richard] . . ."

How about trombonist "Frog" Joseph?

"No," Vappie says. "It's a different Joseph. Joseph is like Smith. There are a lot of separate families."

Don Vappie (his family's original name was Vappaille) was born in uptown New Orleans on January 30, 1956—a troubled time in post–World War II American history. It was just two years after the Supreme Court's historic decision on *Brown vs. Board of Education of Topeka*, ruling school segregation unconstitutional. In New Orleans, the decision ultimately led to serious riots in the Central Business District in November 1960. These in turn led to the resignation of Mayor DeLesseps "Chep" Morrison in 1961. While New Orleans does not seem to have experienced the racial violence that occurred in some other American cities with large black populations in the 1960s, it is not difficult to understand how black children growing up at that time could have been affected by the problems of desegregating.

Blacks of a certain age have often criticized musicians like Louis Armstrong of "Uncle Tomming."

"It was a different time and all," Vappie admits, "but for people in my generation, we came up not wanting to be that way. I even saw some of the old musicians as basically tomming for the white folks. I mean, I didn't really know Preservation Hall [founded in 1961] existed. Sometimes you would see things, you know. Sometimes the older black musicians at that time would have nothing to do with young black musicians. They'd more readily take in a young white musician, and it might have been because deep down or somewhere back in their memory was stored the fact that 'if I let this little young white guy get in here, he might help me get to somewhere else. There's nothing this young black dude can do for me.'

"It's very easy, man, to fall into a situation like that, especially when you live in a place like New Orleans where the people who come to New Orleans sometimes expect to see a stereotype of what they imagine is going to be here. And because they expect it and have money and are bringing it in, people who hire musicians sometimes look for that image. So they can say, 'Hey look, we have what you're looking for.'"

And that would be?

"Old black musicians," he explains. "It could also be young black musicians, on the street. You go in the bookstore and look at books about New Orleans. All the pictures of black people—90 percent or more—are going to be [in] poor neighborhoods, little kids on the streets with no shoes on, dancing in the street or dancing behind a brass band. But all the pictures of white people in these books are *Southern Living* [an upscale magazine]—look at my house on St. Charles Avenue, how nice it is. It's almost like black people don't have nice houses, and there aren't poor white kids in the streets with no shoes on.

"So, that should explain what I'm trying to say. There's an image of what people want to see.

"Sometimes, assimilating and stereotyping is a choice for people. But you can do it and not act like Stepin Fetchit while you're doing it. Or start spreading your legs or bugging your eyes—'Oh, look at me playing the banjo, my, my'—and that kind of stuff. Man, I see that going on today.

"There were times when I just walked out of jobs," he adds. "I know, if I lived sixty years ago or something and had a job, I couldn't just walk away from it like that because the opportunities were just not there. It was a different time.

"When I came up, I had both my father and my mother telling me, 'You can do whatever you want. You can do and be whoever you want to be.' I always had that in my head. My father didn't realize it—he's not with me anymore, he died in '89—but he was always offering to help. 'Do you need some money, do you need this, do you need that?' I knew he didn't have it. He was always there, and I told him that. Finally, I think he understood. The fact that he was there was like a safety net for me. I took a lot of chances I wouldn't have taken if I didn't have a safety net. If I lost everything I could go back to my parents' house. A lot of people don't have that."

Vappie got an early start in music. He began piano at age five, soon graduating to trumpet and baritone horn in school bands. As a freshman in high school he took up the electric bass and, a year later, the guitar. He and cousin Stanley Joseph started a garage band.

"We played pop music in high school," he recalls. "There was some jazz. That's what people don't understand. No matter what you play, if you are in New Orleans, you have to play some jazz. You have to know some traditional jazz—'Bourbon Street Parade,' 'Saints,' 'Washington and Lee Swing,' 'Second Line,' 'Joe Avery Blues'—so you know some of that, regardless. Music in New Orleans has a sort of social purpose. If you were going to play a party, you had to know certain things. You had to play all the pop stuff, too."

After graduating from high school in 1973, Vappie attended Loyola University on a music scholarship. He soon became disenchanted with the program and left school. He was married young and had a daughter. At about that time he helped start a very popular R&B and pop-music band, Trac One, in the city. A number of other members of that band—Stanley Joseph, bassist Mark Brooks, reedman Pierre Poree, trumpeter Tracy Griffin—have since become notable performers on the local music scene. Vappie played with the band for five years, during which time he also worked as a guitarist with the Dick Stabile Orchestra at the Fairmont (formerly Roosevelt) Hotel. [The Fairmont was renovated after Katrina and rechristened the Roosevelt in 2009.]

"[Stabile] used to feature me on 'Rhapsody in Blue,'" Vappie remembers. "That was a time when they were taking these tunes and making them pop. So, I had a guitar solo in there somewhere. That was kind of nice."

He played all kinds of material with Trac One. "That was interesting," he goes on, "but then disco came around and I got bored. I was playing bass and I remember saying that you could teach a chimpanzee to play this line because it was over and over for like twenty minutes. That's when I quit. I sold all my instruments except my string bass . . . and I bought them all back in about three months. I realized that I couldn't give up playing music. Maybe I could give up playing in the band, but I couldn't give up playing music."

He decided to try school again, enrolling at Xavier University. "Xavier was okay," he says. "I'm sort of an outspoken person, so I asked the guy,

Mr. Fernandez—he's died too, but he was a really nice guy—'If you're going to rehearse the saxophones the whole rehearsal, why don't you just call a section rehearsal so I don't have to lug this big amplifier in and waste my time? I could be studying something else.'

"And he told me, 'Look, Vappie, you've got to learn how we do things around here. This is not Loyola.' So, I figured, they don't need me here," Vappie laughs, adding, "I left again."

Around 1980 Vappie began performing with a lot of traditional jazz bands around New Orleans, playing with the likes of Teddy Riley, Lloyd Lambert, Placide Adams, and Danny Barker, among others. He remembers Barker fondly.

"We kind of played the same instruments. I first met him on a job for [drummer] Bob French, who called me to play bass. Danny was playing banjo. I remember we played 'I Can't Give You Anything but Love,' and I had a bass solo and played the melody. Danny was just looking at me, and on the break he says, 'You know, man, keep doing that. None of the bass players play the melody. That was great.'

"Over time, we worked together, and he pulled a fast one on me a couple of times." Vappie laughs heartily as he recalls one such instance, saying, "We were at Ascona, Switzerland, and we were talking—I used to like to listen to him talk, about anything—and we walked into this jewelry store. I don't know why. He tells the lady, 'My friend here is interested in this piece of jewelry,' and he pointed to something in there. And he looks at me, and he looks at the woman—I guess she was good-looking. She starts talking to me—and he was gone! The cat just disappeared! I say to myself, 'He puts me here and she thinks I'm interested in . . . and I wasn't interested in anything!'"

Vappie laughs again, saying, "That was pretty good. He was a nice cat. You know, I do a lot of that Creole music, and I always think of him when I do that."

After a few years of gigging around town, Vappie started his own trad band—Papa Don's New Orleans Jazz Band. The band was together about four years (1980–1984) and recorded a CD during the process.

When asked if the "Papa Don" nickname is borrowed from "Papa John" Joseph, he replied, "Actually, it is. I went to his funeral [in 1965]. I didn't know he was a musician since I was still a kid. When I started playing the New Orleans thing and pretty much focusing on the tourist trade, working on the boats downtown, I took the title 'Papa.' It's sort of an affectionate title. I don't use it anymore because that kind of thing has been overused to the point that people move to town and call themselves 'Cousin Joe' and 'Rowboat Jack,' and it's become sort of a joke. But I called my grandfather 'Papa.' There were people in the family you call 'Papa' because they were sort of the elders, so to speak. Yeah, that's where I got the name."

In 1988, Vappie began playing at Preservation Hall and was soon traveling with their bands, an experience that he calls "amazing."

"Until five or six years ago—now my beard is kind of gray—people would say, 'You're too young to be here,'" he smiles. He still plays at the Hall two nights a week.

By the early 1990s Vappie was traveling to New York to play banjo and guitar with the Lincoln Center Jazz Orchestra, and he was also featured with a band from New Orleans, with Wendell Brunious, Don Suhor, Steve Pistorius, Richard Moten, and Stanley Joseph, on the *Smithsonian's Folk Master* program on National Public Radio. He had begun to write transcriptions of some classic jazz tunes, which he admits may have been the "initial seed" leading to the creation of his Creole Jazz Serenaders.

But the real turning point seems to have been a Jelly Roll Morton concert back home with clarinetist Michael White. "It was at the Palm Court Café, maybe '94, but I think it was '95," he recalls. "After that concert, I remember speaking with [trumpeter] Jamil [Sharif] and saying, 'You know, man, I can do a better job than this.' I had actually written out 'Black Bottom Stomp' for myself, just to see. Because, after reading the one they had at Lincoln Center, I thought I could do a better job—and that's not putting down the guy who did the one at Lincoln Center, whoever it was. I just felt like, I'm actually coming out of this, I mean, I come from the same place that this music comes from."

Thus was born the Creole Jazz Serenaders in 1995. The band played its first New Orleans Jazz and Heritage Festival in the following year (and every year since) and recorded their first CD, the well-received *Creole Blues*, in 1997. Vappie, who plays banjo (both tenor and six-string), guitar, and does the vocals (in French on the Creole tunes), has written/transcribed the whole of the band's book.

Don Vappie was a featured banjo soloist at the JazzAscona Festival, Ascona, Switzerland, June 2007.

It should be noted that a significant member of the CJS team is Vappie's wife, Milly, whom he married in 1991. They met at a conference in New Orleans, where she was representing the South Carolina Humanities Council and he was part of the musical entertainment.

Educated as a historian, Milly also grew up with music. "I played piano and organ in high school, and my family sang," she says. "I also played baritone in the high school band, which was really unusual for a girl."

At this, Don, who also once played baritone horn, adds with a laugh, "We're such a good match because we have similar embouchures.

"Usually I end up doing what Milly tells me to do," he says. "She picks a lot of the music we play. In fact, she's written lyrics to some of them—original lyrics to old songs."

"There are just some songs that say, 'I need lyrics,'" Milly confirms. "One of them was a King Oliver song, 'I'm Going Away to Wear You Off My Mind.' It needs lyrics—and I can hear them. Another was the McKinney's Cotton Pickers' 'Will You, Won't You.' I wrote lyrics for that one. Every year I do this. I get the music together for Jazzfest because we do a new program every year. I listen to a lot of music and write down songs that I think are interesting. Last year, when Don was away, I had three or four pages of songs. Then I try to pin Don down, and we sit down and listen to them over a period of time. We have to narrow it down to songs he can rearrange for seven pieces. Some of them are great tunes, but you just can't do them, because they might have twelve pieces in the band.

"Last year at Jazzfest, we did some Ellington, Fletcher Henderson, Luis Russell, Fats Waller, McKinney's Cotton Pickers, and always Creole tunes. That's another thing. I'd like Don to try to write an original Creole jazz tune and work with Sybil Kein—she's our Creole scholar—to get it in the French patois."

In December 1997, the band recorded its second CD, the impressive *In Search of King Oliver*, for Robert Parker. It was produced by Will Allen. For acoustic reasons it was recorded in St. Joan of Arc Church in New Orleans (where, as it happened, Don Vappie had attended elementary school), and most of the musicians played historic instruments.

"I wrote all of that out," Vappie says. "To me, that's just classic stuff. It's like all orchestras aren't going to play Beethoven's *Fifth* the same way. We play this music, and I don't tell, like [clarinetist] Tom Fischer, 'Hey, Johnny Dodds had a breath here, he slurred that note that way.' In fact, in all of the Oliver stuff I didn't put any articulation in it at all. I should have," he says, smiling, "but I was in a hurry.

"I just said, 'Hey, here's the music, let's play it, interpret it.' Each guy is free to interpret what's there. It's like an actor reading a script—he's got to interpret it."

"You can't 're-create' what somebody else did," Milly adds. "The only way you're really going to hear it as close as you possibly can is if you write out what was played. We try to be honest about this. We're not going to say that we re-create it. We're saying that we're going to play for you what we hear they played and not just read the notes but put the spirit and energy into it."

In the spring of 1998, the CJS performed a series of concerts at Le Petit Théâtre du Vieux Carré in New Orleans, "Jelly Roll's Big New Band." The program included the music of Morton, his own arrangements, and some of his compositions never before recorded or performed in public —all of which are now in the Bill Russell Collection at the Historic New Orleans Collection (HNOC). These were memorable concerts, as evidenced by the subsequent attention given them by Howard Reich of the *Chicago Tribune.* Don Vappie was the program's music director, and Milly Vappie researched the music at the HNOC.

"Jelly Roll Morton is grossly misunderstood, in my opinion," she says firmly. "When we were talking about that concert, I can remember when I heard 'Ganjam' I actually got chilled. It brought tears to my eyes. After we played that song the first time at the read-through, you could hear a pin drop when the band finished. It was so quiet. Everybody who heard it— even the band—it was like they were in shock or in awe. It was really a special experience. To hear what Jelly did with that piece, to me, it was a really tragic moment to realize that, yes, this man had so much more to give."

"The small band stuff I think he recorded with one of his last General recordings," Don adds. "Our instructions were to play it as written, and that was Jelly's arrangements. It sounds very different from the recent CD of his last recording session—'My Home Is in a Southern Town,' 'Mama's Got a Baby,' 'Climax Rag.' You've got to wonder if Jelly would have them read what he wrote. They didn't even let him hire the band. His orchestration on 'Climax Rag' is four horns, but it sounds like ten the way he voiced it. I've listened to recordings of other bands doing 'Climax Rag' and it's thin, just doesn't have the meat of Jelly's. His voicings are just great. I love 'em.

"It's about the same thing that Bunk Johnson went through," Vappie goes on, characteristically. "They bring him up there, they get a couple of guys, they choose the musicians. Bunk says, 'Hey, I didn't like any of those guys.' But that seems to be a trend now. In New Orleans, there's at least two clubs that do it that way."

It is not easy to keep a good seven-piece band together these days, as Banu Gibson and any number of other New Orleans bandleaders will testify. The Serenaders have done some traveling, and they had a steady local gig at Storyville District until the club's budget was cut. At times, Vappie becomes very discouraged. But, he says, "Jamil [Sharif] is one of those guys who says, 'Man, don't stop.' He's my cheerleader.

"Is there a future for this music?" Vappie asks rhetorically.

"There's a future for it in my life because I'm going to continue doing this," he asserts firmly, answering his own question. "It hasn't been a big financial success. In fact, it costs money to do this, but it is so satisfying. We played a concert the other day [at the New Orleans Jazz National Historical Park's Visitors' Center], and it was so satisfying. I only wish I could finance enough time to get everybody to rehearse more. I cannot say enough about the members of the band—Stanley Joseph [drums], Larry Sieberth [piano], Tom Fischer [reeds], Jamil Sharif [trumpet], Alonzo Bowens [tenor saxophone], Jim Singleton [bass]—giving me their rehearsal time to do this stuff. When I do something at Lincoln Center, they can always put you up for a week and you rehearse every day for five days. That's nice. One very encouraging thing is that every year when we play at Jazzfest we have a huge number of young people in the tent. It's always packed, and there are always a lot of young people.

"You know," he says, "starting the CJS and doing that music—the band hasn't gotten that much work but a lot of critical acclaim—it just broke open these wide doors for me."

Indeed, Vappie seems to be very busy. Apart from his traveling abroad as a featured single, education seems to be a significant part of his personal mission. He was adjunct professor at the University of New Orleans for two years, teaching traditional and early jazz combo. He also does transcriptions for educational purposes.

"Lincoln Center has put a sort of education program together to provide things for schools," he notes. "Warner Brothers published four of them last year—'Black Bottom Stomp,' 'The Chant,' 'Grandpa's Spells,' and 'Potato Had Blues.' They were edited by Chuck Israels, so, if you find something wrong with them, speak to the editor," he says with a laugh.

The Lincoln Center Jazz Orchestra also played his transcriptions of Armstrong's "Twelfth Street Rag" in last December's [1999] concert.

"Don has been doing, for the last three years, the Hot Springs [Arkansas] Classical Music Festival," Milly adds. "They've been having him do on the last night a classic jazz jam for the students. They're classical music students in college or graduate school who come in on scholarships and work with mentors. Don takes some of his transcriptions for this jam, and these kids, of course, play real well. They read well, but you have to lead them. It's been very popular, and they want to do it every year. They've never played jazz, but they always enjoy it so much.

"We actually did a school program," she goes on. "It was a huge auditorium in Montgomery, Alabama, and all the kids were high school age. I remember thinking, 'How are they going to react to this?' I was standing at the back, and there were these young boys—probably freshmen or sophomores, at the 'cool' stage of their life—sitting at the back and clearly looking bored. And they're making the introductions, talking about traditional jazz, and I knew these guys were thinking straw hats and striped jackets. They were just so bored and so ready to be bored.

"Then all of a sudden the band walks out—a group of young guys in suits—and started to play 'The Chant.' And all of sudden they go, 'Wow!' and for the rest of the concert they were tuned in to the band. And when Don was going to show them how to do some second-line, the kids in the back went, 'I want to do it.' So, it was a complete turnaround from this indifference and I-am-ready-to-be-bored attitude. This is a direction that I would love to see us go—more educational programs, whether it's workshops, seminars, educational performances. When we started the Serenaders we even had in our little promo thing that, when we travel, we should like to be able to do an educational performance free."

Vappie has been a frequent guest performer at Lincoln Center under Wynton Marsalis, he has toured with Marsalis's band, and he has recorded with him (the 1999 Sony CD *Mr. Jelly Lord*). Marsalis is a controversial figure, partly because of his prominent role in Ken Burns's recent documentary film *JAZZ*, but Vappie clearly respects his musicianship.

"People are going to say I'm being nice because he's giving me work," he laughs. "I actually think he's very, very intelligent, and he's got a really special gift. It may not be as much a gift as it is something that he's really developed. He can articulate musically things he thinks almost immediately, and he's got a phenomenal ear. I think his mind works so fast. I think he's maturing, too. He'll see things in people now that maybe he didn't see before.

"For me, when I get around Wynton's band," he goes on, "it takes me a week or so. I can fit in right away, I know, but to hear those guys . . . you really got to open your ears. It's sort of like getting off the plane and renting a car in London. You're driving on the other side of the street, man. You're going in the same direction, but . . . you got to really open up and be aware of what's going on. Even though you know how to drive, things are coming at you from different directions." He chuckles, adding, "Then you might run into an American coming to you from the other side.

"Herlin [Riley] brings it all together. He's a phenomenal drummer. A nice cat, man. All of 'em, I enjoyed all of 'em. And [reedman] Victor [Goines], when Victor was going back and forth with Bob Wilber [in the December Lincoln Center concert]. I mean, Bob sounded great. Victor sounded great. Bob's right where Bechet maybe would have been. He's right there in that period. And Victor would be there, and then he would kind of take it somewhere and at times Bob was like, 'Hey maybe I'll go out there.' He'd check it out.

"Victor is such a fine clarinetist. He never got his due. I love his sound. I always get on him and say, 'Man, you had to quit the Serenaders to join Wynton's band. Man, that's bullshit.'" Vappie laughs heartily, going on, "The Lincoln Center band—Wynton's group, all those guys, the whole orchestra—they're really talented. It's a real inspiration for me whenever I work with them."

As for the future, Vappie pauses and reflects, "Sometimes you have to sit back and look at the situation. There was a time when my individuality wanted to express itself in a certain way, but at the same time I wanted to advance myself. I looked at it and said, 'What I need to do is try to blend into this world where I can get some financial independence to assert my individuality without being punished for it. In our world, in America, you've got to have some money and a certain amount of financial independence to try anything.

"Even with the Serenaders right now, there's a lot of stuff we could do. The band has really gone way past the *Creole Blues* CD as far as what we're doing. That's why we need to do a couple more, to show how diverse we've become. I'd like to keep the direction we're going in, but broaden it. That's one of my plans. I want to do some original music with the band and maybe even take some of the tunes that are there and rearrange them, open them up. One way or the other we're going to record at least two more CDs within the next six months, I would say." [A CJS CD, *Swing Out*, was released in 2005 along with the aforementioned *Banjo à La Creole*, which included CJS sidemen as well.]

To which Milly adds, "We'd love to. The band members are always coming up and saying, 'We need to do another CD. When are we going to do another CD? We have so much music that Don has written out and we have accumulated. We probably have eighty songs that he has transcribed.

"For us," she concludes, "classic jazz implies that what those musicians did should get the same kind of respect as the classical composers do."

4

TIM LAUGHLIN
Second Banana or Heir Apparent?

✳ ✳ ✳

Pete Fountain, a living legend in New Orleans, will be 80 years old in July 2010. While he continues to perform on a considerably reduced basis, his health has become increasingly fragile, especially since Hurricane Katrina destroyed his home and its most treasured contents and memorabilia in 2005.

Since that time, Tim Laughlin has appeared on stage with Pete regularly at his casino gigs in nearby Bay St. Louis, Mississippi, as well as at his annual performances with the Half-Fast Walking Club on Mardi Gras, at the French Quarter Festival, and at the New Orleans Jazz and Heritage Festival. It is pretty clear that Fountain considers Laughlin his heir apparent, and he says as much publicly.

Laughlin, now 48, has been an admirer and close friend of Fountain since he first met him at the age of 17. He even plays the gold-keyed Leblanc clarinet with which Pete recorded some forty albums and that Pete entrusted to him in 2009. (Fountain, a disciple of the great Irving Fazola, had also given Tim one of Faz's later clarinets.)

Laughlin has come a long way since that first meeting with Fountain. Indeed, his name may now be nearly as familiar to jazz fans in the city (and beyond) as that of the master himself. He records almost annually, and his recordings now regularly feature at least some of his original compositions. His very successful 2003 CD, The Isle of Orleans, consisted entirely of his own tunes, many of which are now played and/or recorded by other bands. His latest CD, A Royal Street Serenade (2009), includes an original called "For Pete's Sake," a tribute to guess who.

Laughlin has strayed a bit in a few of his recent recordings, yet his excellent playing remains in the tradition of New Orleanians Fazola and Fountain.

It is pretty clear that he continues to be fundamentally, as he would put it, "New Orleans" in his playing.

The following interview was conducted on October 23, 1996, and published in The Mississippi Rag *in March 1997.*

THIRTY-THREE-YEAR-OLD TIM LAUGHLIN IS A RISING young star among New Orleans clarinet players—a not insignificant distinction given the venerable tradition the city has had (and continues to have) in spawning outstanding practitioners of that particular jazz instrument. Known from his long association with the popular Dukes of Dixieland as well as for more than a dozen recordings (several as leader or featured artist) over the past decade, Laughlin has experienced rapid growth as an up-and-coming talent. So much so, indeed, that veteran clarinetist and recording partner Jack Maheu calls Laughlin's progress and potential "scary."

Laughlin recently severed his relationship with the Dukes, deciding to strike out on his own in search of his musical identity. Caught between national and European tours last October [1996], he took time from what is becoming a very busy schedule to explain his decision and discuss his plans for the future.

Tim Laughlin is a native New Orleanian. "I'm a Touro baby," he says, referring to his birthplace and the local hospital made famous by Muggsy Spanier in the late 1930s. And he's solidly in the great New Orleans clarinet tradition.

Taking up the instrument at the relatively tender age of nine, Tim took lessons from the late Bill Bourgeois, one-time Sharkey Bonano sideman. "He was a nice guy and a real wise man," Tim reminisces. "I never knew that he knew guys like Eddie Miller and [Irving] Fazola. He taught Faz how to play jazz. Faz was a reader, but he was a shy kid. He and Bill went down to a place—I forget the name—where there was a jam session, and they let younger musicians sit in with the older musicians. Bill and Faz would sit in, and Bill would play a jazz chorus during the

Tim Laughlin playing with Connie Jones's band at the French Quarter Festival, April 2009.

ensemble. Fazola, who had an incredible ear, could hear that and just mimic it back, and that's how he got started playing jazz.

"Eddie Miller also learned from Bill," he goes on, "because he [Bourgeois] took lessons from a man named Santo Giuffre who was the Albert system teacher back then. Bill took the lessons and would run to Eddie's house and show him what he learned. So Eddie picked it up that way. I don't know if Eddie played Albert, Faz did, but it sounded like it.

"Some people accuse me of playing an Albert system because Fazola played it. [Pete] Fountain doesn't, but he studied under Fazola and has Fazola's sound. I think the Albert system is fatter, to simply describe it.

It's wide open. A Boehm [system] is more legit, more centered. I didn't really notice until somebody told me that."

But it was Fountain who really turned Laughlin on to jazz. "Ma bought me a Pete Fountain album, the *Mardi Gras* album, for Christmas and I wore that thing out. It's still one of my favorite albums. Mardi Gras music that swings—you can't beat that."

Laughlin will never forget his first meeting with Fountain. "We were having dinner at the Hilton. It was my 17th birthday. I realized Pete was up there playing, so I snuck out when I got full enough, and all my family and friends didn't know where I went. I was like a phantom, there one minute and gone the next. I went up to see him and was talking to the doorman, and his son came out. I introduced myself and told him I was a clarinet player, and I asked if there was any chance I could meet him. He said, 'Yeah, I'll arrange it.' After the show ended, he came out with some autographed pictures and an album, and I thought that would be it. So I said, 'I guess he can't see me.' He said, 'No, no, no, just wait over there, he'll be right out.' So I waited for about twenty minutes—it seemed like an eternity. I ran back down and told my family I'm going to meet Pete Fountain, and ran back up. I waited a few more minutes. Then the door opened, and there was Pete in blue jeans and a T-shirt. I was expecting him to be in a suit since he just got done playing. He invited me in, and we talked for about fifteen minutes. He knew Bill [Bourgeois] and laid some reeds on me. He asked, 'Do you have this album?' He signed it and gave it to me. So, it was quite a night to remember. I met a legend on my 17th birthday. He says, 'Come by any time if you want to hear the music.' So I did.

"The next time I went, I said, 'Mr. Fountain said I could come in and hear him any time.' The doorman asked if I was 18, and I said no. He said, 'We can't let you in because you're too young.' He got me a chair so I could sit and listen, which is all I wanted to do anyway. They always had a chair waiting for me. It was like my seat, and I'd watch everybody go in. And they would bring me a beer. That was the weird part of it. I was too young to get in, but they would bring me a beer and I could nurse that for a couple hours. It was so New Orleans . . ." he laughs.

As time passed, the relationship between the two clarinetists developed into a good friendship. "One time," Laughlin remembers, "he took me down to the Christian Brothers convention, down at the ballroom, and the stage was set up, the band ready to play, and Pete comes on. He comes to me during one of his solos and says, 'Do you want to come up and sit on the stage?' I'm like, 'Jeez, this is great.' So, he helps me up—you know, he's a strong dude—and I sat next to Lloyd Ellis, his guitar player. For like a whole hour I was entranced. Then he came up to me during 'A Closer Walk'—I guess he was a little liquored up with wine—and says, 'Do you want to play a little bit?' Being 17, I chickened out and said something really stupid like, 'How does it go?' So, he played it for me, and I said, 'I guess I'd better sit this one out.' It scared the bejesus out of me. I'm kind of glad I passed.

"Ever since that we've had a friendship, about sixteen years, and I'm playing with him every Mardi Gras. I play second banana. That's my relationship with Pete. He's been kind of a 'cool uncle' to me. He's what we call a 'good cat.' I'm one of the few clarinet players he has this kind of relationship with. He's more or less kind of taken me under his wing. He's always kidding with me, saying, 'somebody's got to take my place.' I don't see anyone taking his place. I'm just honored to have known him this long. All kidding aside, it's pretty humbling."

Like other teenagers of his generation, Laughlin listened to rock music. "I loved the Beatles," he says, "but I didn't buy their albums. I bought only jazz, or asked for it. Jazz and big band, that was my focus. My friends never teased me. They always thought it was pretty cool."

Laughlin picked up the alto saxophone in seventh grade and played in the stage band in high school, but clarinet was always his primary instrument. "I really didn't listen to the earlier players like Johnny Dodds or George Lewis," he says, "because I was more of an admirer of the sweeter players or melodic players like Benny Goodman, Fountain, and Artie Shaw. That's where my ears went, as far as my playing and my style are concerned."

After high school, Laughlin tried college for a year and found it was not for him. He was working as a production assistant at WWL-TV, the local CBS affiliate, when he decided to join the musicians' union. "Murphy Campo [trumpeter and bandleader] told me to join the union because that's where all the good musicians were. I'd been getting all these rock-and-roll musicians to play 'Shine,' and they'd have to read it. It was really hard work for me. Joining the union networked me. It was the best thing I ever did. What I would do—if I ever got a gig when I was in the union—I would hire as many leaders as possible to be sidemen. They got to hear me play, and in turn they would hire me. If you hire sidemen, they're never going to hire you—so you hire leaders. Besides, leaders love being sidemen. That was my way of getting the word out.

"I got a call from trumpeter Tommy Yetta to do a tour in Ecuador. It paid little or nothing, but I wanted to go. It was one of the best tours I ever took—a free trip to the Galapagos Islands. I met two leaders there, [pianist] Steve Pistorius and [trombonist] Scotty Hill, who eventually booked me in their bands. That's how I met them. It takes time to meet everybody. When you're from New Orleans, it's kind of like a green light for a lot of guys. If you tell them that you're from New Orleans, they don't look at you with the fish eye if you want to play with them. They think you've done your homework. In my case, I knew a lot of tunes because I was listening from a very early age. I worked with Steve Pistorius for about three years, on and off, at Mahogany Hall [on Bourbon Street].

"It was there that I found out that the Dukes were reorganizing. I heard that they had hired [drummer] Richard Taylor to lead the band. I had known him for a while, so I knew where his head was at. I knew that he respected the music. You know, he heard the original band in Chicago [his hometown]. So, I told the manager that I would be interested in trying out. I played with them for a week, and they said, 'The job is yours if you want it.' That was about 1989 or 1990."

Laughlin enjoyed his tenure with the revitalized Dukes. "We started playing Dixieland tunes in the spirit of the old band," he says. "We didn't copy their arrangements, but we knew what the original Dukes were about. I listened to them as a kid. They were one of the best bands, as far as pure New Orleans Dixieland sound. Incredible players, like Jack Maheu, Frank and Freddie [Assunto] and Stanley Mendelson, who I talked to not long ago. It was fun. We thought of good arrangements without being campy, and we all had a part of them.

"Our first recording, *Hearing Is Believing,* sold really well. Then we did *A Salute to Jelly Roll Morton,* and that was on video. [Pianist] Tom McDermott did most of those arrangements. [Trumpeter] Kevin [Clark] did the arranging for *A Salute to Bob Crosby and the Bob Cats*, and for the Bix album [*Sound of Bix*], we all had a piece in that one.

"The band has been through a lot of changes. I took a couple of breaks to do some touring myself. Evan Christopher played for about three or four months—now he's with Jim Cullum—and Jeffrey Walker played for about a year. What finally happened is I missed a couple of tours because of my commitments here in town and my touring schedule. It killed me to do that, but I had to tell them I couldn't keep doing it. Needless to say, they weren't too happy about it. So, I made the decision to quit the band and devote all my time to my touring and my band. I wanted the band to find somebody who would stay steady with them, not come and go like I was doing. I don't like the idea of that. That's why I made the decision. If they want me to sub a night or two here, I'll be glad to do it. I'm going to keep my Dukes shirt. . . . I really love those guys. They're like brothers."

So, what's next? "A lot of my time will be spent on touring and writing," he says. "It'll be nice. The Dukes work seven nights a week, and sometimes it really gets to you after a while. It gets to where you don't have a life."

On the other hand, there is a steady paycheck. "Yes, but that's one of the reasons I'm leaving. I can afford to. I'm not married, no kids, low overhead. [Tim and his wife Juliet were married on December 7, 2008.] There's enough work in the convention business to keep me busy and have money in the pocket. And I play a brunch every Sunday at the Hilton. They've been really good to me. If I want to go on tour, I just make sure that I have it covered. This will be my tenth year there. They see it as a long-term commitment, and so do I. It's one thing I can count on as well as the tours."

Laughlin has been reflecting upon his musical identity of late, and he hopes that his new situation will help him establish his own sound.

"The last five years or so," he says, "I've listened to guys like Kenny Davern and Bob Wilber. I've learned a lot from the Soprano Summit albums. That's been like 'clinic' to me. It's opened my ears to a lot of things. [Cornetist and bandleader] Connie Jones has been a major influence on me. I've studied under Jack Maheu; he's taught me a helluva lot. I still go and hear Pete. I heard him just the other night, and he sounds great. He's like Wilber, never makes a mistake. He's always right there. He has that sound still—the sound is richer and richer.

"I've also listened to a lot of Benny Carter in the last year or two, and I've gotten into his playing. I really like his approach. One of my favorite albums is one of him and Oscar Peterson. My playing is basically New Orleans, but if I can incorporate this style of playing in it, eventually your personality comes out.

"I was always told that eventually your personality will come through the horn. It may be twenty days from now, maybe two years, maybe twenty years. But when you find it, you know it. Once you have it, you'll have it the rest of your life. Your style. I think I'm almost at that point. Not that I'm not going to be growing anymore. I'm going to be growing for the rest of my life. But stating my identifiable sound—hearing me play and saying that's Tim Laughlin—I'm almost there. I'm starting to get comfortable with hearing myself, to where I can say, 'Yeah, I really like that.'

"I just bought an Art Tatum and Buddy DeFranco album. That's really scary. I nicknamed it 'Chops Are Us.' Man, I didn't know that it was humanly possible, not that I wanted to make that part of my playing. But I'm saying, 'Wow, it's amazing what can be done with a pipe, a tube with holes in it. . . .'

"I got a chance to meet DeFranco in high school. I auditioned for the all-state band and I got lead chair. My reading was so-so, but I had a good lead-alto sound. So, they picked me. DeFranco was the clinician, and I knew who he was. It scared me to death. But he was really soft-spoken. He was like Clint Eastwood playing clarinet, a kind of 'high plains drifter' who hardly said two words and just scalded everyone. We did stuff he did from the Dorsey band and we did some kind of up-to-date tunes. He gave everybody a spotlight, and he took some spotlight himself. That really opened my ears to what was out there. But it still wasn't a school I wanted to go to.

"I stayed pretty much in a traditional bag, but now it's kind of different. I think it's time for myself, not for the musical community, to move on to other things. 'Muskrat Ramble' has been done to death. What else can you do? You can always still enjoy playing it. But I just want to record some of my own tunes, and I have ideas of songs out there—standards— that no one else has tried and I'm hoping to do that on my next project."

Laughlin has been very busy in the studio over the past five years. In addition to his recordings with the Dukes of Dixieland and other groups, he has done five CDs as leader or co-leader. The first, *New Orleans' Own* (1992), featured a seven-piece band, "kind of Bob Crosby–style," he says, "with some New Orleans standards. Jim Cullum did the liner notes and linked me with Faz and Eddie Miller." The next, *New Orleans Rhythm* (1993), featured Laughlin and the fine rhythm section that toured Germany with him in 1993. Another German tour (1994) inspired an excellent recording with fellow clarinetist Jack Maheu (*Swing That Music*, 1995, on Jazzology and issued in Germany on the Hey Now label), about which Laughlin says, "I really wasn't sure how this one would turn out, but I was really happy with everything we worked out in the studio. And that's been well received too. We still play our arrangements when I sit in with Jack at Fritzel's."

Then came another collaborative effort with multi-reedman Tom Fischer for still another trip to Germany (*New Orleans Swing*, 1995).

"The reason I called it *New Orleans Swing* is because we are both swing players and swing lovers. This was fun. I think we stretched out a bit more on this. It wasn't as tight-knit as the Jack Maheu album. One of the reasons we went to Germany was to showcase a different band each time. One of them was with Maheu—two clarinets, the master and the student. Tom Fischer played soprano saxophone, alto, and clarinet so that gave another dimension to it. In fact, Tom and I will be doing another one for a tour of Germany coming up in March [1997]. We'll be doing that next week, on October 28."

But the most ambitious undertaking so far is his most recent recording, *Blue Orleans*, on the (renovated) Good Time Jazz label (1996). "This is one that I'd had in mind for some time," says Laughlin. "I hired a total of seventeen musicians to play a role in the album which I nicknamed 'Blood 'n Guts.' I've always liked the two-trombone sound. Two of the tunes are originals, one is the first tune I wrote, 'Blue Orleans,' and the other is the second, 'King of the Mardi Gras.' I never really thought of myself as a composer, but I did it anyway—and lo and behold. . . ."

And his upcoming album? "I want to get a modern rhythm section," he says. "This won't be a bebop album. It will be me with a little different rhythm section, with a certain edge to it. I haven't quite picked who

I'll have, but I have an idea. There are some great players here in New Orleans, guys who I can get along with. There is a difference between a great player and a great player who you care to work with in the studio. So, I have to be careful about that. [The group will be] similar to what the Oscar Peterson–Benny Carter thing was. I'm not going to have it so tight, where it's like a riff album. I want to avoid that. I just want to play the tunes with great players because I think that will make my playing come out at its best. For the most part I just want it to be totally free. Whenever I play with a modern group or a modern piano player, I have different ideas—totally—than I would with a trad group. Ideas open up." [The CD that Laughlin is probably referring to here did not appear until 2001. It is called *Straight Ahead* and features pianist Peter Martin with John Eubanks on guitar and the late Bunchy Johnson on drums.]

While once hesitant to think of himself as a composer, Laughlin is getting into writing and seems to enjoy it. "Yeah," he affirms, "somebody said 'amateurs borrow, professionals steal.' Nothing is original anymore. You do get a melodic sense after a while, how you think. Right now I'm trying to create a writing style where there is a consistency in all of my writing. It's like playing. You want people to recognize your sound, your style. You get into a groove, and your personality comes out in the music. In my writing I can hear small elements of other tunes I've played, but I put my own spin on it. Even though the chords may be similar, the melody is totally original. That's what's fun to do. So I've got about six tunes written so far and am working on a number of others for my next project.

"I want to write a regular 12-bar blues to have that in there, but I've some ballads, too. One of them—I hesitate to mention the name because it's always confused with Richard Rodgers's 'My Romance'—I call 'Our Romance.' And there's another ballad I wrote, called 'All I Ask of You.'

"I've had people tell me that every time they listen to 'Blue Orleans' they hear something new. That's what I want, to challenge the listener to new harmonies or rhythms. I want to do a funky little New Orleans tune like 'When My Dreamboat Comes Home.' That probably won't be it, but it will have a nice little funky groove to it. I want people to know that I'm from New Orleans, without sounding trad. For the most part, my objective is to identify my sound. I want the public to like it for what it is and want more of it. This is my next step in what I'm doing.

"It's hard to say where you're going. I have no agenda because this is jazz. I may grow in another different direction in a couple years. I'd like to become one of the guys to hear when people come to New Orleans.

"I just started lyrics for my tunes. It's a whole other thought process. I thought that part of my brain didn't work, but I put words to both 'Blue Orleans' and 'King of the Mardi Gras"—they're pretty funny. It's about experience. That's the good thing about traveling, you experience the world. And the more you experience the world, the easier it is to write, I think. You can't stay in New Orleans and write."

In addition to his writing, recording, and regular Hilton gig in New Orleans, Laughlin's schedule includes a good bit of travel.

"I'm going to be doing a lot of touring this year in Europe and the States," he says. "I'm doing the Sun Valley Festival in October with the Blue Orleans band, nine pieces. It's hard to tour with nine pieces. I may be opening for Fats Domino with that band in March at the Hilton.

"With this new album idea I have, I'd like to get on more jazz stations, on more formats, and get more air play. That is a band I can tour with. I would like to tour, do more festivals, and maybe get on an all-star circuit with the festivals.

"When I went to Sacramento, I noticed that they had three all-star bands: New York, L.A., and the Midwest, but no New Orleans. I find that odd since there are so many great musicians in New Orleans. There really wasn't much difference, stylistically, between the three bands. You could hear a little bit between the Midwest and New York, but they were all wonderful. I listened to them as much as possible because those were the top cats. But I think there should be a New Orleans all-star band, and it doesn't have to be trad either. Incidentally, I will be back at the Sacramento Jazz Festival with [drummer] Hal Smith and his California Swing Cats at the end of May. We're going to do a new album, too.

"I'd like to play more of the guest artist role, like I do in England. In December I'll be making my third trip over there. I'll stay about three weeks. It's nice because I don't have to play trad. I can play just what I play, and they feature me. They promote it as a guest artist from New Orleans, a young clarinet player. The Gambit Jazzmen, Pete Lay's band— they're a good bunch of guys. I'm also doing a gig with Neville Dickie, a pianist over there. He's comparable to Butch Thompson over here, really one of the finer players. I'd like to do more of that, but I think the more I play and the more people hear me . . . who knows where it will take me? I'm just having a great time doing it."

Laughlin, who stands well under six feet tall, concludes in his characteristically cheerful and impish way: "I can't believe I do this for a living. I always wanted to. It was either play professional basketball or this. . . ."

5

IRVIN MAYFIELD
Boy Wonder

※ ※ ※

Sometimes people live long enough to fulfill the promise of their youth, and sometimes they don't. Some individuals eventually achieve their youthful dreams of success, but many certainly do not. Such is life.

The following conversation, recorded on March 23, 1996, demonstrates that trumpeter, bandleader, composer, educator, entrepreneur, and civic leader Irvin Mayfield, then just 18, had a game plan for his life that is now coming to fruition. In fact, one could arguably make the case that, at the relatively tender age of 33, he has already achieved his boyhood goals. It is likely, however, that Mayfield himself would strongly disagree. For him, there is much more to be done.

This interview was conducted in the upstairs bedroom of his childhood home on—significantly—Music Street in the Gentilly neighborhood of New Orleans, at the very beginning of his professional musical career and well before he was able to support himself by his music. Yet it reveals most of the personal traits that still characterize him today: intelligence, impatient ambition, perfectionism, leadership skills, sense of humor, and—not least—a certain cockiness and sometimes controversial behavior. It also shows his loyalty and devotion to his friends, family, mentors, and hometown—not to mention his father specifically, a onetime army drill sergeant who lost his life in the flooding of Hurricane Katrina.

Mayfield's accomplishments to date are little short of overwhelming. He first came to my attention as a precocious teenage performer with the traditional Algiers Brass Band. But he ultimately went on to found the award-winning combo Los Hombres Calientes and the 2010 Grammy-winning New Orleans Jazz Orchestra, as well as leading his own quintet. His commissioned compositions include The Half-Past Autumn Suite, Strange Fruit, All the

Saints, The Art of Passion *(performed with the distinguished Minnesota Orchestra, for which he was recently appointed artistic director for jazz), and,* most recently, *The Elysian Fields Jazz Suite, a tribute to the victims of Katrina, including his own father.*

Mayfield's devotion to his hometown is reflected by his membership on numerous boards in the city, including serving as chairman of the board of the New Orleans Public Library. In 2003 Mayfield was appointed to the post of cultural ambassador for the city of New Orleans and the state of Louisiana. And, as of this writing, he announced that he would not run for mayor in the 2010 elections despite considerable public support for his candidacy. Perhaps ironically for one who left college after three semesters at the University of New Orleans, he was recently appointed professor and artistic director of New Orleans jazz at UNO.

In the spring of 2009, he opened a posh new jazz club in the Royal Sonesta Hotel in the French Quarter, Irvin Mayfield's Playhouse. There, he proudly announces, "jazz is back on Bourbon Street."

In late March 2010, President Barack Obama appointed Mayfield to the National Council on the Arts, the advisory body to the National Endowment of the Arts. His list of accomplishments goes on and on.

But now to the interview that took place more than a decade ago. Mayfield's remarks were liberally sprinkled with wry smiles and outright guffaws —as well as numerous telephone interruptions—that could not be represented in this rigorously truncated transcription.

TJ: Let's begin at the beginning. Where and when were you born?

IM: I'm a New Orleanian to my heart. I was born December 23, 1977, two days before Christmas, which deprives me of Christmas presents. I have four brothers, and I'm the youngest. The brother who is one year older than me plays tenor sax. He's autistic. We both started off in the Algiers Brass Band when we were nine. He played trumpet at the time. We emulated Frank Cooper and Ruddley Thibodaux.

TJ: So do you come from a musical family?

Irvin Mayfield leads the New Orleans Jazz Orchestra at the New Orleans Jazz and Heritage Festival, April 2005.

IM: I'd say more of an artistic family. Each one of my brothers has some type of art—either they can draw or they can play an instrument. My oldest brother can play, like, every instrument. My dad played trumpet. The other day [bassist] Walter Payton was telling me how my dad used to stand out front of the band when he was at Cohen High School and play these solos. They say he had real strong chops. Maybe there's some genetics there.

TJ: Your musical education. You were already playing at nine. When did you first pick up a trumpet, and was it your first instrument?

IM: Yes, trumpet was my first instrument. I wanted to play the trumpet because I had a friend who I emulated. He could do everything so well. He was smart. I guess he was cute. All the girls liked him. A straight-A student. He started playing the trumpet, and I came home and told my dad, "I want to play the thing with the buttons, like Jeffrey plays." His name was Jeffrey Fazand. My dad said, "If I buy you this horn, you are not going to stop playing." I was about nine then, so not long after that I started playing with the Algiers Brass Band—maybe 10 or 11. I picked up the trumpet and, after two weeks, it wasn't as much fun. My dad said, "Oh no, you play." Man, I hated that. Oooh, I hated practicing.

TJ: Did you take lessons in school?

IM: I was in the school band, and, if you've ever been in the school band, it was pretty random. . . . I just enjoyed playing with Jeffrey, and my brother started playing a year after me. He started surpassing me, man. We were known as the Mayfield Brothers and were on this church circuit around New Orleans, wearing these white suits. We played all over: City Hall, many churches, Baptist, Catholic. . . .

TJ: This must have been good experience.

IM: I didn't have any stage fright. We practiced twelve hours. My dad would wake us up at 7 o'clock. I had extreme confidence. The experience was pretty interesting.

TJ: Then you went on to NOCCA [New Orleans Center for the Creative Arts]?

IM: Oh yeah . . . God . . . Playing with Algiers, I learned a lot of traditional stuff and learned a lot of things from ear. But getting into NOCCA was a cultural shock. Man, I can't describe to you the effect of going to NOCCA.

TJ: How old were you when you started there?

IM: Fourteen. I was in ninth grade. It's actually supposed to be a three-year program, but they let me in in ninth. I knew Jason Marsalis from nursery school. When I got to NOCCA, these cats were serious! These cats were diligent! Kenyatta Beazley—he's in New York now—graduated from NOCCA. He's my rival. He's one year older than me, and he lets me know every time he picks up that trumpet. Now I was in the first level. There are three levels at NOCCA. There is the extremely high level. Nicholas [Payton] was in third level, and Adonis Rose was his drummer. There were some really heavy hitters, man. I'm in level one with Jason Marsalis. I was used to dealing with basic forms of music, which traditional is. It's a basic form of jazz. I thought I was great, man, because I was the youngest guy playing all this traditional stuff. My ego was big, man. But it was a serious culture shock, man. Clyde Kerr totally changed my life. I got all my piano skills from Clyde Kerr. He could play the piano just as well as he could play the trumpet. I had never heard the piano played like that. [Clyde Kerr passed away in August 2010 at the age of 67.] And then I had to learn theory! And I had to learn about Brahms and Bach and Beethoven and Chopin and Tchaikovsky and Mahler and Stravinsky and . . . I made a 30 on my first test. That was a rough trial.

TJ: What does it feel like to be part of the NOCCA tradition that produced the likes of the Marsalises, the Jordans, Terence Blanchard, and Nicholas Payton?

IM: Man, it's rough. You have to be really serious. You can't do it for the money, you can't do it for the fame. You'd better be in it for the music. You feel good because you're a part of it, but then it's, like, I better contribute something to this music or . . .

TJ: Do you feel pressure?

IM: Do I feel pressure? God . . . If I can get Jason to respect what I'm doing, I feel great. These people are not just educated musically. If you talk to Nicholas, he's an internationally educated person. I have so much to learn. I could talk all day about NOCCA. It's an inspiration. I don't want to just die and leave, some guy who was here. I want to contribute something to the music, and that's really hard. That's why I'm always in these controversies. If you get to know what people think about me in the brass band area, I'm controversial, man. I'm not going to condone anything that people allow themselves to be complacent. I'm not like that. You look at these brass bands—I'm talking about all these [new] brass bands . . .

TJ: You don't think they're working hard enough at their craft?

IM: Working hard enough? They haven't started working yet! You pick up an instrument, you get a gig, you go to Europe—you know, this is life. . . . You're not going to tell me that somebody who picks up a trumpet in one year can learn a certain scale and go out there and try to improvise and people call him a musician. Those people are not musicians. Nicholas is a musician. Ellis [Marsalis] is a musician. Adonis Rose is a musician. I'm not tolerating that, man. People are still telling me to get something to fall back on. I'm not accepting it, man. I'm going to do this. I'm not making my "debut" at Snug Harbor [as advertised]. I've been playing at Donna's for almost a year now.

You know, the music and the industry are two completely different things. I think I'm breaking into this industry because I have an understanding of that. Just because Nicholas can play, that doesn't mean that he is making nearly what Wynton Marsalis is making—that has nothing to do with that. That's something I learned at NOCCA from Clyde Kerr.

I was at a wedding, and someone asked Wynton, "How can I break into the music business?" Wynton says, "Break into a practice room." People need to work harder at what they do. Why would you ask me to come into a club and play, you know, and not be serious? That's one aspect of it.

When I went to NOCCA there were no bells in the classroom. You did not have to go to class . . . because learning did not start in that classroom and it did not end in that classroom. And practicing hasn't ended yet, now. I'm practicing mentally all the time, thinking three or four things at one time. That's the thing about NOCCA, man. It's rough, but you begin to love it because you realize what it is.

TJ: After NOCCA you had a chance to go to Juilliard or was it The New School?

IM: It was the New School, and then I was going to transfer to Juilliard. Why do something just because it's good to do? Man, have you seen the ads that Calvin Klein has put out lately? And people buy that it's in . . . It's like going to New York—I wasn't ready for that. I mean Nicholas was ready for that at a certain age, and he went for it and did it. Nicholas is living here too. Terence is living here . . . and Donald Harrison is here. . . .

TJ: Where is Marlon Jordan these days?

IM: Marlon lives down the street, about a block down on Music Street. He's teaching school right now. He's had a few problems because he got a lot of press early. You know what that can do if you're not focused on what you want to do. Wynton can handle that. He's one of those types of people. But Marlon got into a lot of financial problems, but he's back home now. Hopefully, I'm going to start studying some things on trumpet with him.

TJ: Is he 30 yet?

IM: No, not Marlon. Terence is actually a few years younger than Wynton.

TJ: So you decided—with some pressure from Mr. Marsalis—to stay home?

IM: There wasn't even pressure, man. We were at the Big Easy awards, and Jason was up for up-and-coming emerging artist, right? My mother and him are good friends. Jason's mother and my mother have a kinship and they know each other and they go way back. My mother was talking to Ellis about me going off to New York, and he said, "I know, but you got to let them do that." Then he told me, "Hey, man, maybe you might want to consider staying down here and getting some stuff together at UNO. You can decide on what you want to do rather than just going up to New York and doing what everyone else is doing." That's all I would have done. I don't know what my peers are doing in New York now. I have a gig. I have a chance to work with [pianist] Dwight Fitch, I get to play with Adonis Rose, I mean . . . Can you imagine what it's like to stand in front of this rhythm section? Roland Guerin, Germaine Bazzle, and Kermit Ruffins and Corey Henry are coming in. And I get paid for this, man! I'd have done it for free, seriously! Now I had a chance to do this down here. If I had been in New York, I would have had to stand in a big long line at one of these clubs and play—you know, take a solo, and no one is listening and no one cares. Down here I have a chance. I'm going to start doing some things with [pianist] Henry Butler when he comes down. I can't wait, man. Henry Butler . . . Davell Crawford, me and him went to school together. He went to NOCCA. You can't experience this kind of stuff anywhere else. I just think, maybe more cats will stay home and be *serious*.

TJ: Maybe more are coming home. . . .

IM: Yeah. New Orleans is kind of on a [run.] I'm not sure about the governor right now, but the mayor has been doing a lot of things. A lot of things are happening with the arts. Senator Bagneris—he's my girlfriend's uncle—is always up for keeping things. . . . Things are getting better in New Orleans. I have time anyway. As long as I get to play and as long as I'm developing, it doesn't matter where you are. New Orleans has a lot of recognition now. You know, I've been to Europe several times. New Orleans music . . . So that must say something if everybody else is recognizing this music. Maybe we need to start paying a little bit more attention to New Orleans and stop paying attention to everyone else.

TJ: Who are your musical idols? You've got a lot of CDs over there, I see. When did you start listening seriously, outside of pop music?

IM: [*long pause*] I wouldn't know where to start, man. When I started, I was in ninth grade. I was at NOCCA. Music is heard and not seen. The more music you hear, the better off you are. You can't contribute anything to this language unless you know the language immensely—and that's the thing about Jason. Jason has . . . [*looks at his CD cabinet*], well, multiply that by thirty! You begin to understand what he has at home that he can reach and grab—not to talk about the things he has given away. Jason has given me a pile of CDs. It's so funny, 'cause it's our whole world. I check out Miles [Davis]. I'm still trying to get into Miles. . . . Coltrane, every CD he has created. . . .

TJ: You're not just listening to trumpet players?

IM: Oh, man, no. Jazz is not just about trumpet players. Music is not just about trumpet players. I mean, Jelly Roll Morton . . . Louis Armstrong, my guy . . .

TJ: It's nice to hear your awareness of your musical roots. Nicholas and Wynton are aware of that. How about Terence Blanchard?

IM: Yes, Terence was here a year ago. I was in the studio with the Olympia Brass Band with [trumpeter] Milton Batiste, and Terence and [saxophonist] Donald Harrison were playing with the brass band. Terence marched in the band at St. Aug [St. Augustine High School] and at Kennedy [Kennedy High School]. He had that marching band aspect . . . and Nicholas, too.

TJ: How important are the roots, like Oliver and Armstrong?

IM: Man, if you haven't checked out Pops, you are nothing! And then there are cats before Pops. Wynton can name them back to King Oliver, back to Buddy Bolden. . . . I'm still learning Louis. Man, [Nicholas] Payton can give you that excitement. Payton can give you that straight Louis Armstrong excitement.

There are other composers who didn't do jazz that are as bad, such as Ravel and Debussy. Jason did an interpretation of *The Rite of Spring* by Stravinsky on drums! Man, that was the most interesting thing I have ever heard! Ever heard of this guy John Cage? Music is music, man. Why limit yourself?

TJ: So do you think someday you will record something "classical"?

IM: I hope so. I certainly hope so. I am working on something actually on Monday with a singer—me and her were scholarship winners. Her name is Jennifer Wise. She graduated from NOCCA. She's at UNO now. We are going to do a duet. I need to get a piccolo trumpet because I definitely want to do some Baroque stuff. You know, Wynton does that wonderfully, and I think Payton could do it if he wanted to. I think Payton is just doing so much now. I really want to get into a lot of that stuff, but I still have a lot to learn about it. I studied with Ron Benko, the principal trumpet player for the Louisiana Philharmonic.

TJ: What are your stylistic preferences?

IM: Playing stuff I can't do. If I can't do it, I like it. I really have no interest in doing anything I can do. [There are] some cats who say, "I don't know what it is—these beboppers . . . ," which is really an ignorant statement because we don't just play bebop because when you're talking about bebop you're talking about one period. There's hard bop. When you get into naming things, what is jazz kind of thing . . . Jazz is just the blues.

There are marketing things now, which I like because actually I am a very corporate person. You know, I have a production company. That's something I like to do, man. I'm not one of these bitter musicians talking about "the industry." Hopefully, one day I can be in the industry. I love the industry.

But nothing is what it seems. These brass bands . . . I talk to the leader of the Algiers Brass Band about this all the time, but I hear these little bands like—not the Little Rascals because they have pretty much a traditional repertoire, they can go way back. . . . There's a little guy in the Sixth Ward right now, [trombonist] Corey Henry's little brother. We call him "Teedy Man." Man, this kid can play some snares! Wynton said to him, "Learn your instrument, son." Nicholas was raised up there in that environment. Nicholas came from the Tremé area. The first time Mr. Kerr heard Nicholas, he was playing trombone in a brass band. It's about growing. I'd love to go play with [avant-garde saxophonist] Kidd Jordan and be spontaneous. Let's not have a form. Let's just play and create as we go along. That's good, too. But then I like to play with Ellis who says, "Well, let's deal with the forms and learn these forms and try to understand what these musicians did so you can create something." And I like playing with Mr. Kerr who says, "Let's be spontaneous and let's deal with the forms also." Then I like to deal with Mr. Benko who says, "Learn your instrument and deal with technique."

No one wants to do business down here. Because everybody is so slow. You must have noticed this.

TJ: But the rat race up north is a drag, too.

IM: Yeah, it's a drag, but there's room for improvement. If everybody's trying to improve, everything's fine with me. When it's the same way. You play with these bands out here that just give these 1-2-3 notes—they only play in two keys, and all the songs sound alike. What's new about that?

TJ: Where can we hear you now, besides Snug Harbor on Thursday?

IM: Well, I'm at Donna's every Friday. I'll be at the Little People's Place on Barracks, a nice little club.

TJ: Let's finish up by talking about the future. You're up for a Big Easy Award?

IM: Emerging artist, yeah. If you take that for what it is . . . I appreciate it, but it's funny. I do appreciate things. I would be seriously upset if I didn't see my name in the paper. When you get your name in the paper and get to say all these things, you may as well say them. When you think about music as making a living, it's hard for you to imagine that you can make a living at something you enjoy doing. It's like, I'm aiming for this thing, but I don't know what it is. When I think of the Big Easy Award, it's basically popular. It's not really about who's the best. It's about who's the most popular. That's why Kermit Ruffins is going to win all the awards he's nominated for—which he should—because he's the most popular. Nicholas might not win because he's not that popular. I think I got more press than Nicholas. It's scary. Sometimes you say, "Well, what if I did just traditional music?" I could probably mainstream with that. I know I could go to Europe several times. Let's say, if I did funk, if I started singing . . . I got in an argument with a good friend of mine the other day about that. He says, "The only reason you practice so hard is to impress Wynton. Wynton comes down here and he says, 'y'all okay,' he's not giving you any gigs." I said, "That's the whole problem! We don't want to improve. We're about making a dollar without understanding we can make the dollar *and* improve and be happy. The best feeling to me, man, is to know I can play. And the worst is when you know that somebody is playing better than you are and knowing that you should be playing much better. It's inside, man. You know, it's nice to be up for the Big Easy Awards because hopefully it can help to get what I want to do. Hopefully I can win. Okay, I want to win! Jason won last year. I'm going to win, hopefully. [And he did win, of course.]

TJ: Wynton Marsalis seems to be one of your role models.

IM: Oh yeah, Wynton. Just as far as trumpet players, it would be Wynton, Terence, Nicholas.

TJ: How about adult men, maybe not even musicians?

IM: That's a good question, actually. Yes, my dad . . . He hasn't said, "OK, you've done it." I can't exactly support myself just yet. I guess you don't really feel like you're doing everything until you can say,

"This is what I want to do." I don't want to depend on anybody. As long as I'm in this house, I don't get to feel like I'm god or anything yet. Until Ellis says, "Hey, you sound great." But I don't think Ellis will ever say that. His son is Wynton Marsalis. He doesn't tell Wynton he sounds great! We were asking him the other day about what did he think about Wynton and how does it feel to be playing with him. He told us something like, "He's a good musician. I like playing with him."

TJ: So New Orleans will always be home?

IM: Yeah, well . . . I'm kind of hoping that I can maybe have three homes. Maybe a home in Europe, a home in New York, and a home in New Orleans.

TJ: You want to see the world?

IM: Yeah, I don't want to be trapped in a small space. Man, it does something to your mind when you think like that. One thing I'm trying to do right now is get a lot of young cats . . . I'm taking a lot of my friends to Greece. I was in Switzerland and I met these cats from Italy and . . . If you can swing, you can swing.

TJ: How did you get this Greek connection?

IM: It actually came when I went in the studio with Davell [Crawford]. The guy, Gary Edwards—The Sound of New Orleans [label]—has a studio and produces and makes CDs for a lot of New Orleans groups. He needed a band for Greece, and I was always coming into the studio when I was doing this Coolbone CD. I made the whole CD happen. That's me. So I knew this was a guy I wanted to get to know. I had already been to Switzerland, the Ascona festival. He knew I could generate things in Europe, so he gave us this trip to Greece.

TJ: When was that?

IM: That was last summer. We went for the Silk Cut Brass Band—that's our T-shirts right there. . . . I think this will be my last brass band trip this year. I really want to start doing what I want to do. I'm hoping the Silk Cut people will give me a chance and will sponsor me to do a concert there. Yeah, that's what I want to do. To get a lot of young cats . . . I want to try to take these New Orleans cats [with me]. I think now that jazz is bursting at the seams. Greece was another world. I loved it, man. That's why I'm not hesitant to go back.

We haven't discussed this yet, but this is a project we want to start working on: to get these cats together in the studio—all the cats who can play their instruments correctly and are making marks on the music of New Orleans and on the world, like Nicholas, Adonis, and hopefully [guitarist] Mark Whitfield—so we can do the stuff correctly. That's what Nicholas has done. He has done stuff correctly. That's one thing I hope to do. I'm going to get some young cats in the studio. My band, we're going to start trying to do the stuff right.

TJ: So what kinds of things would you be playing?

IM: I would lay down some traditional stuff. We'll get some of the cats from the Algiers Brass Band in there, get some from Tremé [Brass Band], you know, involve everybody. This cat Chad Gales who's playing with me right now is playing alto. He's 19. He's basically the only saxophone player I know in New Orleans right now that is willing to deal with this that is young. He's serious. There's only one trombone player that I know that is serious about playing the trombone. His name is Stephen Walker. He's 17. I'm really just trying to understand why my peers aren't serious about it. They're not serious about it because they can't do it.

TJ: You've got to have some talent, too.

IM: They just don't want to work. Since they're not working already, they feel that we are trying to leave them out. I'm not leaving anybody out. I'm just saying, "OK, get serious." I like to get things moving and everything working together. I don't like to lay back and let other people do it.

6

LUCIEN BARBARIN, LEROY JONES, HERLIN RILEY, GREGG STAFFORD, JOE TORREGANO, AND DR. MICHAEL WHITE

Danny's Boys Grow Up

✽ ✽ ✽

Born and raised in New Orleans, guitarist-banjoist-vocalist-author Danny Barker (1909–1994) not only distinguished himself in national and international jazz circles but has become a legend in his hometown. He left New Orleans for a jazz career in New York in 1930, but like so many local musicians, he and his wife of more than sixty years, singer Blue Lu Barker, returned thirty-five years later. He remained in the Crescent City until his death, which was commemorated by one of the city's largest jazz funerals ever.

Upon his return to New Orleans, Barker became deeply concerned by the paucity of youngsters interested in jazz. He vowed to rectify that situation. It chanced that he was invited by the Reverend Andrew Darby of Fairview Baptist Church (in the city's Seventh Ward) to form a band of neighborhood youth. Joined by a relative, Charles Barbarin Sr., he gathered a group of kids ranging in age from nine to 13 in 1970 and began teaching them New Orleans traditions, especially in music.

The result was the Fairview Baptist Church Christian Band. It made its public debut at the New Orleans Jazz and Heritage Festival in April 1971. Over the years, the band included scores of youngsters, several of whom became professional musicians. The following interviews highlight a half dozen of them who have made a name for themselves in the jazz world.

Don Marquis and I conducted the interviews in the summer and autumn of 2004. Since the interviewees were speaking about their experiences after an interval of some three decades or more, it is reasonable to expect discrepancies about dates and other details—as well as some repetition—from one to the other. We also spoke briefly to each individual in February 2006 about his Hurricane Katrina experiences. The whole was then published in two parts in the May and June 2006 issues of The Mississippi Rag. *Those articles have been modified and abridged considerably for this publication.*

LUCIEN BARBARIN

"I was born here in New Orleans at Charity Hospital like a lot of us. They say if you are born in Charity you are a real New Orleanian. It was July 17, 1956. My parents were Charles and Elizabeth Barbarin. My great-grandfather was Isidore Barbarin.

"When I first started back in 1964 or '65, I can recall my uncle Paul. My father used to bring me and my brother Charles by his house a lot. He'd show us his drums and would show us a little bit of stuff on the drums. But you gotta remember I was pretty young back then. I wanted to be just like him. Then Paul decided he wanted to get us some drums, and he made a small bass drum for my brother—he wasn't big enough to carry a big bass drum—and I had a snare drum. I used my belt to strap it around my waist. I was so little I had to tie the snare drum strap around my waist rather than the shoulder. About a year or two later Paul had us out performing with the Onward Brass Band. In '66 I can remember a parade with Paul and my brother on the streets in the French Quarter. I'll never forget that. Charles is a year and a half older than I am.

"Then, after Paul died in 1969, Danny Barker took over me and my brother. That's when we got the Fairview band started. I can remember, when it first started, my cousin Danny brought me over by the Mims' house, Ernie Cagnolatti's house. I remember sitting over there. We didn't know any songs or anything. I think that's when I first met Leroy [Jones] too. The Cagnolattis lived in the neighborhood around the St. Bernard Project. I don't know what you call that area back then. The Seventh Ward? And you gotta remember that Leroy lived around the block from the Cagnolattis. I'm assuming it was in '69. I was 13 and playing snare drum. That was my first instrument.

"I started playing the baritone [horn] in grade school. When we first started with the Fairview, it was me, my brother, and Leroy Jones that I can recall. There was some other kids that I can't remember exactly. We didn't know too many songs, so Danny got with us and he showed us 'A Closer Walk,' 'Bye and Bye,' a lot of church hymns, not too many traditional jazz songs. I guess it was the next year that he decided to get more guys together. That must have been back in '70.

"It was just me and my brother at first. Danny knew we had the potential to play because it was in us. There was no church involvement at that time. It was just a group of little guys that Danny put together. Then we wound up having rehearsals in Leroy's garage. I don't know if the church was involved, maybe the next year. We rehearsed for a while, then we went to Reverend Darby's church. We played a lot of different Baptist churches, when this was still the Fairview band—a lot of Baptist churches. I wasn't Baptist then. I was Catholic. I was exposed to something I had never witnessed before.

"My father [Charles Sr.] was always there with us. He and Danny brought in another guy, Joe Gordon, who was a clarinet player. He showed us some songs. We learned a lot of songs from Joe and my father.

"We played all the Baptist churches for about a year, all parades. We used to do a parade every Easter with the Fairview—in the St. Bernard Project—and I looked forward to doing that every year. It was exciting, just to be in the band. As a young kid, you were having a ball, a lot of energy, wanting to play all the time. After about a year I started playing the trombone. I put the snare drum down. I think I just took a liking to the trombone. I was about 15 and went to Clark Senior High School.

"I remember we played at the Kennedy Center [in Washington, D.C.]. That was the first time we ever traveled. The first time I was even on an airplane. And it was a ball, I tell you. I can't recall what the function was. I think the Olympia Brass Band was there also. Leroy's more up on the history than I am. I don't [dwell] on the past too much, I [dwell] on the future.

"It's brought me a long way, I tell ya, where I am right now, today. It was very important because it exposed me to a lot of music when a lot of people were saying this music was dying. I can't see that. It's going to live on. I don't care if it's European kids playing it. This is New Orleans music. New Orleans is so unique.

"I can't remember when Preservation Hall got started. The musicians there had to start playing when they were young also. I mean, you can't wait until you're 60 or 70 years old to play at Preservation Hall. That's what I tell a lot of the tourists who tell me I'm too young to be playing this [music]. There's a lot of young musicians out there playing today. Nicholas [Payton] is keeping the tradition alive, I would say, even though he's playing different styles. It doesn't matter. It's still related. You want to make sure that they know the traditional jazz. A lot of them still today don't want to learn because they're a new generation. It's not hip, and it's not a shake-your-booty kind of thing. That's where the money is, shake your booty. Shake it down to the ground, shake it all night [*laughs*]. You can't play a private function without knowing 'Darktown Strutters' Ball' or 'Ain't She Sweet,' and a lot of these kids don't know those songs.

"So when the Fairview got too many musicians, Danny decided to split the band up. He took the guys that had been in the band the longest and started two bands. So he said, 'what can I name this band? I'm going to name this band the Hurricane Brass Band because when you come down the streets playing, it sounds like a hurricane.' Because it was so loud and full of energy. And we could play all day. So the Hurricane Brass Band formed because there were too many of us. Kids coming from all over. Before you knew it, we must have had twenty musicians in that garage. Herlin [Riley] came in around that time.

"My next step was with the New Orleans Jazz basketball team, with Joe Gordon. And I got these sort of pretensions in me that I could play that trombone. So he hired me to play with that particular band. I was still in school. I guess I did that for just one year with him.

"And from there I started out working on Bourbon Street. Got a call with [drummer] June Gardner, at the Famous Door. Gardner, Curtis Mitchell, Olivia Charlot, Harold Cooper on clarinet, and I think we had Wendell and John Brunious every now and then. We also had Chris Clifton. Six musicians. We played six hours then on Bourbon Street, with continuous entertainment. The Last Straws was also playing. They would come on after us. They had three bands then, I think.

"I'll tell you a story. When Harry [Connick Jr.] first put his band together, back in 1990 or '91, I got a call from his musical director Ben

Wolfe. Shannon Powell was the one that recommended me because he had been working with Harry before, when he just had the rhythm section. Shannon, Ben Wolfe, the bass player who no longer works with Harry. So Ben said Harry was putting a big band together and asked if I would like to play in the band. I said, 'Hey, man, that's an honor. I'd love to play in the band.' He asked Leroy too, and he had just recently gotten married. After a while, he [Leroy] decided to be a part of the band. There were two other guys who got in the band that I recommended: Craig Klein and Mark Mullins [both trombonists]. That was the trombone section from New Orleans. The thing about it is me and Craig used to get together and we'd practice, and we'd read duets together every now and then. Just to try to keep my reading up. But when the band got together and Ben pulled out the music—remember I didn't know any of these guys except the ones from New Orleans. The music was very hard for me. I must say it was really hard [chuckles]. This was a helluva experience I went through.

"We rehearsed [the charts] a few times, and I say once again that my reading wasn't that great. I was just a little too proud. I had a lot of pride in myself and I didn't want to embarrass myself. So me being a man, I'm standing up and said to myself that I must go and tell Harry that I'm not a great reader. So during the rehearsal, he's sitting out in the auditorium and I told him, 'Man, Harry, I cannot read this music.' He said, 'Man, it's no problem. Don't worry about it. You're going to learn the music, don't worry about it. It's going to be okay.' So I said all right. So I left it alone and went back in the section and tried to learn my part as much as I could. I was playing the third part. And the third trombone's notes is very strange. No lead, and the notes didn't sound right to me. I had to train my ear really, really good to make sure I could hear those notes. I'd say, is that the right note, and the guy sitting next to me would say, yeah, that's the right note, don't worry about it. So that went on for a while.

"But before that—and I'll never forget this because it's something I bring up to a lot of the musicians today that's been in the band with Harry for the last fourteen years—I can recall some of the things that Danny [Barker] would tell me. Danny would say, when you're in a big band, you've got different groups: all the straight guys hang together, all the smokers hang together, all the winos hang together, all the drugheads

Lucien Barbarin leads his Sunday Night Swingsters at the Palm Court Jazz Café, New Orleans, March 2010. Drummer Gerald French is in the background.

hang together. So I was between all of them. I could hang with all of them! [*Laughs heartily.*] And it was true. It was actually true. I'd never experienced that before, being in a big band.

"So we was rehearsing the blues, just playing the blues, getting the feel of the band. So Leroy took the first solo on the blues, and he played that horn, I tell ya. And I came behind him. And what I played wasn't that great, I thought. I thought I could have done much better. When Harry came he asked what we were playing. So we played the blues again, then next Leroy's solo. So this time when I solo, I pick my plunger [mute] and I play it nasty. I growled and I played that wah-wah, and I played. So the rehearsal's over with, and now here's a band meeting. The manager wants to know how the band is getting along, remember don't put no bad name out about Harry, and so on. So now Harry you say something: 'Okay, guys, this band is going to be great. Did you hear that solo that Lucien played on that blues? That's the way I want my band to sound—just like that!' Man, all those guys. I can see those guys when I played the first solo—they had their heads down, the sax section. A lot of those guys from New York, New Jersey, Philadelphia, Chicago, and them guys was nodding their heads, saying, man, that boy's sad, he can't blow that horn. I took notice of that. He denies today that he said that, but I knew he said it. When Harry said this is the way I want my band to sound, that's when everything just . . . Those guys was like, oh, man. . . .'"

Today, Lucien travels around the world and also leads the Sunday night band at the Palm Court Jazz Café in New Orleans. He has a son named Paul Barbarin, about whom he says, "He's graduated from high school. He's still playing the drums off and on. [In fact, he now often plays with his father.] You see, I wasn't forced to play the instruments that I play now. I decided this is what I want to do. So I'm not forcing my son. If he wants to do it, he can do it. And I'll provide him with as much information as I can. He's always told me that he wants to play the drums and wants to play music for a living and wanted to play music with me. That made me feel great, real good. My other son, he put the instrument down. He's in the air force and made that a career. He's not playing music anymore."

Barbarin lives in a two-story home in Slidell, Louisiana, just east of New Orleans. The area was badly devastated by flooding during the Katrina episode, including the first floor of his home. Yet he and his family were able to survive by living on the second floor.

It has been at least four generations in the Barbarin family playing this music, and, says Lucien, "It's still in our blood."

LEROY JONES

"I am the very first member of the Fairview Baptist Church Christian Marching Band, which was the first name we had. Later it was condensed to the Fairview Brass Band or the Fairview Band. It started in my parents' garage at 1316 St. Denis Street, which was maybe fifty feet away from the Fairview Baptist Church on the corner of Buchanan and St. Denis. I was born February 20, 1958.

"I began to take trumpet lessons in the school band at St. Leo the Great Elementary School at the age of 10 in 1968. I had my first opportunity to play, as a professional musician, in 1971 by the relationship I established with Danny Barker. Danny and Blue Lu lived just around the corner on Sere Street, just a little over a block from my parents' place. Danny was a member of the Fairview Baptist Church, both he and his wife, and at that time, 1970–71, the pastor of the church, Reverend Andrew Darby, asked Danny if he could recruit some young musicians to start a youth band.

"Danny used to drive his car by the garage where I lived. When I would come home from school, after I had done my homework, I would go into the garage and practice for four hours, sometimes five hours a day. Actually, he could hear me around the corner because I had a tremendous sound at the time. I played very loud and powerful. One day he rolled up, the garage door was open, and he got out of his car. I always found him to be a fascinating man because of his very cool demeanor. I knew he was a musician. He was very gracious, but I really didn't know who he was. When he came up to the garage door and introduced himself, he asked me if I wanted to play in a brass band that the church was putting together. I said, 'Of course, but I think we need to ask my parents if it's okay.' Of course it was okay. He met my mother and dad.

"I knew some of the fellows who eventually became members of the first band, people like Harry Sterling, Morris Carmbs, Ronald Evans, and Gary Proctor were all members of the church. We were all around the same age. Harry Sterling and I were born in the same year. Gary Proctor was maybe a year older. Morris Carmbs is a couple of years older than myself. Derek Cagnolatti, who was the grandson of [trumpeter] Ernest Cagnolatti, was a couple of years younger than myself and some other youngsters in the neighborhood: the Mims brothers, Thomas and Gene. We were in elementary school together. Gene was a year younger. Thomas and I were the same age. So the band basically started with the kids in the neighborhood.

"I had the opportunity to be introduced to Joe Torregano, Anthony

'Tuba Fats' Lacen, Gregg Stafford—musicians who were already established musicians and members of the local musicians' union and a few years older than us. They were already teenagers. Actually, when I met Gregg Stafford, he was a freshman at Southern University of New Orleans working on his degree in music education. Joe Torregano was a little bit older. He was also getting a degree in music education. Tuba Fats was an even older member who had already had experience playing with brass bands, some of the more well known bands in the city like Tuxedo and the Olympia and people like that. I also got to meet the Barbarin brothers, Charles who played bass drum and Lucien who played snare drum at the time. Their father, Charles Barbarin Sr., was our chaperone for the most part and someone who kept us in line because we were under age. But he was also, like Danny, very fond of children and had a lot of patience because we were little rascals. So we all established a healthy relationship and everybody was really, really excited about playing music and putting this band together. We had rehearsals in the garage at 1316 St. Denis Street.

"We had tutors that came over. I met [saxophonist] Earl Turbinton for the first time. He came there and gave us some pointers. There was a guy named Joe Gordon, who is dead now, a clarinet player who came over and gave us some pointers. People like Gregg Stafford and Joe Torregano came after these gentlemen were there because we were fresh into this new world of playing jazz and New Orleans brass band music.

"I had the opportunity to meet Herlin Riley. At that time Herlin played trumpet. His mother, Miss Bee, would drop him off when we had rehearsal once a week. We started out with maybe eight, ten members, then we had twelve members. Eventually we had as many as twenty-five to thirty guys in the band. We had enough people in the band to do two or three gigs a day. There was a lot of talent in that band, so the musicality was not on a low level at all—especially considering how young we were. Because we were young we had a lot of energy. So we could play five- or six-hour parades on Sundays, and we did funerals and social and pleasure club events. We became quite popular.

"I remember my first parade was the Easter parade for the Fairview Baptist Church. We would march from St. Denis and Buchanan up to St. Bernard Avenue, go up Milton Street through the [St. Bernard] project, go all around the center street, come back. The pastor, Reverend Darby, and the congregation and the parents would all come out, and a lot of other youngsters who came just to witness it. One of them was a young fellow by the name of Raymond Johnson, no relation to Raymond 'Puppy' Johnson, who lived just around the corner—their house was next door to the Cagnolattis'. That young fellow and his family were members of the church also. But he was, like, four years old when he first came. He didn't even have his adult teeth. By the time he was eight years old he was already trying to play, but he wasn't quite ready to work with us 'big guys.' Eventually, I understand, he did play with the second Fairview band, another generation of the Fairview band.

"The band became so popular that we were getting some attention from the local press and from other jazz enthusiasts like [photographer] Jules Cahn, and Allan Jaffe [bassist and proprietor of Preservation Hall] befriended us. We had instruments that were donated to us by Allan. At one point the garage was full of instruments in good playing condition—sousaphones, euphoniums, clarinets, old trombones, drums. . . . I was blessed and fortunate. My parents could afford to get me an instrument. The kids who did have instruments—during that time the music programs in the junior and senior high schools loaned horns to kids. Unfortunately, that doesn't exist anymore. But when the kids joined the Fairview band, everybody had something they could play. For me, I had the opportunity to dabble around with all the instruments in the garage. It was an incredible experience.

"For me, I think if I would not have met Danny, I would have been a musician. I would have been a professional musician, but the musical direction I would have taken would have been slightly different. I think that I would not have had the love and affection for New Orleans music and New Orleans jazz that I do if it had not been for Danny Barker. It would have been contemporary jazz because I was already listening to contemporary sounds. Believe it or not, my first inspiration—other than Louis Armstrong because I knew who [he] was before I even played an instrument, he was a household name—was the popular music of the time. People like Hugh Masekela, Herb Alpert and the Tijuana Brass—I can't believe it.

"I had an old jukebox in the garage and I'd play LPs, and I had some

Freddie Hubbard. It was before I really got serious in listening to different jazz artists, even instrumentalists other than trumpet players. Some words of wisdom I got from Danny that I didn't understand until some years later: He said, 'Get you some Louis Armstrong records, get you some Charlie Parker records. Listen to how they're playing, that's breathing,' and I didn't really understand that fully. It's the breathing, the breath controlling the instrument. I was 13. I didn't understand that sort of technique, and all the stuff that comes with it that enables you to play quickly and enables you to be fluent when you're playing. . . . I never forget him saying that to me. But I listened like he asked me to and of course I was in awe of all of this playing, especially when listening to Parker play the bebop lines that were very foreign to me.

"Danny taught all of us, especially myself, about musician etiquette, how to carry yourself, how to dress as a musician, being on time. . . . You know, when you're on stage, smile because the worst thing in the world is for the people in the audience to look up, and you've got a sour face. He said, 'You make them feel good when you look like you're feeling good, even when you're feeling bad.' It's the old show-must-go-on thing. Those things have stayed with me throughout my career. And Danny taught me and all of the guys how to manage money as young musicians.

"I was appointed leader of the [Fairview] band because Danny saw that I had leadership qualities and he saw that I was serious about music as a youngster. Danny had very good insight into people. He could read you. He'd been around.

"We had great camaraderie between us guys in the band—even the new fellows who came later. It was almost like immediate family with us. We were kids, and we were having fun too. The most important thing is that all of us *loved* to play music—we would play for nothing. We didn't have to get a paper route; we didn't have to shine shoes; and my dad didn't have to give me an allowance anymore if he didn't want to because I'd go out on a weekend and make me 40–50 bucks! [*Laughs heartily.*] For a 13-year-old in 1971 that was good bread. So we got accustomed to making money quite early.

"My responsibilities as leader? Well, as you know, the trumpet player is the lead, so he calls the numbers. That was one of my jobs, and to think of what numbers to call after that. Because we need continuity, which is

Leroy Jones leads his New Orleans–Helsinki Connection at the Visitors' Center of the New Orleans Jazz National Historical Park, March 2008. The guitarist is Todd Duke.

another thing that Danny taught us. Be thinking about what you're going to do next while you're doing a number. When Gregg Stafford came into the band, I learned from him too because he had more experience. The first numbers that I ever learned were the hymns from the Baptist church, the spirituals. Of course we learned 'Joe Avery's Piece,' 'Second Line,' we had to do that. But it was a collective thing calling the tunes.

"The Fairview band traveled, but not as much as the Hurricane did. Right after Louie [Armstrong] died, in 1971, there was a tribute at the Kennedy Center and we were there. Fats Houston was there. It seems like it was fall because I remember it was a bit chilly. Another big event that the band did was to travel to New Roads, Louisiana, to perform at this 'festival of life.' You've probably heard about that thing. They had big stars. It was like a rock festival. We were the brass band part in there. We used the church bus to go on these short trips. We had chaperones of course. I will never forget that gig. My mom was there and Mr. Barbarin —they were the two chaperones. When we got there all the people were naked, butt naked. [*Big laugh.*] I was so embarrassed 'cause I was 14 and with my mom. We were going to be there four days. We walked around a bit, but basically it was a bunch of hippies. I think there was some drug deals going on because the state troopers came in and someone else said that the Hell's Angels were coming in to crash the party. So 'Rev' [Reverend Darby] of course got us out of there. We spent a good four or five hours there, and then we split. That was around 1972.

The Hurricane Brass Band and Later

"The Hurricane Brass Band was an extension of the Fairview Brass Band. The original band sort of disbanded in 1974 after running from about 1971 to 1974. I was 16 in 1974. Danny was getting a lot of flack from the musicians' union, from certain members who were spreading false rumors that Danny was exploiting us and using us to make money for his own personal gain. Which was never, ever true! Danny would give his last dime for us. He loved children. Him and Blue Lu were the sweetest people I ever knew. Danny explained to us at a meeting, saying he had to cut us all loose, that we'd gotten old enough now to run our own affairs. There's a big difference between 12 and 16. He said we should change the name of the band, and he wanted to call us the Hurricane Band 'because when you come up the street you all blow like a hurricane.' So that's how it got started. [Danny] was still a member of the [Fairview] church, and we'd see him, but he didn't have anything to do with us, basically. After that, Charles Barbarin, Lucien's father, was our chaperone while we were still minors.

"Then I met musicians like Kirk Joseph, Charles Joseph, Gregory Davis, and, I almost forgot, saxophonist Kevin Harris who still plays with the Dirty Dozen [Brass Band]. We started doing different things. Tuba Fats was still there. We started venturing away from the traditional repertoire and started making up songs and riffs that hadn't been played yet —Tuba Fats was very instrumental in that—certain riffs on the sousaphone or tuba that they still use in these so-called contemporary brass bands today. We were doing this then.

"And at that time we switched over to more of a comfortable attire, and we had T-shirts made with 'Leroy Jones Hurricane Brass Band, New Orleans, Louisiana,' with all the information like they would put on the bass drum. Between 1974 and 1976 we were the hottest thing on the street. There were a lot of older musicians who were very jealous of us. I gave Milton Batiste a run for his money back in those days. I admired his power and the way he would soar over the top of the band. The Olympia Brass Band was one of my favorite bands. There's a recording they did in 1971 or 1972 with Paul Crawford on trombone, Wendell Eugene, and Fats Houston was grand marshal [*The Olympia Brass Band of New Orleans*, Audiophile AP 108]. They did it in the studio so the sound quality is really nice. I heard that album when I was about 12 years old, and I was so inspired. Olympia seemed to have this thing, with Milton having the trumpet lead.

"We had an opportunity to record in 1975, my first LP [*Leroy Jones and His Hurricane Marching Brass Band of New Orleans*, Lo An Records, recorded March 1–2, 1975]. Actually, the first LP that I was ever recorded on was also in 1975 with the St. Augustine High School band. But Jules Cahn took an interest in us and decided that we should document the sound of the band. So the members of the Hurricane Brass Band, which in essence was the Fairview band with some new faces, did a live recording session in the backyard of Al Rose, his house over on the lakefront. It was a very nice session actually. My only regret is that I wish we could have recorded it differently, miked it better to catch all the nuances better. It actually sounded better live than it did on the recording. Nevertheless, it's a great thing to have because it's history.

"After that we played gigs locally and had an opportunity to go up and play the Smithsonian Institution's Festival of Folklore in 1976. We made an appearance in a film called *The Minstrel Man*. Basically a black cast and a musical. It was released in 1975 or '76. I wish I could find that film.

"We had several great opportunities to meet other famous musicians. Of course up in D.C. at the Kennedy Center. And we used to meet artists coming in to perform concerts like at the Municipal Auditorium or the Saenger Theater. We had the opportunity to meet Quincy Jones back in 1976 when he was touring, and the Brothers Johnson who were the opening act for Quincy. We got to meet Quincy because we would meet the artists at the airport. They always used to have a brass band to meet famous people, especially musicians. So he invited us to play during the intermission of his concert at the Saenger. We played for about twenty minutes, and they gave us a little bit of money—the manager set it up. Quincy said that he liked us. I gave him a signed copy of the Hurricane Brass Band LP, and he probably remembers that time because he's got a memory like an elephant. That was the same year we played at the Smithsonian, 1976, but earlier in the year. When we went up to play the Smithsonian festival, the manager contacted me and had us play at the Kennedy Center. We were there two weeks. So we did it again in Washington for Quincy. Then we met Frank Zappa, who came into New Orleans. They played at the Civic Auditorium in St. Bernard Parish. They invited us—just the horns—to play the final number with Zappa, believe it or not. I wish I had someone there to take a picture because we were on the stage with Frank Zappa. He had a young guy in his band at that time named George Duke, a pianist who is very well known now, and Frank Zappa's wife was in the band as well. And a saxophone player—I'll never forget—they just called him 'Napoleon.' He was the cat that was thrilled with that brass band sound. He's the one that told Frank to get us up there—myself, Kevin Harris, I think Gregory Davis, Michael Johnson, the trombone player, and maybe Lucien too. At that time Lucien was playing the trombone. In the Hurricane band, Lucien switched over because on the record Charles Barbarin is playing bass drum and Puppy [Johnson] is playing snare."

Leroy has kept busy playing New Orleans venues such as Maison Bourbon, Palm Court Café, Preservation Hall, and Donna's Bar and Grill. He also performs and travels with Harry Connick Jr.'s big band and plays festivals all over the world. In 2002 Jones recorded a CD called *Back to My Roots* (LJ-90112) in which he paid a musical tribute to Danny Barker, who, he writes in the liner notes, introduced him to New Orleans brass band music and traditional jazz at the age of 13. He paid further tribute to the Fairview and Hurricane bands with the CD *Memories of the Fairview and Hurricane Band*, released in 2005.

He and his wife, trombonist Katja Toivola, evacuated New Orleans two days before Hurricane Katrina struck the city, going first to Houston, then to Dallas, where they stayed for about six weeks. When they returned to New Orleans, they discovered that their rented house in the Gentilly neighborhood had taken on three feet of water.

"Miraculously, we were able to salvage a few of our possessions," he says. "I was able to retain three trumpets that I had left behind, but the cases were inundated with mold and had a horrible smell."

Since October 2005, the Joneses have been living with friends in the French Quarter while completing the purchase of a house in the Tremé neighborhood. "Katja and I are back to stay," Jones asserts. "I would have to say that we've done better than most and maybe not quite as well as others."

HERLIN RILEY

"I was born right here in the Lower Ninth Ward of New Orleans on February 15, 1957, to a musical family called the Lastie family. My grandfather's name was Frank Lastie. He was one of the first people to play drums in the church, and his sons were all musicians. Melvin played the trumpet and cornet, David played the saxophone, and Walter also played the drums. So they were all my major influences. Joe Lastie was another brother, but he wasn't a musician. But his son, Joe, is now a drummer and plays at Preservation Hall. He's my first cousin. My mother's name is Betty Lastie, Betty Lastie Williams is her name, or Riley Williams, I guess. She plays piano and sings gospel music. She is known as 'Miss Bee.' For a while, she worked with my uncles David and Walter—they called him 'Popee'—and did some gigs with them as a singer. That's basically my family.

"How I come to meet Danny Barker and those guys? My grandfather, Frank Lastie, had a concession stand at Pontchartrain Park Golf Course, and one of the ladies that worked with him—Rosemary Victoria—was a cousin of Leroy's parents, I don't know whether mother's or father's side. As a young kid I worked at the concession stand and would practice and play the trumpet around there in spare time when nobody was around. I was about 12 or 13.

"I played trumpet at school. This was like 1970 or '71. So Miss Rosemary would hear me practicing. She said to my grandfather one day, 'There's some real young kids who have a band together and they practice out on St. Denis Street by this guy's house. I think Herlin would be interested to play with them.' One night my grandfather brought me by there and introduced me to Leroy and to the other guys, and that's when I met Mr. Barker. I was so amazed to see, at that particular time in my life, that there were other kids my age who were also interested in playing jazz music. I was interested in jazz because I grew up with my grandfather and uncles and they were always playing. I don't think I played very much that first night. So Mr. Barker said, 'Pull your horn out, son, and play a little something.' I don't remember what I played, but I just kind of fell in. To make a long story short, it was fascinating to me that all those kids were my age and they were interested in playing jazz music. Because all the kids at that time were trying to play James Brown or whatever was the latest stuff. But these kids were interested in the tradition of the music, and I was tuned into that tradition.

"When [my grandfather Frank] was 13 or 14, he was thrown into the waifs' home. He was in the home with Louis Armstrong. When I was young he would tell me these stories. We were sitting around the table, just like we're sitting here, and he would pick up two butter knives or whatever and he'd beat out rhythms on the table for me—in the traditional style. [*Herlin gives some examples.*] Then he would challenge me to do it, to play those rhythms. Then he would kick back in the chair and get a big laugh out of me trying so hard and so seriously trying to play those rhythms. So from those times I was in touch and in tune with the feeling of early traditional jazz music—because of my grandfather.

"I joined the Fairview in 1972, after Jazzfest that year and following their trip to Washington, D.C. I think it was 1972. The reason I can remember that is because my uncle Melvin passed away in 1972, in December. A few months prior to that, he and I went to Danny Barker's house because by then I had been playing with the Fairview band. He had known Danny Barker for a long time, and they had shared times together in New York City.

"That's why I'm here right now, because of my love and respect for Mr. Barker. What I've come to realize over the years is that jazz music is bigger than any individual. Jazz music is the queen bee, and the musicians are, like, the workers.

"So when I got to meet Leroy and Gregg and Tuba Fats and Michael White and all those guys, I had already had an idea of how the music was to sound like and how it was supposed to feel. So when I began to play I kind of fit right in, you know. None of us could really play at the time, but we had enough musical knowledge to play a tune and to make it feel good. Mr. Barker and Mr. Charlie Barbarin would always encourage us to play. Mr. Barker would encourage us to do whatever we wanted to do. If we found an instrument we liked and could play it a little bit, he'd say, 'Yeah, yeah.'

"I played trumpet at first, but I would always mess with the drums. I knew how to play that style because of my grandfather. I would do little things, as kids do. Can you do this? Can you do that? I got something on you that you can't do! That kind of thing. I did the same thing in high school when I played the trumpet. I would challenge the other drummers. They could always play these open-stroke rolls and the paradiddles and that stuff, but they could never play the traditional New Orleans parade beat, with press rolls and that kind of stuff. I would challenge them, and they would challenge me to do other things. As a result, they were giving me lessons that I didn't even know. They'd say, 'Man, you can play a press roll, but can you play a five-stroke roll or a seven-stroke roll? Can you play a flam?' I was getting lessons and didn't know it.

"And during that time, I remember, Leroy would play the trumpet. I was fascinated by him because he sounded and his feel was so much like Louis Armstrong to me at that particular time. His sound has changed over the years and evolved, but back then, when he was a child, he was so much like Louis Armstrong to me. He played the trumpet, but he would also play the tuba a little bit.

"When I went in the band, Leroy, Gregg, Lucien and Charles Barbarin were there. I remember Leroy, Lucien, and Gregg all played tuba on occasion. I think I was in the band about three years."

When asked why he switched from trumpet to drums, Herlin said, "Well, I could always play the drums. The drums have been part of me,

Herlin Riley with the Palm Court All-Stars at the Palm Court Jazz Café, New Orleans, May 2010. The bassist is Jesse Boyd.

from being three years old. The drums were always part of my life. When I got to be about 12 years old, my uncle Melvin sent me a trumpet from New York City. No, I was younger than that. I was 10. Then I started playing the trumpet too. I was trying to be serious as a trumpet player, but drums were always part of my background. So when I got to meet Mr. Barker and Leroy and those guys, everybody was playing different instruments. A lot of guys were switching up. Lucien would switch up and play the snare drum or the bass drum, and then he would also play the tuba every now and then. I was so fascinated that all these guys were so talented. Mr. Charles [Barbarin] would always encourage us, and he would tell us, 'Now make sure you find the blue notes.' I'd say, 'What are you talking about?' And he'd say, 'the flatted third and the flatted seventh, you know, the minor third and flatted seventh; those are the blue notes. When you're playing, put some blue notes in there.'"

Did he think being a trumpet player helped him as a drummer? "Absolutely. Absolutely. My approach to playing the drums is not as something to beat on. When I'm playing a drum solo, I'm singing the melody to myself and I try to play over what I'm singing so everybody knows where we are at a particular time and place in the music. But I'm out there to please myself and my fellow band members. I play music for the joy of playing, whether there's an audience or not.

[My influences were] "first off, grandfather Frank Lastie and my uncle Walter Lastie. Then, James Black. Ernie Elly. Smokey Johnson. Freddie Kohlman, though I didn't hear him a lot. I heard Louie Barbarin toward the end of his career. Frank Parker. Most of the modern drummers, like Art Blakey, Max Roach, Tony Williams, Elvin Jones, Kenny Clarke. Each one of those guys, I took different things from their playing. Buddy Rich. I've never seen anybody that has that kind of command of the instrument. He was definitely one of my influences.

[My formal musical education began at George Washington Carver High School], "under the direction of Ms. Yvonne Bush. She was a fascinating woman, and she still is. She was born in '29, so she's 76. She's another one that touched my life. I was very fortunate to have her when I did. She was another one that encouraged you to explore everything you could do musically. Then I went to Mississippi Valley State. It's in the delta, near Greenwood [Mississippi]. I only stayed there for two semesters or so, and then I came back and went to Southern University here in New Orleans and I studied under Mr. Kidd Jordan at the time. I didn't stay there very long either. I started playing at the 500 Club and I got married and had a child and had to find a way to make ends meet. So I went to work. I went to college for a very short time. I was trying to be a music major. Actually, I went to school to do exactly what I'm doing! But I'm limited in my theoretical knowledge of harmony and that kind of stuff. When it comes to writing, there are different aspects of writing that I don't understand.

"I have begun to teach a little bit, though that was not my intended vocation. But as I've gotten more recognized, I've been called upon to mentor kids and to give lessons. At first I rejected it and didn't want to do it. Then I realized someone took time out and taught me. Mr. Barker is one of the people in my life that took out time and showed me about the music. Right now, it's an obligation and a responsibility for myself—and for other guys my age—to teach the other guys about the music, so that the art form is perpetuated. I have written one book for New Orleans drummers entitled *New Orleans Second Line Drumming.*

"I joined Wynton [Marsalis]'s band in 1988. My very first time meeting him was in 1981. I was in London doing a show called *One Mo' Time.* We played at the West End Theatre there for six months. When I got off work, I'd go to a place called Ronnie Scott's. I got a drum lesson from Elvin Jones there.

"Wynton has incorporated the New Orleans style in his show. Not to toot my own horn, but a lot of that has to do with myself and Reginald Veal, the bass player. We're both from New Orleans, and we joined the band together in '88. You know, Wynton didn't really respect the New Orleans tradition as a young kid growing up. He's come to respect it now as an older, more seasoned guy because when Reginald and I joined the band he started incorporating more of the New Orleans style in his music. So that's a part of the music now. Incidentally, we did a traditional jazz funeral for both Elvin Jones and Lionel Hampton in New York, and Wynton looked to me for directions as to how to set it up.

"Wynton, you know, is very smart. He's kind of read up, and he's done his homework. We may have been kind of like the spark that sent him in that direction. He knows that I'm very strong in that tradition, and he doesn't mind asking, 'Hey, man, what do you think we should do here?' He knows I play on the street. When I come home, I can't wait to get on the street and play with Uncle Lionel [Batiste]. I've been very fortunate to play all kinds of music. One thing that contributes to that is the fact that we live in New Orleans, and New Orleans is a small community and the pool of musicians is small. The better musicians are the ones who get the most calls, and you may get calls in different genres or styles. That for me has been one of the most profound aspects of living in New Orleans, that I was raised here and could do so many different types of gigs here in this city."

Herlin Riley, when not on the road with Wynton Marsalis or pianist Ahmad Jamal or performing at festivals around the world, can be heard at New Orleans night spots such as the Palm Court Café and Snug Harbor. His house, located in the Upper Ninth Ward near the Industrial Canal, was heavily damaged by Katrina flooding, and its repair is well underway.

In the meantime, he continues to tour and appear in local clubs when in town. He and fellow New Orleans drummer Shannon Powell were honored with the prestigious Ascona Jazz Award at the famed Ascona (Switzerland) Jazz Festival in the summer of 2010.

GREGG STAFFORD

"I'm a New Orleans native, born and raised here, mostly in the Central City-Uptown area. My birth date is July 6, 1953. I started playing brass band music around 1969 with the E. Gibson band. So, by the time I saw Danny Barker and the Fairview band, I was already playing music with that well-established Uptown band which was led by Johnny Wimberly. All those old guys were my heroes: Jack Willis, Teddy Riley, Louis Cottrell. They became my friends.

"I started with the Fairview in 1972 and from listening to Mr. Barker I think the band started in late 1970. I had never seen any type of band composed entirely of young kids until I saw the Fairview. Doc Paulin always used teenagers in high school, but they were a select few. I played with Doc Paulin maybe once or twice. You might see one or two in the Gibson band. John McNeill had a band and you'd see somebody like [trombonist] Freddie Lonzo. Some of the guys that worked in McNeill's band worked in the Gibson band.

"My way of looking at it is the church is always part of the community or the neighborhood. Whether I'm from Uptown or Downtown I look at the church as being the strongest pillar or institution in any community. But I came from Uptown and I travel to Downtown to rehearse in Leroy's garage as a member of the Fairview Baptist Church Band, I know that we are a group of kids playing music who represent the church. We were all kids coming from different areas of town. My church was St. John Institutional Missionary Baptist Church [Buddy Bolden's church, too]. That's where I was baptized.

"We were all different denominations. There were guys in the band who were Catholics, like Lucien and Charles. Kids coming from all over the city—Ninth Ward, Carrollton, Uptown, Gentilly, coming from every direction. Parents would drop us off. We were coming from different backgrounds, denominations, and schools. But we were all playing under the jurisdiction of the church. None of us had any reason to be at Fairview except for the band.

"I was working at the Perkins Pancake Parlor which was right across the street from Dixieland Hall [in the French Quarter]. On my breaks I'd go listen at Jack Willis, Teddy Riley, because those were the musicians who were playing at Dixieland Hall as opposed to those who were playing at Preservation Hall. Papa French, Louie Cottrell, Louie Barbarin, Jeanette Kimball, Freddie Kohlman, Frog [Joseph]—they were all at Dixieland Hall. I was working my way through college. I used to work the midnight shift. I started out as a dish-washer, then a short-order cook, then a waiter. Dixieland Hall closed at something like 12:30. I'd come to work at eleven and take my first break about a quarter to twelve, and sometimes I'd pull a double shift. On Thursdays I'd work from 3:00 to 11:00. I'd take my break somewhere around nine o'clock and go listen to the music.

"At the time Mr. Barker was working at the Maison Bourbon with Worthia Thomas. When he got off, he'd come to Perkins Pancake Parlor and have breakfast. Bourbon Street was the old Bourbon Street, so the busiest time in the restaurant would be between 3:00 and 5:30. It was a 24-hour restaurant and was flooded with the barkers, strippers, policemen on duty. Louie Prima would come through there, Al Hirt, Pork Chop . . . so I met a lot of people there. Thomas Jefferson didn't want anybody to wait on him but me. 'Night people,' Mr. Barker used to call them. 'Show Boy' [Worthia Thomas] used to come in, and I'd wait on him. He mentioned the fact that Danny had a kids' band. He said, 'the banjo player that works with me, I'll bring him down here and introduce him to you.' And that's what he did. He brought Mr. Barker down, like, three nights later.

"I'd never heard of him. I'd seen him when the kids were marching at the Southern Christian Leadership Conference parade. When I saw him I had no idea that he was working up the street. When Show Boy brought him in and introduced him to me personally, Danny looked at me and started asking me questions, trying to feel me out. He said they had rehearsals every Thursday night on Sere Street, on the other side of the St. Bernard Project. He said they had a little gig coming up, a political rally, so I went. When I got there, he introduced me to Leroy, Lucien, Charles, and the rest of the guys in the band. After I joined I brought Joe

[Torregano] and Tuba Fats because Tuba was working with me in bands Uptown. So that's when we all became members. When I brought Tuba, Mr. Barker looked at him and said he'd never seen nobody that big before and said that's a kids' band.

"At the time Mr. Barker was a member of Reverend Darby's church. There were times when we couldn't all fit in Leroy's garage, and Reverend Darby would open the church up. It's very common among Baptist ministers to go around to other churches to preach, and sometimes he would bring us.

"As far as supervising the kids, that was Mr. Barker and Mr. Charles Barbarin. A lot of the time Mr. Barker could not be with us. Mr. Barbarin was with us all the time. He was dedicated as well.

"We played the church parade every Easter for Fairview Baptist, and we did a lot of performances inside churches. We were very busy playing for church musicals and church services. Sometimes we got paid, and sometimes we just did it basically as a service to the church. And Mr. Barker was able to get some funds for the band. There were a lot of kids, but sometimes we'd get $5 apiece, $3 apiece, $7 apiece, but we were happy. We were happy about being able to play and happy about being exposed to a lot of new experiences.

"Most of us had our own instruments because we were already in school bands. There was a time when a lot of kids wanted to join the band. I remember one time when we arrived at rehearsal, Mr. Barker told us we were fortunate to have received a whole case of instruments from New York. Some friends of Mr. Barker who had heard about the band and had sent trumpets down, drums, saxophones, and clarinets. Mr. Barker was able to give instruments to some kids who didn't have them. That's when we started really stretching out to where we could have two or three bands.

"I was in the band all the way until the time when Mr. Barker had to cut us loose. You know he split up the band. He would send Leroy with one group and he would send me with another group because he knew I was capable of handling the songs because of my experience with the Gibson band. Sometimes we'd go three different ways. He'd send Herlin Riley, who played trumpet then, out as a leader sometimes. All under the name of the Fairview Baptist Church band name.

"I can remember one specific trip we did. I don't remember exactly where it was, but I know it was a good three-hour drive by school bus. It was a church picnic or campsite that we played at and on the way back to New Orleans—I know it was across the lake—the bus had some electrical problems. The lights went out, and we were stranded on the highway for a while. The bus driver hailed a trucker and the bus was attached to the truck and he towed us all the way into . . . a service station in Metairie. We were so glad to see the lights of the city because we were stuck on that dark highway for at least two hours. That was one of our outside engagements. There was one engagement—which I didn't make—that the band went to Angola [the state penitentiary] to perform for the prisoners.

"The most important thing that I can bring out is that [Barker] was very dedicated to helping kids, especially young musicians. That went beyond the brass band. If he knew there was a young kid who was promising and coming along, he made a point to meet him. Davell Crawford, you know. When he first heard about Davell, he hired him to play with the Jazz Hounds. Give him a feel of the music. John Boutte, he brought him in just to sing. He was very dedicated to New Orleans traditional jazz being around for ever. He was just a very fair person. I call him the genie of New Orleans music. He had this very deep sense of foresight. He had a strong sense of intuition, wisdom. He was very articulate about what he felt. And vision. He was very much concerned about history, history of music, history of the development of jazz. He was very well informed about a lot of things. So you're given the chance to understand your people's history. When Mr. Barker started lecturing to us at rehearsals about how important the brass bands were and what they stood for, besides just playing the music, it is pretty much the community for fellowship with one another through the churches and the organizations. He said this is a very proud heritage and it is something that you must protect and preserve. It's part of your family history and your ethnic history. Prior to my meeting Mr. Barker, I had never heard about that before. It was just going through the motions with E. Gibson. My great-uncle was very high in the hierarchy in the Knights of Pythias and the Odd Fellows, and I'd see him with his uniform on. When he passed, it looked like he belonged to *all* of them.

"I think I pretty much understand what preceded our becoming the

Fairview band. Tuba Fats knew because he played the parades with me with the likes of Pythias and the Odd Fellows. The other guys in the Fairview Baptist band never experienced those kinds of parades.

Danny Barker's Last Days and His Jazz Funeral

"I remember the last few months before [Danny] passed and the last time I saw him in good health. I went off to Mexico to play with Preservation Hall, and he was having his complications with his stomach at the time, and I noticed that he wasn't bringing the banjo any more to the Palm Court. He was bringing his light-weight guitar, and I asked him if he wasn't going to play the banjo anymore. He kinda looked sideways at me and said, 'Well, the banjo is a little too heavy for me. I haven't been feeling well at all. I've been having problems with my stomach.' I had just come back from Helsinki then, the first week of December, and Nina [Buck] was about to close the restaurant down for the Christmas holidays. So I asked him if he had gone to see a doctor. He looked at me and laughed and said, 'Now you're telling *me* what to do.' I told him that I was concerned and it seemed that something was not right. He agreed and said, 'Okay, I'll do that. I'll make an appointment to see the doctor.' So the restaurant closed down, and I was going through some changes at the same time because my drummer was very sick. I called Mr. Barker a week later to see if he had gone to the doctor. He said, 'Yeah, I've gotta wait until the test results come back.' But that last night that we played at the Palm Court, he looked at me and says, 'You and me.' I couldn't understand what he was saying because he looked straight into my eyes. He says, 'You and me, always. Me and you.' And he walked out the door. That was the last time I performed with him.

"Then I went to Mexico. And my drummer took a turn for the worse, and my mother called me and said I might have to come back home because your drummer is very ill. Then she said, 'Oh, Mr. Barker called for you. He wanted information about you, and I told him I didn't have any information because you hadn't called me back to say where you were staying.' She says, 'Mr. Barker wants you to call him. He hasn't been feeling well at all.' When I did call him, he said, 'I just wanted to thank you. You didn't have to do that for me.' Because before I left, I had told

Resa Lambert [of Preservation Hall] and asked some questions and said I come there some nights and there's nobody on banjo because you can't find a banjo player. I said that Mr. Barker was sitting at home doing nothing. So they called him for the last two jobs—the last two Fridays—at Preservation Hall. I guess she told him that I had suggested they call him. So he called me and thanked me and he took the job.

"When I did call him I asked him how he was feeling. He said, 'Oh well, things are not too good. The doctor says I have the Big C.' So I asked him where it was located, and he said in his pancreas. 'But the doctor says, you know, sometimes you . . . maybe seven years more.' I didn't know if he was just trying to throw me off. He said, 'The reason I wanted to talk to you is that I want you to take over the band when you come back. I told her [Nina] to wait until you come back and you'll take over the band.' So I said, 'Okay, Mr. Barker.' He asked if I was willing to do that, and I said, 'Most of the time, when I'm there, I'm calling the songs anyway.'

"About a week before I came back he called me and wanted to know *specifically* when I was getting back. I told him that I would be back in about two weeks. 'Nina's talking about firing the band again because the band is playing all these slow songs that [pianist] Walter [Lewis] is calling,' and I told him to just wait until I come back. So I had to give her a specific date.

"When I came back I went straight to see him because I was told he was at Touro Hospital. But when I got to Touro they told me he had been released and was at home. So I went straight to his house. At the time he still was able to talk and was coherent about where he was and what was going on. 'Call Nina and tell her you're back,' he said. So I called her the next day, and we discussed what he had talked about."

Gregg went on to explain how Danny had become "upset" with the deterioration of the funeral tradition in New Orleans. The music had become too loud and too fast. Funerals had become "disrespectful" of the tradition. "We had many conversations about that before he became sick," said Gregg. When he did become very ill, Danny's daughter Sylvia and wife Lu asked Gregg to take care of the music for the funeral. Gregg recalled finding Danny lying on the couch in a weakened state upon his return from Mexico. Lu and Sylvia were in the kitchen discussing what to do at the funeral. During his conversation with Gregg, Danny suddenly stopped and said, "Shhh . . . Go in there [the kitchen] and see what they're talking about." He sensed something, and, in fact, they were discussing what to do at the funeral.

On the following Sunday, Gregg had his brunch gig with Michael White at the Intercontinental Hotel. After the gig, White went directly to Barker's home (Gregg was to follow), and as he arrived, he was told that Danny had just died. White called Gregg at the hotel and gave him the news. "Sylvia and Miss Lu then said there would be no music at the funeral, that Danny hadn't wanted it," Gregg says. "I was very surprised." There was a meeting with Lu, Sylvia, Tom Dent, Lolis Elie, Fred Johnson, and Gregg on the following day. "I've always said that the music sets the tone for the funeral," Gregg continues. "So I told them, 'I guarantee, if I do the music, everything will go the way it's supposed to go, the way Danny would have wanted it. I would see that all the musicians were properly dressed: black suit, black caps, white shirt, black tie, and black shoes. This occasion would be like that for a four-star general. We need to give back to him what he gave us.'"

Famed bassist Milt Hinton was at Danny Barker's funeral. "I saw him standing next to Lu," Gregg says, "with tears just rolling down his face." Clarinetist Willie Humphrey was also in attendance. Afterwards, he asked Gregg, "Did you put all of this together?" When Gregg said he was in charge of the music, Humphrey said, "Great job. Wonderful funeral."

The modern brass bands were there too, but not properly dressed. They learned how a proper funeral should be done. "You know," says Gregg, "you can't read about that in books in the school system."

Gregg Stafford is one of the busiest musicians in town today. He still leads the Jazz Hounds, and he is the leader of the Heritage Hall Jazz Band, which he took over when trumpeter Teddy Riley died. He's also the leader of the Young Tuxedo Brass Band, which he inherited from Herman Sherman, and is a regular at Preservation Hall and a member of Michael White's Liberty Jazz Band. He's long been deeply involved in the so-called second-line culture, having founded a social group called the Black Men of Labor. In 2004, he was elected king of the Lady Jetsetters social and pleasure club. Beyond all of this, he travels widely throughout the world as a featured guest artist.

Stafford lives on Second Street in Central City, having escaped Katrina floodwaters, he says, "by about 3 or 4 blocks." He evacuated to Baton Rouge, where he stayed with his sister. "My house was spared from the wrath of the storm," he admits, but he lost his back deck and several big trees and had to replace his roof. He returned to the city one month later, but the elementary school where he teaches was still closed. "So I'm enjoying unemployment and playing some." He was in Scandinavia for a month, then went to Paris with Michael White in late October [2005] before completing the year in New York City for the annual New Year's holiday gig with White at the Village Vanguard.

JOE TORREGANO

"I was born here in New Orleans February 28, 1952. It doesn't seem like thirty-three years ago that we were in the Fairview Baptist Church Band practicing in Leroy Jones's garage on Monday nights at 1316 St. Denis Street. I can remember that like it was yesterday.

"I got started musically at the age of four. I took piano lessons from a lady named Ms. Annabelle Jones. Unfortunately, Ms. Jones passed when I was almost 12, no 10. I went about a year before my mother could find another piano teacher. I took piano lessons from her. It was mandatory in our house that you started taking piano lessons at the age of four. There were four boys, and we all took piano lessons. I later took piano lessons with another person that I later played with professionally, Ms. Olivia Charlot Cook. We later played with June Gardner's band at the Famous Door in the '70s and off and on through the years. She also taught my brother Louis on organ as well as piano. I'm the first renegade jazz musician out of the bunch.

"When I came up, my father didn't play—[except] sometime barrelhouse piano. But his father, Joseph Torregano, was the trumpet player in the original Excelsior Brass Band. His godfather was Tats Alexander, so he knew all the brass band guys. My father would sometimes take me to the weekend parades and we'd watch the bands, and I had a good idea of musicians.

"At the age of 12 I switched to clarinet—a very similar story between myself and Pete Fountain. We both suffered from respiratory ailments as children. Doctors recommended that people with respiratory problems if possible take clarinet, flute, saxophone—wind instruments, particularly woodwind instruments. So I studied under Mr. Carey Lavigne privately from, like, January 1965 up until 1971. Through him I was also able to study with Willie Humphrey, who taught at the same studio. It was a little studio at Aubrey and Rocheblave called Crescent City Music School. It's not there anymore. A lot of the black public school band directors taught there. They operated in the evenings, after school, and all day Saturday from something like 8:30 to 5:00 or 5:30. They had a wide range of students who took lessons there. In fact, that's how Michael White and I met. Michael took lessons from Mr. Hampton, who directed St. Augustine's [high school] band. We never took lessons together—I'm two years older than Michael—but we've known each other since 1967.

"I played in the school band at Andrew J. Bell Junior High School under the direction of the late Donald W. Richardson. I played clarinet and bass clarinet and, because of my private lessons, I progressed rather quickly. Most of the people in my class had been playing clarinet since the fourth grade. I didn't start until I was in seventh grade. But the private lessons put me in the Klosé method, which is the collegiate method. It's almost like a telephone book, very thick. It covers all the scales, breathing exercises, the arpeggios, introduces chords and a lot of solo work and technical drills to build up your speed and technique. Mr. Humphrey, surprisingly, didn't talk anything about jazz. He always said that that would come once you learned the instrument. Having played in the navy band himself, he drilled me on Sousa and other marches because he said the marches were where the technique was and if you want to play this instrument you've got to have technique. So I've always been grateful to him for that. A lot of people have told me that I play with a lot more technique than some of the early clarinet players like George Lewis or Johnny Dodds or whatever. That's just the way I was taught. It's probably kept me around a lot longer because God knows I've suffered with carpal tunnel syndrome for about the last six years and I've also had reconstructive surgery in my mouth twice. So it's amazing that I can still play at all. I also have tennis elbow in the left arm.

"From there I went to McDonogh High School on Esplanade Avenue. I attended there when they first integrated that high school in 1967. I was band captain my junior year. Unfortunately, in my senior year in high school, my father suffered a heart attack so that kind of limited my band activities for the first half of the year. I wasn't taking band as a class because I was in the COE program, which is Cooperative Office Education. You go to school half a day, and then you'd have a job. My job was secretary in the personnel department of the now-defunct Jackson Brewery on Decatur Street. It was a very interesting two years [1969–1971, through first year of college]. Coincidentally, typing and playing the clarinet—I started both at almost the same time—and even today I come to work and do one if not both every day. I think the coordination that goes with typing coincided with the coordination of being a clarinet player and helped me.

"After leaving high school I attended Southern University in New Orleans on a music scholarship. After one year I gave up my music scholarship and assumed an academic scholarship. In 1975 I graduated with a B.A. degree in music education. I was in the first music graduating class in SUNO's history. While I was there I got to study with Kidd Jordan, one of the great modern jazz saxophonists. I played in the big band there, when he started his jazz program, and we had some real good jazz musicians. John Longo played first trumpet and later went on to play with the Mercer Ellington band. Wendell Brunious played trumpet in the band for a while. Richard Knox played piano. Roger Lewis played baritone sax. Freddie Shepherd was on tenor sax. I played baritone and tenor in the band. Reggie Houston was in the band. The saxophone section looked like a who's who of saxophone players.

"While I was at SUNO there was a trumpet player in the music program named Archie Robinson, and he used to play in Doc Paulin's brass band. He knew I was interested in playing New Orleans jazz. He called me and said that they needed somebody, so I showed up. It was a two-hour parade on a Sunday afternoon, and I didn't know anybody in the band but Archie . . . and Archie didn't even show up for the gig! I got the wonderful salary of $8 for my first professional job, which wasn't a bad wage in 1971. I didn't complain. I played with Doc for six or seven months. He had three bands. It turned out that [one of his] trumpet players was Gregg Stafford, and it was the first time I met Tuba Fats Lacen. Gregg mentioned that there was another band getting started by a guy named Leroy Jones called the Fairview Baptist Church Band. He said I should try to come to a rehearsal. I talked to my parents about it, and they said it was okay. At the time I was about 19.

"So I showed up and got to meet Danny Barker for the first time and his nephew Charles Barbarin, who had two sons, Charles and Lucien, playing in the band. And I met this 13-year-old trumpet player, Leroy Jones. I tell people that Leroy at 13 was playing stuff that I had never heard anybody that young play before, and I had heard a lot of musicians. It was an exceptionally large brass band, sometimes reaching twenty-two to twenty-five people. I was in the band from May of '71, maybe, until August of '72. We'd have four clarinet players, sometimes five. One of them became a very great tenor saxophone player: Branford Marsalis. He was playing clarinet then. The other four, besides myself, were Donald Gaspard, Thomas and Gene Mims—they both are doctors now—and Branford. Branford and I had a relationship because we could talk music. The others really weren't as interested. They weren't aspiring to be serious musicians. Among the saxophone players, we had two or three altos. The trumpet section was pretty good. We had Greg Davis, who is now with the Dirty Dozen, Gregg Stafford, Leroy of course, and Herlin Riley was a trumpet player in the band. And we had Tuba Fats and a couple other tuba players, sometimes maybe three or four trombone players, two or three snare drum players, and a bass drum.

"We did a lot of parades, but I don't recall doing a funeral. The ages of the guys in the band would range from, like, 13 to Tuba Fats who was probably 20 at that time. Most of them played in school bands. We rehearsed every Monday night religiously. The rehearsal was kind of laid back. We would go over the songs we were supposed to know, then every now and then Gregg and Tuba and myself might show them something new because we were playing with some of the older guys in bands like the Gibson band and Doc Paulin's band. And we might listen to a record and work on something from that. Myself, Leroy, Tuba, Gregg, Charlie, and Lucien, the six of us stuck together as friends at that time. It was nothing for us to come down to old Dixieland Hall and listen to Louie Cottrell's band and Jack Willis and those guys, Frog Joseph and Alvin Alcorn. We'd hang out by Maison Bourbon, and I tell people I think we wore the paint off the street sign. It was one of my favorite places to go.

Joe Torregano's group honors the late trumpeter Harry "Sweets" Edison in a performance at the Sheraton Hotel, New Orleans, April 1999. *From left to right:* Ellis Marsalis, Torregano, and Troy "Trombone Shorty" Andrews. The bassist in the background is unidentified.

Preservation Hall was always nice to us. They would always let us in, and every now and then, maybe Sunday night late, they might let us sit in. We got to see a lot of the legends, people like Kid Thomas, Emanuel Sayles, Louis Nelson, Harold Dejan, Milton Batiste, Raymond Burke. They were all real good guys to me coming up. Mr. Barker especially loved to talk about the days of Jelly Roll Morton and King Oliver, and I loved to listen.

"Our rehearsals were rather informal. As I look back on them now, I guess our repertoire got up to maybe twenty-four, twenty-five songs with that group. When I was in the band, Danny was not always at rehearsals because he was playing with George Finola's band at Maison Bourbon. Sometimes he would come, but could not stay long because he had to leave to go to work. And a lot of times we'd leave rehearsal and come down and stand outside to hear him play. Charlie's dad would kind of supervise rehearsals. He'd give guys rides if they needed it, and he did a lot of booking of the band.

"The summer of '72 became a problem with complaints from some of the older brass bands saying that we were starting to take work away from them. So much that we were told that an ultimatum was given to us, if you were going to work in hotels or convention halls, you need to join the musicians' union. I think Danny was against us becoming union members because of our age and all. I was the first one to leave the band and join the union. I left during the Jazz Festival that year. Gregg, a trombone player who died really young, Michael Myers, and myself sat in with Andrew Morgan's Tuxedo Brass Band. Man, when we got back to play with the Fairview band, we got our butts chewed out by Danny. So I gave Danny a reason not to like me. But you want to learn, you want to play, and you have to take the chance of sitting in.

"When I play tenor sax in a brass band today, I play like Emanuel Paul played in the Eureka Brass Band and the Olympia Brass Band. That's one reason why I was able to secure a spot in Andrew Hall's Society Brass Band because, one, I can read and, two, I understand tradition and I can play that old style on the saxophone.

"Many of the younger guys today wouldn't stand outside a club for four hours like I used to do and listen to people play an instrument that they played. When I was in high school and college—especially in college—I'd listen to Al Cooper, Clarence Ford, Tony Mitchell, Albert Burbank, Louie Cottrell, Cornbread Thomas, Willie Humphrey, anybody who would pick up a clarinet I would listen to. Most of the time when you hear me play, I call myself a gumbo clarinet player because you hear a little bit of every other clarinet player that I ever listened to when I was coming up. I knew Eddie Miller, who played with the Bob Crosby band, and he introduced Michael White and me to Kenny Davern and Barney Bigard. He called us his protégés. When I finally joined the union and these guys took nights off, I was the one they called because I was the only young clarinet player in town at that time. Michael White wasn't in the union yet, and he didn't join the Fairview band until probably '73. So he was a little behind, and there was no Tim Laughlin, no Ryan Burrage, you know. When Michael started doing more, he went in a different direction musically. He was more George Lewis style, and I tended to get more into some swing things.

"I did eight years in the Olympia Brass Band, and thirty-two years later I'm still a member of the Young Tuxedo Brass Band. I play mostly tenor with them now. I've gone on to work with Benny Jones and the Tremé Brass Band, Storyville Stompers, with Jamil Sharif at Maison Bourbon—I've probably played with every jazz band in town except for the Dukes of Dixieland. You know, when I formed my first professional band, Danny Barker was my banjo player. I had a real good band: Richard Payne on bass, Walter Lewis on piano, Lester Caliste on trombone, Gregg on trumpet, myself, and Leroy 'Boogie' Breaux, who just passed. That was from 1974 to 1976. We used to call it the Tremé Ragtime. My kindergarten teacher wrote a song called 'Tremé Ragtime.' I never played the song, but when she died I played it at her funeral. I was very honored that my kindergarten teacher followed my career.

"Thirty years ago I started teaching. I started as a middle school/elementary school band director. I'd go to four elementary schools a week and one middle school. I am presently a high school band director at East St. John High School in Reserve, Louisiana. In my teaching career I've had the pleasure of teaching some very fine musicians: Shannon Powell, Kim Prevost, who once played clarinet, Dwayne Burns, Troy Andrews— for three years at Gregory Junior High—Christian Scott, Lumar Leblanc of the Soul Rebels, Kirk Joseph, Gerald French . . . and one major league baseball player, Gerald Williams. About twelve years ago I went to Japan with John Brunious, and the drummer in the band was Gerald French. I'm traveling with my students now. And I took the Excelsior Brass Band to Salzburg, Austria, three or four years ago, and I took Troy Andrews with me on trombone. Oh, I forgot one! Victor Goines, who is now director of jazz studies at Juilliard. [Goines is no longer at Juilliard, having been appointed director of jazz studies in the School of Music at Northwestern University in 2007.] He's also my cousin.

"Then fifteen years ago . . . I joined the reserve division of the New Orleans Police Department. The city of New Orleans has been very good to me as a clarinet player. I've been very fortunate to have gone to Europe twenty-six times, I've played for three U.S. presidents, records, movies, TV commercials. . . . That's my way of saying thank you. I've always told people I was in the right place at the right time. And I've never forgotten the people who took an interest in me, to develop me. I had an interest in being a police officer since I was a kid."

Joe Torregano now leads the Excelsior Brass Band. Asked if he was responsible for getting that name back on the street, he says, "I can't take total credit for reorganizing the band. Teddy Riley ran the band. After Teddy passed, they asked me to run it, especially since my grandfather was in the band. We try to keep it as a traditional band, just like Teddy ran it. We don't get into the marches and dirges like, maybe, society bands, but we do try to keep it a very traditional repertoire. My grandfather played trumpet in the band. He died about two months after my dad was born. But they named me after him. I had another cousin, Lionel Torregano, who played snare drum in some of the brass bands in the '40s and '50s. Harold Dejan talked about him a lot, but I never knew him.

"I also currently have a quartet, with my youngest brother Michael on piano. [Their CD, *Joseph Torregano, a Jazzman at 50!* was released in 2002.] Right now Frank Oxley is playing drums with us. Frank and I grew up together in the junior high school band, and we've known each other for forty years. Al Bernard is my bass player now. He's a great bass player. We play kind of Benny Goodman swing, with New Orleans music. I got to play with Benny in Los Angeles and met him again later in New Orleans.

"I've seen so many musicians come and go in my 33-year period. When Tuba Fats died [in 2004], it was extremely hard for me because he was the first one of our group to pass on. I had just seen him two or three weeks before, and he was looking pretty good then. Then I got the e-mail saying he was dead. Then to see how, in my opinion, disrespectful the funeral was handled. Unfortunately, the music has never been the same since Tuba passed. They don't come up with the same intensity, very disorganized, and they're fussing and fighting among themselves."

Prior to Katrina, Torregano lived in the Gentilly neighborhood. He and his family headed for Texas on August 28, the day before the storm hit New Orleans, but traffic congestion forced them to go to Greenwood, Mississippi. They stayed there for five days before going on to State College, Pennsylvania, to drop off Joe's daughter Jennifer at her mother's. Then to LaPlace, Louisiana, where he stayed with a colleague.

"I finally made it back to my home in New Orleans about four weeks after the storm to find the water settled at nearly ten feet inside the house for about three weeks, and a tree came through the rear of the house severing a gas line. I couldn't enter the house until the fifth week, and the loss was total. I had the keys on my alto saxophone fall off in my hands, my piano buckled and split in half, and five clarinets and my tenor saxophone suffered water damage." He lost memorabilia, too.

"I didn't remove anything from my house until Thanksgiving week when we were off for a week's vacation. I bought a new home in LaPlace and moved in January 3 [2006]. I still own the home in Gentilly but have no plans for it as yet."

Torregano still lives in LaPlace and continued to teach at East St. John High School until retiring, for health reasons, in the spring of 2010.

DR. MICHAEL WHITE

White was not a member of the original Fairview band, not joining until the later generation of the band. A native New Orleanian, he was born on November 29, 1954, in the Ninth Ward below the Industrial Canal. Later, he and his family moved to the Carrollton neighborhood, a few blocks from Lincoln Park (where Buddy Bolden once played). Still later, the family moved to Liberty Street across the street from the cemetery where a famous family member, Willie "Kaiser" Joseph, is buried.

The Joseph family is that of "Papa John" Joseph, brother of Kaiser, and no relation to Waldren "Frog" Joseph. They came from St. James Parish. When asked if he knew Papa John, White replied, "I don't know a lot about him, but I remember going to a party and there was a figure in my mind that at the time seemed ancient. I think that was him, and I have a very clear picture in my mind of when that was. It was in the early '60s, but I was so small that I don't know for sure if that was him or not. My mother tells me that I did go to something, a family gathering at some-one's house, where he was. When he died in '65, I was, like, 10. My family didn't really deal with the music and the musician part too much. So I didn't know any of these people growing up. He had a niece, Ollie, that used to look a lot like him. She would tell me a lot about him. I knew one of his sisters, Ida, who lived on Washington Avenue. But she was really old. She told me a lot of things about how the family used to play differ-ent instruments and would gather on weekends, on Sundays, and play.

"In terms of Papa John, there were so many coincidences and simi-larities that it was frightening. I lived on Liberty Street a long time. His

[barber] shop was on First and Liberty, and at one time he lived somewhere on Liberty Street. He played clarinet too at one point. 'Course
you mentioned the saxophone—the first saxophone—and all of that. He
also played mandolin and guitar. Our birthdays were very similar. I got
to know a little more about him in Japan because of the people who had
seen him in '63, on that trip with George Lewis. So it was really kind of
strange—a lot of coincidences—but collectively they're so many of them
that they're strange. It's really, really weird.

"I'm related to a lot of musicians who are out there today: [drummer]
Stanley Joseph, [bassist] Richard Moten, [pianist] Thaddeus Richard,
and [multi-instrumentalist] Don Vappie. If you go back to Thibodaux
and St. James Parish, we have a lot of relatives out there. I did a thing
in Donaldsonville that honored [saxophonist] Plas Johnson, King Oliver,
and Bill Summer, and Homer Richard, one of the older musicians—he's
in his 80s and played piano and lot of the R&B guys knew him—and I
talked shop afterwards. In talking to him and his son, I detected a certain
kind of pride in the idea of being musicians. I certainly know that Papa
John was extremely proud of being a musician. A lot of musicians told
me that he represented the highest standards and values in music. They
said that one time he was living in the project which was a different thing
then—more like apartments—if you knocked on his door, he would not
come to the door without a tie on. He was like a teacher for a lot of musicians out of the barbershop. Some people told me they used to stay there
if they didn't have anywhere to stay, the musicians used to rehearse at
the shop, and of course he used to book jobs out of the shop. [He] had a
little sign, Musicians Headquarters, on the barbershop. Yeah, there was
quite a lot of pride that I detected, and I think somewhere down the line
in the genes that kind of came to me. I have four or five younger cousins
playing today."

White started out with Doc Paulin's Brass Band when he was in college. In 1975, a year after being with Paulin, he met Danny Barker, who
told him about the Fairview band. "When I started with Fairview," he
recalls, "it kind of reminds me of when I was in the Boy Scouts. We had
Mr. Barbarin in charge and at that time about ten, eleven boys. We used
to have regular rehearsals on Thursday nights at Fairview Church. On a
couple of occasions during my time Danny Barker came over, and I re-

Michael White and Gregg Stafford perform with White's Young Tuxedo Jazz Band at the Old Algiers River Festival, New Orleans, April 2008.

member one time he brought a musician who was in town to talk to us. It turned out that it was Jonah Jones. But, for the most part, he told me that he didn't have too much to do with the band because of the incident with the union.

"I knew about the first generation before I met Danny because I was going to the same music school as Joseph Torregano. I probably first heard about them through him, but I may have also read something about them in the paper.

"The reality is that I met Danny Barker in the fall of 1975, and it was 1976 before I got with the Fairview. I'll never forget, I had this sort of spiritual connection with the music, and a lot of things that happened are kind of strange coincidences that I can't explain. My meeting with Danny was one of them. I was sitting in the library [at Xavier University] at the time, in a room which is actually where I teach today. At the time it was part of the library, now it's considered the music building. I was looking at a book and had a swivel chair and was kind of moving around looking at the book. There were pictures of different people, and I was looking at a picture of Danny Barker. I swiveled around and looked up and thought I saw in the frame of the doorway Danny Barker standing up staring at me with a guitar in his hand and something else. I thought I must be losing my mind, so I closed my eyes and turned around and looked up again and there was no one there. So I said, it's my imagination. But then I thought, I'm not crazy, so I went around looking and looking and didn't find anybody. Then, about twenty minutes later, I found him. He had come to teach a class [at the university], and that was his first day and he was lost and was looking for the classroom, which happened to be way upstairs in the top of the library in an almost hidden room. So I met him that very day, but that was 1975. That was my last year [at Xavier], 1975–1976. So I was 20 years old before I joined [the band]. There's no question about that. Anyone who says they remember me before or saw pictures of me before, that is simply not true. There are pictures of this guy, Gene Mims, who used to play clarinet and looked an awful lot like I used to as a kid, and there are people who swear up and down it's me. The first generation, which had people closer to my age—a little older or little younger—was the first generation. When I got in the band, there were people ranging from nine to about 17—and then I was older.

"The kids in the Fairview band were at first sort of like a cute novelty, then people wanted to hire them for jobs. So supposedly some of the union musicians thought they were cutting union bands out of work. They complained to the union, which at that time had certain power and control over situations—which no longer exists. I think they may have brought [Barker] before the union board and questioned him, so I think they either warned him or threatened him with a fine or something like that. So he just stopped, officially, having too much to do with the band. He let Lucien's father, Charles Barbarin, kind of take over. He was like an adult supervisor.

"We basically did three things. We had rehearsals on Thursdays. We used to go out and play in the French Quarter every weekend—Saturdays or Saturdays and Sundays. We would play in the area that was once called the Fish Market Restaurant—I don't know if it still is—right across the street from the Greek's place [the old Mediterranean Café]. We used to play by Al Hirt's old place. We would play for tips, and there were eight or 10 of us. Mr. Barbarin's granddaughter used to come out, and she would be the grand marshal and dance. At that time, we played a lot of basic traditional standards: 'Li'l Liza Jane,' 'Bourbon Street Parade,' 'Saints,' 'Second Line,' a number of songs actually. People who have become professional musicians from the second generation are Harry Sterling—he played tuba with Fairview, but he now plays guitar with Big Al Carson; Edward Paris—calls himself 'Eddie Bo'—plays trombone; Jerry Anderson, Mr. Barbarin's grandson, a drummer who sometimes plays with Kermit Ruffins; Efrem Towns, who plays trumpet with the Dirty Dozen; William Smith, a trumpet player, Dodie Simmons's brother. Stephen Cotton played trumpet, but he stopped playing music and got into the funeral business. There were very few people who kind of survived from the first generation into the second because most of them went with Leroy and formed the Hurricane Brass Band. But there were the two sons of Dave Williams. Nobody ever talks about them anymore. One played trombone, and I don't remember what the other played. He didn't stay that long.

"So there was a point at which the kids were very competitive. You know, it was kind of fun and adventurous to be out in the Quarter playing. It was always nice to get our little tips—that was good money in those days. Occasionally there were other performances. We played at the Jazz Festival, and I remember we played—why, I don't know—out in Metairie on Veterans [Boulevard] for the opening of a movie, *A Bridge Too Far*.

"I think the first and second generations were really the ones that were kind of important in the sense of jazz. Once Danny Barker and the Barbarins were no longer in charge of it, everything kind of changed. It became something completely different, and I don't think any professional musicians came out of that. I joined the union in late '78, and that's when I stopped playing with the band. Once I got out of the band, [Charles Barbarin] was still handling the band, and I would say that the second generation went on until about '79, '80, something like that. Then they changed hands. I think the church organist took over the band, and she had a whole different idea of what the band would be. Her name was Deborah White [now Mrs. Darby]. She made it more like a high school band. From what I can tell, Danny's mission was to try to teach kids about jazz and the jazz heritage. But that's kind of a tough concept—even in New Orleans—because a lot of people don't understand jazz.

"I think [Danny Barker] was a very complex individual. He had different sides. Over the years, I got to know him pretty well. I got to see him in lots of different settings so I probably knew him better, on some level, than most people. I think there was a side of him that was very, very conscious about jazz and jazz history, and I think he did have the vision and insight to see that the talent that produced jazz in the beginning still existed in New Orleans. I think he wanted to try to promote that. It's really kind of funny because I find myself saying this myself. Last week I was doing a seminar for the music teachers in New Orleans public schools and, without thinking of Danny Barker, I found myself saying some of the same things that I think he envisioned. And that is seeing jazz as a social cure, for some of the problems that are going on in the inner city, by offering kids not only a way of making a living but also a way of gaining pride and self-esteem and having something from their past that they can hold on to. To sort of counteract the negative effects of television, the media, radio, MTV, BET, rap video, and all of that. So what I think he saw years ago was that New Orleans could still produce a lot of jazz musicians and the kids had a way of being proud and keeping out of trouble and learning concepts like unity and teamwork that could be a positive force for jazz and also in the lives of these individual kids. I think he had those objectives in mind, and I think that was a great thing. He used to talk to the kids, individually or whenever he would encounter them, quite a lot about history.

"For me, I guess he used to help to keep up a romantic view of jazz—some of the places he had gone, things that he had seen. I was always interested in jazz history, so it was good. He in a lot of ways was like a history book. He had seen so many people, played with so many people, and he could easily and casually talk about people like Louis Armstrong, Jelly Roll Morton, Sidney Bechet to Charlie Parker, Dizzy Gillespie, Cab Calloway, and so many others. So I learned a lot from him in that sense. I learned a lot of things from him, musical things—the sort of things like what to do and what not to do.

"But I had already gotten a lot of those kinds of lessons, in a different way, from Doc Paulin. He preached a lot—not as much about history, of course—about values in life and values in terms of music and professionalism, how you present yourself and what the music means. So they were complementary, in a sense, though very different. There was hardly ever any mention between the two of them. It was almost like they functioned in different worlds. When I started out, one of the things that I found really amazing was there were very much separate worlds or communities, which there still are actually. There are some people that never have contact with people in other worlds. There's a lot going on that people don't know about in jazz in New Orleans because it's hard to see and find. Doc Paulin was in the world of the brass bands, the streets, Uptown, small churches, club parades. Danny Barker wasn't really around that stuff. He was in a different world.

"I have to tell you, when I start talking about spirits and spirituality, a lot of strange things have happened. As it relates to Danny Barker, the thing that's strange is the only class that I teach now at Xavier is the same class he had, and the fact that I teach it in that room where I first saw him. It's strange."

Michael White graduated from Xavier University in 1976 (*magna cum laude* in foreign- language education in French and Spanish). He earned his master's degree in Spanish in 1979 and his Ph.D. in 1984 from Tulane University. Since 1981 he has been a full-time instructor at his alma mater. He was recently appointed to the Rosa and Charles Keller Jr. Endowed Chair in the Arts and Humanities. He teaches a class on jazz and jazz history.

White has performed with many New Orleans jazz legends and several brass bands. He has appeared with Wynton Marsalis at Lincoln Center in New York City and tours extensively abroad in addition to leading his own Liberty Jazz Band and Liberty Brass Band. His recordings on the Basin Street label, *Dancing in the Sky* (2004) and *Blue Crescent* (2008), reveal him as a significant composer in the New Orleans jazz tradition as well as a first-rate instrumentalist in that tradition. In 2008 he was awarded a National Heritage Fellowship (the country's top award in traditional and folk arts) by the National Endowment for the Arts and was named Humanist of the Year in 2010 by the Louisiana Endowment for the Arts.

Until Hurricane Katrina, White lived in Gentilly. He fled to Houston on the day before the hurricane struck. He returned to his home nearly two months later to find dead grass, demolished trees, and the stains of six feet of water in his house. He lost virtually everything: instruments, books, records, photos, memorabilia of all kinds.

"I tried very hard to picture what this would be like, but you can't begin to imagine. The hard part is that there's a lot of history here that can't be replaced. It's all gone. I'm overwhelmed. I wouldn't know where to start."

He returned to Houston, where he was also caring for his 83-year-old mother and an 80-year-old aunt, but came back to New Orleans several months later to resume teaching at Xavier University. As of early February 2006, he says, "For now I'm back home." Yet, as one of the internationally best known traditional jazz clarinetists from New Orleans, he continues to travel and perform extensively both here and abroad.

EPILOGUE

Don Marquis and I were unable to interview Anthony "Tuba Fats" Lacen, who died at his home in New Orleans on January 11, 2004, at the age of 53. A member of the first-generation Fairview band, Tuba Fats subsequently played in numerous other brass bands, eventually leading his own outfit, Tuba Fats' Chosen Few Brass Band. His influence on the modern brass band movement in the city will be felt for a long time.

Accordingly, we dedicated this article to him.

7

JACK MAHEU
The General

.⚜. .⚜. .⚜.

Upon settling permanently in New Orleans some two decades ago, Jack Maheu became one of the most respected and frequently called clarinet players in town. His weekend jam sessions at Fritzel's Jazz Pub on Bourbon Street became legendary.

Maheu brought a lifetime of professional experience as a jazz performer to those sessions. Many a fine young clarinetist—people like Tim Laughlin, Tom Fischer, and Evan Christopher—had an opportunity to sit in and learn from him. His acolytes were not just clarinet players, either. They included the likes of keyboardists John Royen, Tom McDermott, and David Boeddinghaus and trumpeters Kevin Clark and Duke Heitger, among many others. Maheu came to be known as "The General" to many of those young musicians.

Jack Maheu has experienced a number of misfortunes since those Fritzel's days. There were two abortive attempts to start his own jazz clubs, one on Frenchmen Street and the second at the corner of Canal and Claiborne (near Rampart). A significant factor in the failure of the latter was Hurricane Katrina and its attendant flooding, which took place just six months after the club's opening. The club and Maheu's own grand piano were ruined in the disaster.

The clarinetist was on vacation with his children in California when Katrina struck New Orleans, and like so many others, he was dislocated from his home for a period of time. After having heart surgery later that year, he experienced a massive stroke in March 2006. A subsequent fall during rehab led to brain surgery, and he was in and out of hospitals much of that year. His recovery has proceeded at a deliberate pace. He has been residing in an assisted-living facility in New Orleans since 2007.

Maheu has not played professionally since his stroke. Yet it should be

noted that he made a recording for the Jazzology label as part of a quartet—
Jim Hession, piano; Mark Brooks, bass; and Richard Taylor, drums—in his
beloved New Orleans home prior to Katrina (2004). The home has since been
sold, but the CD—entitled My Inspiration*—is scheduled to be released in the*
summer of 2010.

The following interview is the product of lengthy conversations in Febru-
ary 1994 and January 1995, and was published essentially as is in The Mississippi Rag *in May 1995 as a tribute to Maheu on his 65th birthday.*

Veteran clarinetist Jack Maheu—perhaps best known for his long association with the Salt City Five/Six, recordings with the original Dukes of Dixieland, and as a member of the house band in the last manifestation of Eddie Condon's (Club) in New York—moved to New Orleans in 1990. More recently, he has been deeply involved in the design and construction of a large home just off Esplanade Avenue and is establishing himself as a permanent resident of the Crescent City.

Maheu is playing as well as ever, and the weekend jam sessions that he leads with a core trio at Fritzel's European Jazz Pub on Bourbon Street have become one of the hottest happenings on the local jazz scene in recent years. Just last month, a group he put together for the occasion— "Jack Maheu and His Fire in the Pet Shop Callithumpian Jazz Band"— won the French Quarter Festival's Battle of the Bands competition for the third year in a row.

TJ: Jack, what brought you to New Orleans?

JM: Well, things weren't working out anywhere else, and I always knew that I would be coming back here one of these years. I had played here with the Dukes in 1958, in 1960 and 1961 with Muggsy Spanier, and in 1976 I joined Connie Jones for two weeks at the Esplanade Bar. That was the last time I was here. I had some friends here—I knew George Buck [of Jazzology Records]—so I thought I would take a chance.

I landed here in the spring of 1990 with very little money. I met [record producer] Gus Statiras, and he took me up and down the street and introduced me to the players. I stayed with [clarinetist] Jacques Gauthé for a few nights—he was very kind to let me sleep on his daybed—and then I got a room on the corner of Bourbon and Esplanade. I sat in at various places. Everyone was friendly. I was prepared to do menial labor—I had my mind adjusted—but, luckily, I got calls for work.

I went with Jumbo [Al Hirt] for six months and filled in on the riverboats with Eddie Bayard. Then I got a steady job at the Fairmont Hotel [now—again—the Roosevelt Hotel] with a trio in the fall of 1990. John Royen was on piano and Joe Morton on drums. About that time I started at Fritzel's. That would have been in 1991. I was there for a while and then quit for about five or six months, and then I went back and have been there ever since.

TJ: The Fritzel's format is a trio. Tell me about that.

JM: Well, David Boeddinghaus is on piano and Dickie Taylor on drums. When David is out of town with Banu Gibson, I'm fortunate to have such fine players as John Royen, Steve Pistorius, or Tom McDermott to call upon to fill in. When Dickie, who's the leader of the Dukes of Dixieland, is out of town, I can call on guys like Mark Morris or Trevor Richards. I'm very happy to be in that situation.

I was staying busy and there was no reason to leave [New Orleans]. If you want to go on tours, [New Orleans] looks good on the brochures and advertising. I like the weather and pace of life and, surprisingly, I started liking the town. It is "eccentric," a different way of life. It's a party town and a music town, just about everything I want. I have had opportunities for steady work in other places—good-paying jobs and prestige work—but I have not had thoughts about leaving.

TJ: Okay, that gives us an idea of where you are now. Let's do some history and go back to the beginning. When and where were you born?

JM: May 1, 1930, in Troy, New York, but I was raised in Plattsburgh, New York.

TJ: How about your family? Do you have siblings?

JM: That's a long story. I didn't know that I had brothers and sisters until about six years ago. My father and mother split up when I was about three. He moved to California and started another family. They didn't stay in touch, so I didn't know that I had any [siblings]. I have four brothers and two sisters, and they're great people —just absolutely the best. I got a phone call from a gal who, after questioning me about this and that for a while, said, "I'm your sister, Patty." I said, "What?!" Then she told me the whole bit, and it has been like winning the lottery—to find a family like that.

TJ: So, you were then basically raised as an only child by your mother?

JM: Yes, but she remarried when I was about 10.

TJ: Were you raised in a musical environment?

JM: My grandmother was a mandolin virtuoso and studied seriously. But she raised a family and only played locally in upstate New York. I remember the family always used to sing a lot—that was our entertainment, and playing cards. There was no television in those days. I remember that she could always sing the harmony parts, and it used to frustrate me that I couldn't find the notes she would sing. I kept trying to find them and didn't know how she could do that. My grandfather would sing bass and probably my great-aunt sang lead. She had one of those D.A.R. chorus-type voices, and I would try to do the harmony with my grandmother. She also played piano by ear.

TJ: Did you take piano lessons as a kid?

JM: No, I wanted to, but I started on alto saxophone. In the summer of '43. I think I was 12 or 13.

TJ: Did you pick the alto, or did someone encourage you?

JM: My grandfather brought one home from his jewelry store where he had taken it in on trade. And he said, "Here, if you want to be musical." I used to grab everything I could find to play, like little plastic horns. "Here's the real thing," he said. I remember practicing on the porch in Plattsburgh, and the neighbors calling up and complaining.

TJ: Did you start with instruction in school?

JM: Yes, I played in the school band. In my junior and senior years in

Jack Maheu discusses musical details with pianist Jim Hession in a rehearsal for a recording at Maheu's home, April 2004.

high school in Plattsburgh, I started doing solos on stage—things like "Saxophobia" and "Flight of the Bumble Bee." I didn't start clarinet until I left high school.

When I went to college—I went to Plattsburgh State Teachers College, where I was studying art and music—I wanted a smaller instrument to carry around. So, I got a clarinet, and I played in the college band.

TJ: How did jazz come into your life?

JM: I used to listen to records—Benny Goodman, Artie Shaw, and some Dixieland. I had a wind-up Victrola, and I think my first jazz records were the RCA green-label Bunk Johnson and George Lewis. As I remember, that was my first album.

TJ: When did you start playing jazz?

JM: My first job was in 1947. That was before I started on clarinet. It was in Dannemora, New York, and we had a five-piece band. Then I went to college and had my first band in the fall of 1947, a seven-

114

piece band with music stands and a library. We read everything. In the summer of 1948 I met a very good piano player by the name of Al Delano. He's still a very fine piano player—in fact, he toured with my band many times throughout the years. He's one of those excellent players who never got any recognition because he liked Plattsburgh and didn't leave there. He formed a seven- or eight-piece band, and I played saxophone and some clarinet in that band.

Then I applied to Pratt Art Institute in Brooklyn to study commercial art and started there in the fall of 1949. I sold my saxophone and took a few lessons on clarinet. I was listening to Eddie Condon records by this time and heard the radio broadcasts from Nick's in the Village and, after I'd been in Brooklyn a month or two, I saved enough money to go over to New York to Condon's. I loved that music. I remember walking in the door—the stage was in the back—and there were Wild Bill Davison, Pee Wee Russell, Cutty Cutshall, Gene Schroeder, Walter Page, and either George Wettling or Cliff Leeman, and Condon. And, as I walked through the door, they hit "At the Jazz Band Ball"—and I almost fainted. It was so powerful. I was overcome. I couldn't imagine anything so good.

That was the turning point [in my musical life]. Up until that time, I hadn't known how good it could be. You can hear it on records and be thrilled by it, but not until you hear it live . . . Whoa . . . Serious. So, whenever I could, I made trips over to either Nick's or Condon's. Pee Wee Erwin or Phil Napoleon was playing at Nick's, I think. That was a rare treat for me. During the following summer back home, I met [drummer] Bob Cousins and I joined a trio that he was playing in near Plattsburgh. He persuaded me to apply to the music school at the University of Syracuse. I had no idea what I was doing, but I went there as a clarinet major.

The first year there I practiced a lot. I remember days putting in nine hours of practice. I'd have classes in the morning, then practice from noon until ten at night with maybe a short break for dinner. The second year I discovered the joys of playing in the bars and drifted away from my schoolwork. By that time we had formed the Salt City Five and were getting jobs. This was the first real jazz band that I was with. Don Hunt played trumpet, Bob

Cousins played drums, Will Alger played trombone, and Charlie French played piano.

[We were all at the university], but Will had just quit. He took me around to the clubs in Syracuse where bands were playing and was very nice to me. We played some jobs in 1951—frat parties and things like that—but our first steady job was at Memory Lane in January 1952. In June, we were on the Arthur Godfrey Talent Scouts show, and we won that. We got three of his morning shows and a Wednesday night show out of that, which he didn't have to do for us. He liked the band very much and wanted to keep us on as one of his steady groups. But one of the sponsors—it was Chesterfield cigarettes—turned us down.

TJ: And you got other bookings from that?

JM: Yes, we were booked into Child's Paramount on Times Square. We started there November 11, 1952. We played five nights a week, from 6 p.m. until midnight, and by 12:05 we were on our way to Nick's or Condon's. Don Hunt had an excellent ear. He would memorize all their arrangements, and we would go back and practice and play them—especially the ones at Nick's because Phil Napoleon had a lot of things worked out. We were learning, and that's how we learned—by copying.

They used to have these Sunday afternoon jam sessions [at Child's], where they would bring in outside bands—it was dazzling—with people like Bobby Hackett, Vic Dickenson, Coleman Hawkins, Hot Lips Page, Pee Wee Russell, Wild Bill Davison, and on and on. The management would pick out a band from who was available, and we would have both bands there. At the end of each set, both bands would be on the bandstand. One time, they picked the band from Nick's [he laughs heartily] and here we were playing all their arrangements! And [Billy] Maxted said, "You S.O.B.s. . . ." So, the next time, we went down to Nick's, a few days later, Maxted had worked out an arrangement of "Basin Street Blues" in the key of D and he had it all written out with memorized figures [Maheu hums it] . . . He turns around and looks at us sitting there and says, "Copy that one, you pricks . . ." [he laughs again]. But if you know Maxted . . . he was flattered. That was one of our first experiences listening to good live jazz. These guys were really top of the line. This was back in the days when the jazz bands took their music seriously, and they rehearsed and practiced. It was a very good learning experience for us young guys.

Actually, Maxted took one of *our* arrangements—I think it was "Maple Leaf Rag"—and he said, "I hope you don't mind." We hung out a lot with them. Actually, they were glad to see us because they worked from 9:00 to about 4:00 a.m., so when we would come in about 12:30 they'd get us to sit in. So that—plus the Sunday afternoon sessions with all those great jazz names—was a marvelous time of our lives. And a lot of that is on tape, too. We also used to broadcast from Child's Paramount, and I have some of those tapes. I was amazed, when I heard them, how clean our band sounded—it was quite a good band.

TJ: You mentioned Pee Wee Russell at those jam sessions, and I know he was one of your early idols. Did you get to know him at all?

JM: It was very hard to get to know Pee Wee because he was sort of in his own world. I remember one incident. We were standing up there at the end of one of the sets, and all of the brass players were playing and the drummers, and us reed players were standing there side by side and Pee Wee said, "I think I'll practice my low notes now. . . ." I used to hang on every word he said—it was gospel. Actually, I'm on a record with him that we made just before I left Chicago in 1961. I think it was "Tin Roof Blues," and I went first. I was being a little cocky and going to cut Pee Wee, but you don't cut Pee Wee. No one does. He was a master jazz player.

TJ: When did you start going on the road?

JM: We were at Child's for four months and left there in March 1953. We signed up with MCA, and they booked us in various out-of-the-way places. We added a bass player, Dave Marquis. We were then six pieces, a cooperative band, but we called ourselves "Will Alger and the Salt City Five." Six young guys, each with his own idea of how to run a band—quite a picnic. But Will Alger was a major player. If he had ever come down here, he would have caused quite a stir. He had such exuberance in his playing. He was a very funny guy, and played with humor. He was a great ensemble player.

We played in Bermuda at the Princess in 1954. We were there for three months. It was at the end of that year that we made our first record for Jubilee Records, and that turned out pretty well. We made a second 10" LP for Jubilee in 1955. The band on those recordings was made up of Will Alger, Bob Cousins, Frank Frawley on bass, Dick Oakley on cornet, Dave Remington on piano, and myself. Then we played Detroit and the Blue Note in Chicago, and there was a mix-up. There were two bands booked at the same time, and we held them to the contract. Jack Teagarden's band was the other band, and I have a picture with both bands on the stage at the Blue Note. That was when half the band left. Cuz left, Dave Remington left, and Frank Frawley left. That was one of those bleak periods when we couldn't find players and couldn't find work. But we managed to job around for a year or more, nothing eventful that I recall until we went to Vegas. That was in the spring of 1957. That's when I joined the Dukes of Dixieland.

Now the Dukes were playing from midnight to six in the morning, and we were playing from six in the evening to midnight. They had two Dixieland bands going. They wanted Dixieland bands because people would gamble more. It loosened things up more, and people were happier.

TJ: Why did you join the Dukes?

JM: There were always personality problems on the Salt City Six, and I had wanted to make some changes. Will and I weren't getting along. When Hal Cooper quit the Dukes, [trumpeter] Frank Assunto asked me if I wanted to join the band. It was paying about double what I was making, so I said, "It sounds good to me." It worked out fine up until I got bored playing the same tunes over and over again—that's the only thing that bothered me.

On the Salt City Six we had an extensive repertoire of arrangements, hundreds of them, and I was always looking for different things. I kept pushing for different things, stretching the boundaries, exploring things that had not been done before. I finally got my way in the '60s when I rejoined the Salt City Six. I did a lot of the arrangements for the Dukes. In fact, I think all of Volume 7 is my arrangements, which I never got credit for. They gave me a

Christmas bonus, but I never got any credit for the arrangements.

TJ: How many recordings did you make with the Dukes?

JM: When I joined them, they had made Volume 3, which was the first stereo record on the market. Then we made Volumes 4 through 9, and they were selling out. Volume 4 and Volume 5 were number 3 and number 4 on the top ten albums, next to Nat King Cole and Ella Fitzgerald. Then they did Volumes 1 and 2 in stereo, and Hal Cooper is on 1 and 2 in mono. They were years apart.

I remember some funny scenes in the recording studios. This was in the first days of stereophonic recording, and we were in the RCA studio in Chicago [which was] the size of three basketball courts. They had us spread around the room to get the separation of sound and put screens around us. We didn't have headphones, so we had to shout to one another and do fifteen–twenty takes to get the sound that Sid Frey [owner of Audio Fidelity Records] was looking for.

It became a total nightmare. I was good for about three takes, and then I began going downhill. If I got through it without a major blunder, great. So, all my worst stuff is on these records. Freddie [Assunto, trombonist], in trying to get "Slide, Frog, Slide," kept blowing the line at the end of the tape. They didn't do much splicing in those days, so we had to re-do the whole thing—twenty-six takes on "Slide, Frog, Slide"! I remember being three days in the studio from ten in the morning until midnight.

TJ: Were there any high moments, musically, with the Dukes?

JM: Yeah, it was a good band, actually, but we got that Bourbon Street-itis, when you played the same tunes over and over. Like on Volume 7 there were some nice things—"In a Persian Market," "Asleep in the Deep," and a couple marches, all good arrangements—but they'd play them a few times and go back to the old stuff again. They became set in their ways, and, after a year and a half of it, it bothered me. It was time for a rest. That's when I left. It was a show band, and I was young and naïve and didn't realize that you had to put up with it. I wanted just pure jazz and things to be fun. It just wasn't fun anymore. Freddie and Frankie were good players. And that band, when it was on, it sounded good—good jazz—

and got across, people loved it. Frankie paid the band well. He was a fine lead player and soloist, good singer. There just wasn't enough diversity for me.

TJ: Did you then go back directly to the Salt City Six?

JM: No. I left the Dukes in March of 1959 and formed my own band at the Preview Lounge in Chicago and played opposite the Georg Brunis band. That was back in the good old days when they had bands all over town. Norman Murphy was in that band on trumpet, Bob Cousins—my old pal—on drums, John Welch on trombone, Andy Johnson on piano, and Joe Johnson on bass. After the Preview, I formed a trio and played at Sir Gant's Restaurant on Lawrence Avenue with Cousins and Andy Johnson. It was sort of a jam session thing. Guys playing at the Aragon Ballroom just down the street and other places—the Green Mill was two blocks down the street—would come and sit in. We were there about six or eight months, as I recall. Then I joined Muggsy Spanier in 1960 and played with him for about a year and a half. Then Will and I reformed the Salt City Six in 1961.

TJ: How was it playing with Muggsy?

JM: Great, just great. Such a consistently swinging player, hard-driving ensemble player. When we played a new tune, we would play it every night, and every night he would develop his chorus on it. He would polish it, hone it, and get that chorus the way he wanted it, and that would be his chorus on that tune.

TJ: The 1960s was not a great time for traditional jazz, but the Salt City Six seems to have managed pretty well.

JM: There was a time when Wild Bill [Davison] joined us. We were scuffling, but even he couldn't find work. He couldn't play for free! He came to Syracuse with us for $25 a night. Very sad. That was a very slow time. When you're young, when you're behind the eight ball, it's so hard to get going because you don't have money for phone calls, transportation, or anything. That was in 1962, but then we started getting work. We were a six-piece band. We'd do all our show tunes, and then we'd bring Bill on. We had a helluva act, a good show.

Will was on trombone, Paul Squire was on trumpet. Dr. Paulu,

I call him—doctor of space. Playing next to Wild Bill for that year really focused his playing. Bobby Mahan was on piano, Lou Johnston on bass, and Ralph Haupert on drums, in addition to me.

TJ: Wild Bill didn't record with you then, but that was the band that made those Audiophile recordings that have recently been re-released by George Buck on Jazzology, wasn't it?

JM: Yes, that was 1963, when we did the "William Tell Overture." They reissued both of the albums that we recorded in Pittsburgh in September 1963, and there are some tapes around for a third album that we did at the same time and they've been lost. I don't know where they are. When George put out the CD, he put both albums on it and called it *The Original Salt City Six Plays "The Classics"* pertaining to the classical music and jazz classics. The third album we did was medleys of songs. [The Salt City Six and Five came and went over the next few years. It was disbanded for good in 1978.]

TJ: You eventually recorded with Wild Bill in the '70s?

JM: Yes, that was in 1973. *Tie a Yellow Ribbon* was the name of the album, recorded at PCI studios in Rochester. That was where the engineer had a problem getting the distortion out of Wild Bill's microphone. He kept changing microphones and changing things around, doing sound checks, and he couldn't figure out what was wrong. He kept getting this distortion. Come to find out, it was Bill's tone. He was growling—that's his sound!

One of the tunes we did was "Sweet and Lovely" which has a rather difficult bridge. Bill never read very well, we found out, so we wound up making little symbols for which keys to push down. And the same thing with "Tie a Yellow Ribbon" because that was popular then, and we wanted to get that one down. But the parts that he did get, he really came in like gangbusters. He nailed it.

Wild Bill was probably the hottest player that I ever played with. It was absolutely mind-blowing how he could drive a band, his drinking habits notwithstanding. I think Pee Wee Russell was the same way. Their drinking habits tempered their technical facility, but they made up for it with the other things that they did. It worked. Pee Wee was a genius. He was probably one of the all-time greatest jazz players. Probably the best Dixieland band of all time, for raw excitement, was the Condon band with Wild Bill, Pee Wee, Georg Brunis, George Wettling, Gene Schroeder, Walter Page, and Condon. And the Commodore records they made: "That's a Plenty," "Panama Rag" . . . that is the ultimate. If someone wants to know what the best of Dixieland—or any other music for that matter—sounds like, that's what I would recommend to listen to.

TJ: Tell me about the quartet you formed after disbanding the Salt City Six.

JM: Yes, that was the winter and spring of 1978–1979. That was a modern, swing-type thing. We did "Love for Sale," "Blue Monk," "Lover," "Cherokee," and modern swing tunes, a very hard-swinging group.

[It lasted] a little less than a year. We did one tour, but we played mainly in Rochester, four nights a week. It was more for musicians. I loved it. The group was called "Helium." We went into the studio, and I have some tapes. It was a very hard-swinging group, pretty fierce in spots. I had Danny D'Imperio on drums and Steve Alcott on bass. Barry Kiener was on piano. That was my one serious entry into modern music.

TJ: Didn't you start at Condon's in the late '70s?

JM: Yes, I started there December 5, 1979.

TJ: What brought you back to New York?

JM: I never really liked living in New York. I was a small-town guy. Wild Bill used to call me to play down there, but I wouldn't go. So, in the spring of 1979, I was scuffling around Rochester and then got a huge contract with this place on Main Street. I have a seven-piece band lined up, four nights a week, good money, with a nice seven-foot grand piano, but the new owners couldn't get an entertainment license. The city said they didn't want a jazz club too close to the Eastman School of Music because it might corrupt the students, but it turned out that it was really a political thing.

To make a very long story short, they eventually opened the place, without an entertainment license, and it became a gay bar. So, that's when I made the ultimate sacrifice—I said I'd never go back to New York—that's when I called New York. I got the number for Condon's, called, and asked to speak to the manager, and

I think I got Eddie Polcer on the phone. I told him who I was and asked if anyone needed a clarinet player in New York City. Polcer could have just said no and slammed down the phone, but he was gracious enough and polite enough.

"Well," he said, "I don't know you. My partner is Red Balaban, does he know you?" Well, Red vaguely remembered me and, just by chance, their regular clarinet player was leaving and they needed someone.

TJ: Was that Herb Hall?

JM: No, it was Bobby Gordon. And then they said that Wild Bill was scheduled to come in and they wanted to get someone he would like to work with, at least for those two weeks. So, I told them to call Bill for a reference, and he gave me a very nice recommendation. So, two or three days later I headed for New York. Wild Bill came in, it worked out fine, and I stayed for five and a half years.

TJ: Polcer was both playing [trumpet] and managing the club then?

JM: Yes, and [bassist] Red Balaban was the owner and also played in the band.

TJ: Was it he, then, who started the third Condon's?

JM: Yes, he was a friend of the Condon family. They gave him permission to use the name.

TJ: Who else was in the band in those days?

JM: When I went there Connie Kay was playing drums, Jim Andrews and John Bunch switched off on piano, Vic Dickenson on trombone, Balaban, Polcer, and myself. [The year 1985] was the end of "Eddie Condon's." Since then another place called simply "Condon's" got started, but that's not the same thing at all.

TJ: I know Vic Dickenson was one of your favorites. Didn't he die shortly before the club closed?

JM: Yes, we went to his wake. I remember the last day he was in Condon's. It was in the afternoon, and they were having a party for him. They got him up to play—he didn't want to play, he wasn't well, had lost a lot of weight—and he played "Just Friends." Such a gracious man, gracious gentleman. When he was leaving for home—he had his trombone and was walking towards Seventh Avenue—and I said, "Thanks for the lessons, Vic." And that's the last I saw him. He had such beautiful lines in the ensemble—oh, a master. Those were very special times that I played with Vic.

"I remember the last day [at Condon's, in 1985]. The three television stations were there filming and people were standing out in the street. It was a sad day. The historic jazz landmark was closing down. We taped that last afternoon, and I've got that. And just before that, we taped [trumpeter] Billy Butterfield who was there for two weeks. That's in the can, and somebody has them. And he was playing great. I think that's one of the last things he ever did. [Butterfield died in March 1988 at the age of 71.] The first night he was—shall we say—not up to par, but after that he learned that we had a swinging band. We had Dan Barrett on trombone, D'Imperio on drums, John Bunch on piano, and Dave Shapiro on bass. After he heard that, the next night he came ready to play. And play he did! That was in the summer of 1985, maybe a month before they closed.

Jack Maheu spent most of the late 1980s in Florida, where he helped to form the popular Paradise Jazz Band that worked regularly in a club on Marco Island. They recorded in 1988 and toured Germany the following year. But as work opportunities slowed, Maheu decided to move to New Orleans, later admitting, "I should have come here sooner."

TJ: Let's conclude by talking a bit more about the present. I've witnessed some very hot nights in the jam sessions at Fritzel's.

JM: Oh, yes, it's very good to have a place for musical experimentation and expression, for guys to come in and play and listen and learn tunes. I like the room. It's intimate. It's got the feel and atmosphere of a jazz room. I learn tunes. I learn from other guys, and they come in and learn. I just try to keep it commercially viable, keep the crowd interest, and not get too far out. It seems to be paying off, the crowds have been very good, and Dutch [owner, the late Dutch Seutter] seems to be happy. I don't get bored there, that's for sure. There's always something different. The fun of it is having an open mind and an attitude of experimentation—like, let's see what happens. It's musical fun. You can call it Dixieland or New Orleans music or whatever you want. As Condon used to say, "We called it music."

TJ: Just about everyone from around town (and beyond) has sat in at one time or another, and all seem to fit in comfortably.

JM: Everyone has his own musical personality. You can learn from everybody, even players who don't play very well. There are little things they do, a way of playing a phrase or something. I admire the younger players, like Chris Tyle, Orange Kellin, John Gill, Tom Roberts. They have done their homework. They are bringing to light some of those old tunes that no one else might be aware of. I think it is just great. The shame of it is that they don't get the recognition that some of the politically correct groups get. And Eddie Bayard takes an excellent seven-piece jazz band to tour the Middle East and never gets a local mention. Duke Heitger is a great player, and he keeps getting better and better. A good kid, too. Connie Jones is one of my favorite players. I could go on and on.

TJ: How do you see your personal future taking shape, as well as the music scene in New Orleans?

JM: I would like to see more jazz clubs on Bourbon Street or in the French Quarter. I predict that the next two jazz centers in New Orleans will be on Frenchmen Street and Rampart Street. I think Bourbon Street is pretty much washed up, except for a few lonely outposts of jazz. It will take a while, but it will probably go the way that Times Square did. They outpriced themselves. The more money the clubs made, the more the landlords raised the rent—until the clubs had to either put in non-union bands or they became T-shirt shops or some other abomination. Yet there will always be a market for jazz. The most-asked question is, "Where are all the jazz bands?" People come from all over the world expecting the street to be lined with jazz clubs—Dixieland, swing jazz, the blues—and they find very little of it. And they're very disappointed, especially those who remember the New Orleans bands of yesteryear. They have the records, love the sound, and they can't find it.

There is a definite market for it here, but a jazz club must be run by someone who really loves jazz. When Hyp Guinle had the Famous Door, he loved the players, he loved the music, and it showed. It was a successful jazz club for years. That aura spread up and down the street—ten, twelve bands going all day long until the late hours of the morning. I don't know whether I can blame any of that on the complacency of some of the players—when musicians get in the factory-type frame of mind, playing the same tunes over and over because you have a constantly changing crowd. You get the requests for the old warhorses, "Sweet Georgia Brown," "Saints," "St. James," and all that stuff.

I deal with that by not playing those tunes unless someone absolutely insists. As you know, I announce, "We're not here to play what you want to hear, we're here to play what's good for you . . . unless you threaten violence." There are so many songs to keep the band fresh. I feel stagnant when I play something that I've done over and over. This is why I loved the job at Condon's, because it was always, always fresh. You're constantly being tested. You're not being tested when you're playing something that you could play in your sleep. You get bored, and it starts showing on your face. You see the players come alive when you call a tune that they don't know, and the audience can feel the excitement of the players. This is healthy.

TJ: Do you have any recording plans?

JM: I have a lot of recording dates that are pending. I just have to find the time to do them. I have several for George Buck, and some other people have mentioned things that they would like to do. Buck says, "Anytime, pick the players and the time." I'd like to do a record with several different groups, with guys like Dave Boeddinghaus, John Royen, Steve Pistorius, Tom McDermott, and Ronnie Dupont on piano, just to show the various flavors that a group can have. Drummers like Hal Smith, a great drummer, and Jeff Hamilton, a fine player and good piano player too. George has been very gracious about that—plus the fact that he knows I'll sell some. I have been selling those Salt City Six [re-issue] CDs left and right. They are sold out! I can't buy any to sell down at Fritzel's, can't make any money. I wouldn't sell anything I don't like. I won't sell the things I did with Don Ewell. I don't like them. They can sell those at the airport. For some reason—good players, and

Don Ewell is a master player—the whole session just didn't click. Something went wrong. My playing was contrived and lusterless. It didn't happen. Write it off.

You know, I'm learning all the time. I'm learning from other players, learning different tempos on tunes, different tunes. I'll wait to see how a session would turn out now, especially since I have more experience down here playing with these players. I am just sort of curious to see what I can do. Maybe I'm reluctant to find out—that's why I'm dragging my feet on this thing.

In live sessions, where I don't have studio-itis to be concerned with, I seem to relax more. I don't usually play my best in the studio, but I want to see if I can overcome that with the next session. We'll see what happens.

TJ: Are you talking about "performance anxiety?"

JM: Well, performance anxiety is usually good in a live performance. They recommend it. The way I do it, playing in the same place, I feel confident. I don't feel "anxiety"—it's not like walking on the stage at Carnegie Hall. You can maintain that edge by forcing yourself to play tunes that are difficult, wondering whether you are going to get through them or not. It keeps that edge. Like when Tom McDermott comes in, I like to do "Temptation Rag"— that's a challenge. I'd like to do more stuff like that, but I use so many different players that I don't have time to work these things out that I'd like to do. Hopefully, I'll have time for that later on.

TJ: What do you think about the clarinet in jazz? You've managed to survive through one of the most difficult times—the '60s to the '80s—for a jazz clarinetist.

JM: I've heard that rules for managers of motel chains and the like said not to hire clarinet players. Rather than to leave it up to the managers to decide what is good and what is bad, they would rather have a bad tenor [saxophone] player than a mediocre clarinet player. So, generally speaking, clarinet players have become the lost orphans of the music business—except for New Orleans! It's a good clarinet town. It's the only town I've ever been in where the clarinet players get the first calls for the good jobs.

I think it's [due to] the tradition, and Pete Fountain has done great things for this town and for the clarinet. When there are private parties or when people come to town from the riverboats, they like to see the clarinet.

TJ: There are a lot of good young clarinet players in town.

JM: Yes. Tom Fischer is fine, classically trained. He knows music. Timmy Laughlin, of course. He's a fine, fine player and getting better and better—a little scary. Another young player is Brian O'Connell, who has a fine jazz concept. Pee Wee Russell influence, George Lewis, but he has his own sound. I always enjoy working with him. And I should definitely mention the new young clarinetist in town, Evan Christopher, who I feel is a major jazz talent.

One of the problems with the clarinet is that it is so difficult to play it well. You have to put a lot of years into it. A lot of guys can pick up a saxophone, a guitar . . . and in a couple of weeks they can play a job. But here are records and enough good young players carrying on the tradition. I don't think it will die out. The clarinet had its heyday in the '30s. I would like to hear more players being influenced by Artie Shaw, say, rather than—now don't ever misconstrue, we all bow down to George Lewis as we do to Pee Wee Russell—but I think there's life outside Lewis and Russell for clarinet players. Artie Shaw's gorgeous ballads were just dazzling, and Benny Goodman, a player who swings.

TJ: Goodman and Shaw were so influential. How would you compare them?

JM: They are two different approaches, two different strong points. Benny could swing fiercely. Those sextet things were some of the greatest music that's ever been recorded. Shaw showed how ballads could be played. His sixteen bars on "Stardust" is one of the all-time most exceptional pieces of music ever made. But, you see, those are two different styles. Shaw could never quite come up to Benny on the hot tunes, on the fast things, because he had too much of a spread in his tone. It was spread around a little too much to get the same edge on the fast tunes that Benny got. Benny had a more centered sound and could make those runs come out just like a machine gun. Artie had bigtime chops, but he could never get the swing that Benny could.

TJ: Time is running short. Any parting shots?

JM: I'd like to remind people what Leonard Bernstein said—I've read it—that the most exciting sound in music is a good Dixieland band at full tilt. He doesn't say "one of the most," he said, "THE most exciting," and I have to agree—even though my first love is classical and I like modern jazz. It's a glorious, exciting sound, and it should not be made light of or trivialized.

If people would just take the time to search out these records: the Hot Five, the Hot Seven, even Bunk Johnson, the Lawson-Haggart band, and especially the Condon band with Wild Bill and Pee Wee Russell or Edmond Hall, and the Bob Scobey band. Oh, marvelous, that's as good as it can get. If we could get people aware of that sound, demanding that sound, and get it back again on a more consistent basis.

Now and then, down at Fritzel's, we get the right combination and it will click, and you can feel it—all of a sudden, whoa! I know you've seen it there.

TJ: Many times. But I'm afraid that we now have run out of time. Thanks very much, Jack.

JM: It's a pleasure. It's been good therapy. I can now face another day of this house construction.

8

JOHN ROYEN
New Orleans Stridemaster

Stride piano stylist John Royen is probably the best-known solo pianist in New Orleans these days. He has appeared regularly in that capacity at upscale hotel venues such as the Hilton and, more recently, the Intercontinental. But he is also a veteran ensemble player, performing with groups at the Palm Court Jazz Café, Fritzel's Jazz Pub, and, for many years, Preservation Hall. Royen is well known on the jazz festival circuit as well.

Since Hurricane Katrina, Royen has also been working with Pete Fountain two nights a month at the Hollywood Casino in nearby Bay St. Louis, Mississippi. He and his family live some distance north of New Orleans in Folsom, Louisiana, so they were spared much of the destruction of that hurricane as well as her sibling Rita.

Named one of the city's Jazz All-Stars by New Orleans Magazine *in 2008, Royen says, "I'm just trying to keep the idiom alive." His latest solo CD (2008) is called* In the Beginning. *It includes, as he puts it, "a variety of usual trad piano pieces, some rags, Fats [Waller], Jelly Roll, Ellington, James P. Johnson, and so on."*

The following interview was conducted in July 1998 and published in The Mississippi Rag *in September 1999.*

I'VE BEEN TERMED A STRIDE PIANO PLAYER—AND I AM— but I try to get into different musical aspects of traditional jazz. I don't know everything about anything. I know a little bit about a lot of things because I've tried to experience it. I don't play every song that Fats Waller ever wrote or every tune Jelly Roll Morton ever composed, but I've tried to learn a nice eclectic cross-section of all of it."

Thus 44-year-old New Orleans–based pianist John Royen characterized his musical approach in this interview last year [1998]. Royen, an East Coast native, has been living and playing in the Crescent City for more than twenty years. During that time he has become a highly respected piano soloist as well as one of the busiest sidemen in town.

"John is a sensational pianist," says ace drummer Hal Smith, with whom Royen is making plans to form a trio in the near future. "He is immersed in the Harlem stride style, but he sometimes ventures into other territory—Morton, [Joe] Sullivan, blues, and boogie-woogie. Whatever style he performs is played for keeps. John is an excellent musician, a gentleman, and a delightful musical associate."

That's quite a tribute in a city that is blessed with an especially talented crop of "two-handed" piano players.

John Royen grew up in Washington, D.C., where he was introduced to jazz by his father. "My father was with NBC radio [in New York] in the '40s," he says. "He was always involved with people in the arts and entertainment. While he was at Brown University as a young fellow, he was a booking agent on the side. He would book piano players and bands for local college fraternities and sororities at parties around the academic community. Through that he got to know personally various piano players, people like Cliff Jackson. He booked Fats. He booked Willie the Lion [Smith]. And he was a diehard Sidney Bechet [fan]. He loved Bechet's music."

"I remember," he goes on, "when I was about 10 years old, he brought home an RCA collection of big band music. There was one cut of Fats Waller on the whole thing—it was all Artie Shaw and Benny Goodman—and you don't think of Fats in a big band context. This one cut was a piano solo. I freaked out. I just played it over and over again. The Beatles were just coming in and all the other kids were talking about the Beatles . . . and I'm talking about Fats Waller! These kids are, 'Who the hell is Fats Waller?' So, I grew up listening to it. As I grew up, my father would take me around to various piano players as I got past 16 and he could get me into places."

Royen started piano lessons at a tender age, but like so many other young boys, he didn't stick with it. Yet, as he grew up listening to jazz with his father, he was finally bitten by "the bug," as he puts it.

"It was when I was a senior in high school, and it was getting to be too much. I wasn't concentrating on school or anything, so I just decided to try to teach myself. I did remember those fundamental little lessons. Joshua Rifkin had come out with the 'Maple Leaf Rag.' There was sort of a renaissance of ragtime getting started, and I thought that was kind of neat. So, I got it on record. Of course, it was published on paper. What I would do is play the record and match it up with the notes on the paper and piece together the notes. I wasn't that good on reading time—technically, I was pretty awful—but I pieced it together. It took me about three months just to get through this thing. To this day I can't even think of that song anymore," he laughs. "It's like eating chicken every day and you just can't eat any more. I almost get nauseous, but that was my first step in trying to get into the piano."

Soon thereafter Royen began his first formal piano lessons with well-known D.C. pianist John Eaton. "It was John," he says, "who had been in school in New York in his younger years—he studied with Alexander Lipski—who got me into the New York players, the two-handed players, Willie the Lion, James P. Johnson, Fats Waller, all those fellows, and Jelly Roll Morton down here. But what I got [from Eaton] was a very nice eclectic exposure early on of listening to the old great guys and at the same time hearing people like John and other piano players in Washington like Gene Steinbeck. Steinbeck is a wonderful two-handed player, and he's still playing in Washington.

"To be honest with you," he continues, "I was a terrible student. I was so overwhelmed with all that I was discovering that I wasn't concentrating on anything. I'd start to try to focus in and then I would hear this and would be busy listening to that, and I wouldn't sit down and do the homework on the basics. So, I sort of kept developing on my own, with John working with me. John showed me so much in the way of technique, more by osmosis than actual hands-on lessons, by just being around him and exposing me to the various elements of the instrument."

Royen's first professional job was at the National Press Club in Washington, D.C., in 1975. He was still taking lessons from Eaton, who had sent him to work—"on a sort of tutoring basis"—with another Washington pianist, Charlie Howze. "Charlie was sort of a boy wonder in New York at the time John was there, back in the '50s. He was really into the New York piano scene, the old guys that were still living. He introduced me to a whole wealth of material."

Howze was playing at the National Press Club, and when he couldn't make the gig one afternoon, he invited Royen to sit in for him. "I was terrified," John says, "but he said, 'You have enough material under your belt, you can do it.'

"So, I went there and started playing, and halfway through the gig Charlie comes in to check up on me and throws me off the job because I'm not wearing a suit! 'You don't dress like this on a job. I'll take over,' he says.

"I was humiliated by this whole thing, but he called me later in the week and said, 'Look, I want you to finish up the summer for me.' So, I finished up the summer at the National Press Club for him."

While playing at the Press Club, Royen had an opportunity to initiate a relationship with Don Ewell, the man who would become perhaps the most influential jazz pianist in his life. He had met Ewell earlier through Baltimore drummer Bill Riddle, who was a friend of his father. He had even played a little for him at that time, but Ewell "kind of blew it off," Royen remembers. When Ewell came to Washington to play in a concert series at the Press Club, Royen had a chance to hang out with him and Riddle for a couple of days.

"So, it was at that point—I had grown a little since I first met him—he said maybe we can get together sometime and have a seminar. I almost fainted right there. I think things were in a flux for him. I think Don had had a bad accident, and he was still a little shaky from that. Anyway, after that summer I went to Europe for a year."

Having studied two years at American University in D.C., Royen spent a year as a student in Lugano, Switzerland. When he returned from Europe, he headed almost immediately to New Orleans. "When I met Ewell in Washington at the Press Club, he had talked about New Orleans—which is one of the reasons why I decided to come down here to study," he explains. "I had not been to New Orleans before."

Royen enrolled at Loyola University, where he eventually graduated with a degree in business administration. "I was going to study music because I had been encouraged to do so," he says. "I had had a lot of my common curriculum courses from American University, so I could zoom right into [music] theory.

"The first week I got here," he continues, "I had wanted to hear a pianist everybody had told me about, Armand Hug. So, I went down to the Royal Orleans [Hotel] to see him [and learned] Armand had died two days beforehand [March 19, 1977]. And there was Don Ewell at the piano! Don had just come in to take over Armand's job at the Royal Orleans. He was there five nights a week—and I was there five nights a week! I never went to any classes, I never did any studying. Actually, I did well in all my theory courses, but I dropped a lot of courses because I was too busy listening to Don. That's when we got to be very good friends. I was there every night."

But that lasted only six to eight weeks, at which point Ewell moved back to his home in Deerfield Beach, Florida. Yet he returned to New Orleans several times thereafter, and there were opportunities for him and Royen to discuss John's coming to Florida to work with him.

"I went back and forth [to Ewell's home in Florida] several times starting in '79, and it went on for about three years. I would stay down there for like a month at a time and live with him and Mary. I'd clean the pool, cut the grass, and sort of help out around the house. Mary was working during the day at a local newspaper. Don would work with me on the piano. Don's health wasn't all that good at that point. [He] had a horrible cardiovascular condition, and it was getting worse. I was actually with him when he had his last stroke. We were at the dinner table when he had the stroke. He was stunned, and I looked over to Mary. I took him out to the car. They were about nine blocks from the hospital, and I flew like a bat out of hell to the hospital. He had a pretty big stroke. Fortunately, it caused only temporary paralysis in his left hand, and that went away. But he did lose partial vision in the left eye, and that was an annoyance to him to the end. He would see shadows. You know, when you play that kind of two-handed style, it just kind of affected it.

"But I would go down there off and on when things got slow," he goes on. "It was awful, and here I was this young upstart. He would get tired and lie down in the bedroom. He would say, 'You just go ahead and play.' We worked a lot on theory. He'd go to the bedroom and say, 'Go play that

Pianist John Royen at the French Quarter Festival, April 2005. The drummer is Hal Smith.

passage, and here's a kind of chord sequence, play that and I'm going to lie down.' He'd be lying there, and I'd be muddling around with something, and all of a sudden I'd hear him yell, 'Stop!' I'd stop, and he'd say, 'Go, go back,' and I'd go back and he'd say, 'Right there. Take your fourth finger off that A-flat and move it down to the G. . . .' He's correcting my fingering from the bedroom! He's lying down in his bedroom halfway across the house and he's correcting my fingering from three rooms away while I play! I'm just this young pup . . . that's intimidating as hell! And he was intimidating in a lot of ways, but I think I saw through it because I realized how insecure he was. Don's playing was magnificent, but he always felt he was bucking the grain of what people really wanted. I don't know why, but that's the way he was. He would be gruff and growly—he'd growl at me and I'd growl back and everything would settle down and we'd get back to what we were doing."

Next to Don Ewell and John Eaton, Royen considers Willie the Lion Smith the greatest influence on his playing.

"Willie was an incredibly complex piano player in so many ways," he says, "and he amazes me to this day. I saw him the year he died [1973].

My father took me down to Blues Alley [famed jazz club in Georgetown], and I got to go in. Willie at that point was in bad shape. He had grown sloppy and kind of slow, but there was still that persona. I could hear it in his playing—in the middle of something he'd come alive, and wow! For me to see that was really great. There was a quality to Willie's playing where he was willing to take a chance. Willie made everything sound like he wrote it. I believe he died a couple of months after that appearance at Blues Alley. My dad wanted me to see that, and I think it was kind of sad for him, too. He knew all those guys from thirty years back when they still had some energy.

"Don [Ewell] really loved Willie as well. He worked with Willie—the duets and stuff—in his later years. I was listening with Don to the duet album that the two of them did. I wanted to listen to it. He didn't," he laughs. "But finally he joined me. Then he said, 'Listen to this.' They did 'You Took Advantage of Me' and in the last four bars of the front eight measures, Willie threw a very interesting chord substitution in to Don. And on the next chorus Don had already figured out what it was and turned it right around and played it back at Willie. And you can hear Willie laugh on the track.

"I had talked with Francis Squibb, who worked at the Tulane Archive [William Ransom Hogan Jazz Archive] when Curt Jerde was there. He lives in Chicago now, but he was a dear friend of Don's. When Don was going to go out and do the duets with Willie, Don was worried—you know, Willie was up there in age—and said that he didn't want to make Willie look bad if he couldn't keep up because of his health and age. Francis said, 'Keep up, hell, he's going to try to cut your throat. I'm telling you, Don, he's going to try to carve you to shreds if you give him a chance.'

"And he was right. During the session Willie threw this passage at Don, and Don had to wake up, and he turned around and threw it right back at him to let him know he had caught it. He and Don developed a wonderful friendship. It was both social and musical. So, I had the best of both worlds," Royen smiles, "by my association with Don."

Ewell died in 1983, but Royen, between his trips back and forth to Florida, was beginning to establish himself on the New Orleans music scene. He had met native New Orleans pianist Steve Pistorius, and they became good friends. He and Pistorius were hired to play solo piano, on an alternating basis, at the Gazebo in the French Market (in the French Quarter) in 1979, and that started a run of almost eight years for Royen at that venue.

"When Steve went to work with the *One Mo' Time* show," he says, "I stayed at the Gazebo and put in a group of my own, a quartet, and was there until the mid-eighties. It was a great job because it was a great learning experience. If anybody was in town they would come by the Gazebo and sit in. You know, playing solo and playing ensemble are completely different. I learned how to play ensemble, sitting in with people from all over the world, at places like the Gazebo."

In 1980, Fred Starr and John Joyce of Tulane University were putting together the Louisiana Repertory Jazz Ensemble, and they invited Royen to join the group. That proved to be another valuable learning experience.

"I had to play idiomatic to the style that they wanted, which was that early '20s King Oliver–type of group, and that took a lot of discipline," Royen stresses. "I had never applied myself to that area, so that was a growing experience for me as well."

Royen's musical education—or, perhaps better, his on-the-job training —continued when he was asked by Allan Jaffe to sub at Preservation Hall in 1981. Later, when pianist Dave Williams died [March 1982], Royen was asked to replace him in the Kid Thomas Valentine band. That was still another marvelous opportunity to learn.

In addition to Kid Thomas, he was playing with Hall veterans like Emanuel Paul, Emanuel Sayles, Raymond Burke, Louis Nelson, Chester Zardis, Preston Jackson, and the Humphrey brothers.

"I was the youngest regular member of Preservation Hall," he says. "When I came on with them as a regular, I was 27 years old. It was rough. Some of them were three times my age. Kid Thomas couldn't remember the names of half the tunes he played. He would just stomp his foot and start playing. I had like six choruses to figure out what the tune was, what key it was in, and to figure out how to play it for a solo because my solo was coming up right after the banjo," he laughs. "Boy, talk about pressure. But they were just great guys. There wasn't the slightest racial anything going on, with any experience I had at the Hall. I would give anything to have had a tape recorder, remembering all the conversations I had with all of them on the road about their experiences growing up.

There were some tunes that they did where I had no idea how they arrived at that way of playing a tune. I'll never know to this day. What I learned from that was the need to give and take and to be flexible.

"It's been a long road of learning for me," he sighs. "A lot of it has been learning the hard way. I have tried to play with as many different groups—not so much groups as different styles—as I could."

Royen has worked with three of New Orleans' top clarinet players—veterans Jacques Gauthé and Jack Maheu and young hotshot Tim Laughlin. "Gauthé's band was doing a lot of West Coast, sort of Turk Murphy idiom," he notes. "That called for something completely different from Preservation Hall. But working with Jack Maheu has been great, too. When you play with Jack you have to play full tilt. You're in a trio, and you use your left hand stylistically a lot. When Jack knows what he's got, he uses it. I got to tell you, when I come off a job with Jack Maheu, I feel like I earned my money. I'm drained. But that's been a great experience, too."

Royen has recorded extensively with Tim Laughlin and worked for him for about six years at Horizons in the Hilton Hotel. Underlining the pianist's important role in small-group jazz, Laughlin says, "Today, with clubs only hiring trios, John handles the absence of the bass line like a real pro." Royen, he says, was "the backbone of the rhythm section of my band at the New Orleans Hilton."

While Laughlin no longer has a band at the Hilton, Royen continues to play there regularly. "The Hilton is my home base," he says. "I play solo Friday and Saturday at the English Bar on the second floor from 5 to 10 p.m. I also play there on Sunday mornings and during the week if things are full in town. Every Thursday night I'm at Preservation Hall, and on Sunday nights I'm at Fritzel's with [cornetist] Jamie Wight. Then of course I am occasionally on tour with Preservation Hall or Tim [Laughlin] or some other group that wants to hire me," he laughs.

But traveling does not seem to be a high priority with Royen. The more one talks with him, the more one gets the clear impression that his family comes first in his life. He and his wife of nearly sixteen years live with their three children—Jason, 14; Devon, 12; and Jessica, 6—about fifty miles north of the city outside the little town of Folsom, Louisiana.

"We live out in the country," he says. "I don't think I'd want to live anywhere else. There are times when, instead of sitting down at a piano by myself 'til three in the morning and learning every single tune that this guy or that guy wrote or listening to every recording, trying to re-member every recording that this guy did, my family comes first. I think my home life has taken priority over a lot of [that]. Whereas many musi-cians devote every waking moment to it, I just haven't devoted that kind of time to it because my wife and kids have always come first."

Royen reveals at times a self-effacing modesty and, like talented art-ists in many fields, moments of self-doubt. He has, of course, done a good bit of traveling. Yet, despite appearances with various groups throughout Europe as well as in Asia, Latin America, and this country, he still says, "I don't think there are very many people out of New Orleans who are really aware of who I am. I was out at the Sacramento Jazz Festival last summer with Clint Baker's band," he goes on, "and that was really inter-esting because I got such a wonderful response from people out there. That kind of surprised me. I guess I haven't had enough respect for my own playing. I've never thought of myself in the kind of terms that I see other musicians. It's only really been in the last year that I started think-ing, 'You know, I think I've got enough to offer that I can go out there.'"

So, he and drummer Hal Smith are talking about putting together a trio. They plan to do some recording and then perhaps take the group on the road. "There's a wonderful wealth of jazz styling out there and devel-opments musically that I can approach with a trio. In the South—you've got Jelly Roll—there's a wonderful history of developments down here as well as on the East Coast. Baltimore, Washington, people like Joe Turner out of Baltimore, Eubie Blake, New York and all those people . . . Those are all things I've come up with in my playing, and we want to approach that with the trio."

But, as an outstanding piano soloist, Royen is also looking for more solo exposure. He has a fine recording out now (*Solo Tradition*, 1996), and there seems to be more in the pipeline. He is also heard, of course, on the recordings of countless other bandleaders.

"I have enough solo cuts on everybody else's records," he jokes, "that I could make my own CD. I always wind up on somebody's session, and they say, 'Gee, while you're here, why don't you do a solo number?'"

So, reflecting upon his first quarter century in the music business, John Royen—family man and premier pianist—can say (with characteristic humility), "I'm proud of what I have accomplished, considering I've primarily been a self-taught musician. I've come a long way."

Indeed he has, and we look forward to even greater accomplishments in the next twenty-five years.

9

EVAN CHRISTOPHER
Young Man with a Musical Plan

※ ※ ※

Clarinetist Evan Christopher has lived in New Orleans off and on since 1994.
Mixed in have been sojourns in San Antonio, New York City, and—after the
disaster that was Hurricane Katrina—Paris, at the invitation of the French
government.

Long considered a very special talent on clarinet, Christopher, now just
41, is widely recognized both nationally and internationally as a superb in-
strumentalist, composer, bandleader, and featured soloist for, among others,
the Grammy-winning New Orleans Jazz Orchestra. He has also worked and
recorded frequently with pianist-composer Tom McDermott's Latin-flavored
Danza Quartet and with trumpeter Duke Heitger.

As a leader, he recently recorded a fine CD (Delta Bound, 2007) featur-
ing distinguished pianist Dick Hyman and dedicated to the legendary New
Orleans clarinetist Lorenzo Tio Jr. It included several of his own compositions.
His current group, Django à la Créole, was formed during the Paris interlude,
and is also the title of their initial recording (2008). His most recent CD is
scheduled for release in June 2010 on the Arbors label and features the great
Bucky Pizzarelli on guitar. It is called The Remembering Song, *about which*
he says (in the liner notes), "Essentially Delta Bound . . . *was about leav-*
ing New Orleans but staying tied to the city through the music even though I
wasn't sure I'd ever live there again. This record is about being back."

Christopher's abiding interests in musicology and jazz history led him to
undertake graduate study at Tulane University prior to Katrina. He has con-
tinued that study—as his performing schedule has permitted—since return-
ing to the city in late 2007. He has also taught part-time in the music depart-
ment at the University of New Orleans, where he worked with individual jazz
students and directed student jazz ensembles.

The following (slightly revised) article was compiled from interviews over a period from 1995 to 1998. The original piece appeared in the December 1999 issue of The Mississippi Rag.

"E VAN CHRISTOPHER IS A SPECTACULAR PLAYER BY ANY standard, especially considering his youth. He combines musical knowledge with technique and emotional energy—all qualities that a great jazz musician needs. But, above all, he swings." So spoke New Orleans drummer and bandleader Trevor Richards, with whom Christopher has recently recorded, and his words seem to capture the sentiments of most musicians and serious jazz fans who have heard the young clarinetist play. A frank and thoughtful young man who is about to embark on a new stage in his career, Christopher shares some of his personal thoughts and plans for the future in the following interview.

Christopher was born in Long Beach, California, on August 31, 1969, and was raised in nearby Los Alamitos. His birth mother was Thai and his father probably an American serviceman. He was given up for adoption at the age of four months. His adoptive father, a professor at Long Beach State, listened to music of the big band era and his wife was fond of classical music, but neither of them played a musical instrument.

Like many musicians, Evan started out on the piano at age six and then switched to clarinet "at 10 or 11 in the junior high school band." All of his instruction came in school. There were no private lessons. He doesn't remember exactly why he made the switch to clarinet, but he says, "My father is under the impression it was chosen for me because of my physical size. I started school a couple of years early—I guess I was four—and I was always a little smaller. I think that was why the clarinet was chosen for me. I just wanted to be in the band, and I liked [the instrument] immediately."

Music became his passion. "It was almost all I did," he recalls. "I didn't find other things that came as easily to me. I took it for granted a little bit, but, as a result, I didn't pursue other things. And it was something I could do on my own. I remember playing along with the radio a lot, trying to unlock the mysteries of improvisation by myself."

Records also helped him get an appreciation for the proper sound of the instrument. "I was checking records out from the library, pretty much on my own," he says. "I didn't benefit from having peers who shared my musical interests until much later. The first records that I started listening to were early Louie Armstrong—the Hot Five—and Artie Shaw. The Louie Armstrong record was a gift, and a friend of my father's who had an extensive record collection laid some Artie Shaw on me, some of the late '30s Shaw where there was a lot of melody. It was easy to play along with, since I learned the fingerings. The only sounds that I knew to imitate were Johnny Dodds and Artie Shaw. I didn't realize they would stick with me as long as they have."

"I was fortunate," he goes on. "My father had a couple friends who loaned me records and sent me tapes, things like Condon's small groups with Edmond Hall, Peanuts Hucko, and Pee Wee Russell, and Bill Napier with Bob Scobey's band. My evolution on the instrument has been one of technical facility. I gravitated toward the players I could imitate, based on where my technique was. It was the same with the saxophone [which he picked up in high school]."

It was during high school that Evan realized music would be more than a hobby. "Right before leaving high school I was discouraged by people about the music idea, and I was going to enter college as a math major. I found my way around that by transferring to an arts high school [the prestigious Idyllwild School of Music and the Arts in the hills east of Los Angeles] and in essence finished my senior year there. There I had my first classical training on clarinet and was playing chamber music. That was in 1986–87. It was nice to be hanging out with people who were being directed toward the more serious pursuit of a musical career. At Idyllwild I met a jazz player named Marshall Hawkins [a bassist], who became my first instructor in jazz improvisation and jazz piano. Marshall played with Miles Davis briefly after Ron Carter. That was the first time that I really began to take jazz seriously."

"After high school," he continues, "I was looking for and waiting for someone to tell me I couldn't do music. I didn't find anybody that would do that; all I got was positive feedback about it. I went to USC for a year and a half, as a jazz studies major. It was pretty academic and, when the scholarship money got funny, I left. I hooked back up with Marshall and moved to San Diego to play more with [him] and some friends down there. That's when I started working for a living."

At this time he was playing alto sax in bebop groups, but he was also getting more and more calls for "Dixieland-type" jobs on clarinet. "I decided, if I was going to [play Dixieland clarinet], I might as well do it right," he says. "I started listening to the right clarinet players and getting some history and getting some training on the instrument. It became rather consuming. The attitude musically of the types of people I was working with was more positive than that of the guys who were trying to play bebop and straight-ahead and other styles."

Veteran West Coast clarinetist and soprano saxophonist George Probert came to be something of a mentor for young Christopher during that period. "We met for the first time at a festival where his band was appearing and one of the very first bands I was working in was appearing," Evan recalls. "He took me under his wing and made a point of sharing significant recordings with me to gain a better understanding of swing, how to play hot, how to communicate energy by playing time, and how, even if you are playing with bad rhythm sections, you can still present a sense of swing in your playing. I still have tapes that George made for me. The one that probably had the most significant impact on me was the recordings he gave me of Edmond Hall. But he also gave me recordings of Bigard, Pete Brown on alto saxophone, Captain John Handy on saxophone, recordings of Earl Bostic, the Harlem Hamfats, Edmond's brother Herbie Hall—you name it—the early Robichaux band, the early Benny Moten band. So George shared recordings that taught me how to swing."

But Christopher soon realized that he was not quite ready to be out on his own musically. He decided to go back to college in the summer of 1991 for two principal reasons. "Number one," he says, "I wasn't making enough money, and number two, my father's approval. As an educator, it was very important to him that I finish school."

So Evan enrolled in a junior college, where he finished his general education requirements (and studied arranging with Tom Kubis) and then transferred to Cal State Long Beach, where he graduated in 1993 with a B.A. in music. "I managed to graduate *cum laude*, but, just a few months before graduating, I began touring and recording with A. J. Croce and was close to not finishing. Fortunately, I finished the degree in May and the following summer I went on tour . . . and school stuff was behind me."

Christopher worked with Croce, the son of pop singer Jim Croce, for about a year, playing mainly clarinet and alto saxophone. "We played mostly original music, but also some Fats Waller and other cover tunes that he was interested in. It introduced me to some styles—Memphis and Delta blues—and taught me a lot more about rock-and-roll basically."

But, perhaps more important, the Croce interlude introduced him to New Orleans. "I recorded on his first album," he recalls. "We went to Europe a couple of times and did a six-week tour of the East Coast, and that's what brought me to New Orleans for the very first time in June of 1994. We played Tipitina's. I was here for three days and met some people that I had mutual friends with on the West Coast: Chris Tyle and some of the guys from Banu [Gibson]'s band, David Sager, and Duke Heitger. Chris invited me to sub for a week at the Can Can [Club] later that summer, in August 1994. That's when I met Jack Maheu and some of the guys from the Dukes [of Dixieland] who were looking for someone to substitute for Tim Laughlin for a while. I was offered that opportunity to come back and sub for Timmy—which I did.

"So, after going back home," he goes on, "I came back [to New Orleans] in September and played with the Dukes until the end of 1994. It was a fun job, and in that fall I met many other musicians and hooked up with this brass band [the New Orleans Nightcrawlers] and a fun band called Galactic Prophylactic. The thing I like about New Orleans and the music here—no matter what the style is—is it's flavored so much by the culture that surrounds it. There's no other city like it in the United States. But what I've gotten out of being here, feeling more connected to the city and its musical history, is more conviction in my own playing. Living here, being here everyday, manifests itself in more authority and conviction in my playing."

Christopher was an immediate hit in the Crescent City. His name was soon on everyone's lips, musicians and jazz fans alike. In addition to his appearances with the Dukes of Dixieland and, eventually, other local bands, he came to be a regular participant in the weekend jam sessions at Fritzel's on Bourbon Street led by veteran clarinetist Jack Maheu. It was not uncommon during the winter of 1994–95 to hear people ask, "Have you heard that young clarinet player who's sitting in with Jack Maheu?" I remember first being told about Christopher by Dukes' pianist Tom McDermott, who enthused about him as a "killer clarinet player."

The Fritzel's sessions with Maheu and Christopher produced many exciting moments for the lucky audiences that happened to be on hand as well as for the participating musicians themselves. One could sense a special symbiosis developing between the two clarinetists as they continued to play together, a relationship that in fact became something of a mutual admiration society. Maheu openly referred to Christopher as "a major jazz talent," and the latter termed his association with the talented veteran "a tremendous learning experience."

Hearing that Maheu had called him "a very good listener," Evan responded, "if there's one thing that's important about the music that came from [New Orleans] it is the concept of the ensemble. You don't find that in college or among people learning post-swing styles as much as in earlier styles. The activity of creating the music relies on the ensemble more so than in any other style of music. If people say anything about me, I'd like it to be that I'm a good ensemble player."

Evan Christopher brings an electricity—a special energy—to the bandstand. When told that he plays with surprising authority for someone so young, he replied, "thank you, but some people think my concept of time and rhythm is too pushy. I like my swing hot. The bands that I like the most created that energy with temporal relationships, where they placed notes within the time—Jimmie Lunceford's band, Fletcher Henderson, Benny Moten, even Joe Robichaux, thirties' bands like the Harlem Hamfats, or Basie's small groups, Benny Goodman from the mid-thirties, that concept of hot."

Christopher says that the intensity he brings to the stand is no accident. "It's very conscious," he stresses. "I learned that. I learned how to go into a situation and not try to bring out the best in the other musicians, but try to make the musicians around me bring out the best in me. I taught myself how to do that. There are subtle ways," he goes on, "that musicians can lead a listener's attention and even the other musicians' attention to a certain element that they might not have been paying attention to. You can discourage talking during the bass solo. You can use your eyes, and you can give subtle encouragement to draw attention to something that's going on. You can find ways to connect. Upholding a listener's imagination isn't just from the beginning of your solo to the end of your solo. It's from the beginning of a tune to the end of a tune, from the beginning of a set to the end of a set, or from the beginning of an evening to the end of an evening. There are all sorts of levels to work on."

Christopher's full-time residence in New Orleans lasted only a little more than a year (though he still makes frequent return visits to the city), and he admits with regret that he arrived about thirty years too late to meet many jazz pioneers. And who would he have wanted to meet? He pauses, then says, "Well, for instance, to actually have spent time hanging out with some of the people who studied with Lorenzo Tio, some of the clarinet players, some of the Tio dynasty. Or Danny Barker. I moved to New Orleans at the beginning of fall '94, September or so, and I think [clarinetist] Willie Humphrey had just passed away that summer [actually, June 6, 1994]. They were already gone by the time I got here."

Having been approached by Jim Cullum to join his well-known band in San Antonio in the summer of 1995, Christopher auditioned that August. "John Sheridan, the piano player with the Cullum band, remembers it being the shortest audition on record," he laughed. The job was not to begin until later in the year, however. "In November, I returned to San Antonio to be a guest on one of the radio shows," he recalls, and they had done a little press to announce that I would be joining the band at the end of December. So, right after Christmas, before New Year's, I officially joined the band. It was on December 29 or so, 1995."

After two years in the new setting, Christopher was voted "Best New Artist" for 1997 by the readers of the *Current,* a San Antonio news-and-entertainment weekly. As it happened, he was the first non-native musician and first jazz musician to win the honor in the publication's history. He took over the clarinet chair in the Cullum band that had been occupied by a series of first-rate players. (His immediate predecessor was the fine Canadian clarinetist Brian Ogilvie, who now lives and works in New Orleans.)

"When I joined the band," he notes, "they were into their eighth radio season and their thirty-fourth year or so. It was great to have such a solid scene. The band essentially makes their living off tourism to the River Walk area. They work six nights a week, pretty much year-round. They

Evan Christopher performing at the Old Algiers River Festival with
Irvin Mayfield's band, April 2008. Pianist Ronald Markham and bassist Neal Caine are in the background.

don't have to travel more than, on average, three or four days a month.
What a great situation to really get into. . . . [It gave me an opportunity]
to have really quite a bit of freedom and really get some clarinet things,
some concepts of music, under my belt and to work some things out and
get into the minutiae of how I want to sound and how I want to approach
the music. Those were [some of] the good things of being with the Cullum band. The only bad things were the repetition of it all and the fact
that I wasn't having as many outlets to do other types of music and to do
other things."

So, he decided to leave the band after almost exactly three years, in December 1998. As of this writing, [he and his then wife] have stayed on in San Antonio while they plan their next move. Will it be back in the New York area, near her family as well as a lively and highly competitive music scene? Or will it be back to New Orleans, where he has many musical friends and, clearly, a soft spot in his heart?

Speaking of the Crescent City, he says, "I love it. I come back every chance I get. I try to see as many people as I can, and I try to eat some good food. I love the energy of this place."

Or, will it be somewhere else? Time will tell.

In the meantime, Christopher has begun to formulate some ideas about his musical future. While in New Orleans, he began to experiment with the traditional Albert-system clarinet (rather than the Boehm system, which most clarinetists now play). That decision has had a significant impact on his playing in several ways.

Christopher turned to Albert system, in his words, "just to get into the heads of guys like Louis Cottrell and Barney Bigard, just to see if the ideas come out in a certain way because of the technical limitations. And to some degree I found that was true. I also found, because it was a new thing for me, that it got me into trouble more. The improvisation process of getting in and out of trouble became fun. The clichés on Albert system had not yet developed, whereas on Boehm I had become predictable to myself. That was part of the attraction of the Albert system. It was making me work and think a little harder, holding my concentration, because one of the things you develop when you have a rhythm section and repertoire that is the same all the time, is patterns of reactivity. As a jazz musician, you can't receive the same information and pretend that you're hearing it for the first time. So, with a different fingering system, I found that, because my fingers were reacting differently, things would come out differently. Albert has been a very fun experiment for me. Not only that, but it sets me apart from other musicians and puts me closer to the lineage of the tradition that I want to come from. The ideas come out differently, and the range of colors are more exciting to me.

"But what I decided to do," he goes on, "was to really concentrate on coming from more a New Orleans Creole clarinet aesthetic. My research in New Orleans led me to learn about many of the New Orleans Creole clarinet players and about performance practices and things like that. And that led to some of the Creole clarinet players of the French West Indies, specifically Martinique, and melodies from Haiti and players like Alexandre Stellio and Eugene Delouche. When I started learning about them, there was such a remarkable similarity between the sounds of the clarinet.

"If I was going to dictate how people thought of me as a musician, I would be less interested in them thinking of me as a clarinet player who played traditional styles of jazz. I would be more interested in them thinking of me almost as a musician whose roots and influences are deepest in the Creole clarinet tradition as it came through New Orleans as well as the French West Indies. I'd like to see that approach to the instrument be imposed on original music. What form that original music will take, I don't know. I'd still like to play with New Orleans–style jazz bands— don't get me wrong—but I would also like to take the language of the instrument, the way I approach the instrument, and combine it with other musics that are out there—even modern, contemporary forms of music.

"In Martinique, for instance, you can hardly find a band that is playing traditional folk tunes. The new style is called 'zouk,' which is a fusion of popular Western music—disco and rock-and-roll—and the old rhythms of Afro-Caribbean origin. I'd like to see the clarinet be approached in an almost folk idiom—the same way as some of the musicians are being influenced by the Klezmer school of playing. They're not playing Klezmer music. [Clarinetist] Don Byron is a perfect example. You could definitely hear how he approaches the clarinet, as having influences from the Klezmer tradition. He's doing original compositions and collaborations with electric guitars or the music of Raymond Scott. It's really more about the way he approaches the instrument than about playing Klezmer music.

"So that's how I'd like people to think about me. Certainly I'd like for them to know that if there's anybody still alive out there who can play the shit out of old New Orleans–style clarinet, it's that Evan Christopher guy. That's nice.

"I would love to have a reputation like that, but I would also like to get away from the idea that the only thing you can do with a clarinet is play 'My Bucket's Got a Hole in It.'"

And he's already had an opportunity to try out some of his ideas. "On Tom McDermott's *Louisianthology* album [1999] I do a tune with the Nightcrawlers playing Creole clarinet in sort of a pseudo-Caribbean Creole style on top of that brass band. It was on Sidney Bechet's 'The Fish Vendor,' and I think it came out wonderfully. It really opened my ears to the possibilities because my imagination is only good up to a point. Recording that tune gave me something concrete to listen to objectively and say 'there's some possibilities here.'"

As of this writing, most of Christopher's recordings—*Classic Jazz Classics* (1993), *This Side of Evan* (1998), as well as his albums with the Cullum band and, more recently, the Trevor Richards Trio—are in the traditional jazz idiom. But it looks as if something rather different is in the offing.

Christopher did all of the arrangements on his two featured albums and, when asked if he has plans to do any writing in the future, he quickly replied, "Oh yeah, the next album. The producer and I are working on a project of original material. I have opened up my ears to those Afro-Caribbean rhythms of the Martinique things as a point of departure. But I think the aesthetic is still very similar [to traditional jazz]. The compositions are very simple, especially harmonically. I'm going for a certain emotional content with the music. I'm not going for something cerebral. I'm just trying to get into some of the recording technology available to us now to create things that might have a little more interest to a person with more modern ears. I'm trying to make something that's interesting to me.

"Right now, it's on computer. I've sequenced the material at this point. We're going through the process of playing the sequences back through a synthesizer in the studio and recording me with them—to see where I might want to change things compositionally. Then we'll go through the process of figuring out what guitar player is going to be perfect for this project, or what drummer is going to be perfect for the project. But we're not there yet."

One goes away from a conversation with Evan Christopher feeling that this is where he is as an artist now, but it is not where he will always be. He is too talented and ambitious to stand still for long. It will be interesting to watch his career evolve and grow with the passage of time.

10

DUKE HEITGER
New Duke in the Jazz Kingdom

It's going on two decades since trumpeter Duke Heitger took New Orleans by storm, when he arrived in town from Toledo, Ohio. Since then, he has built upon the sterling reputation he established in the Crescent City, his name now familiar to all on the international classic jazz scene as well.

While he still considers New Orleans his "base" (he continues to rent a home in the city), Heitger now spends much of his time in Stuttgart, Germany. He moved there in 2006 when his partner Gundula Straub became pregnant with their first child. Alicia Heitger was born in December of that year. A second daughter, Briana, was born in July 2009. Heitger and his family have returned to New Orleans many times during the past four years, and he says it is their intention to move back permanently.

Heitger now does a great deal of touring, both in Europe and the States, working with some of the top names in jazz on both continents. "I practice far more now than I used to," he admits. He has made numerous recordings since his highly acclaimed CD, Rhythm Is Our Business *(2000). The latest is a duo CD recorded in Germany for the Arbors label (*Doin' the Voom Voom*) with the fine young European pianist Bernd Lhotzky. Several more recording projects are "on the horizon," as he put it.*

In spite of this busy round of activities, Heitger has also managed to complete his master's degree in geology at the University of New Orleans. But don't worry: he's still fully committed to his music.

The interview that follows was completed in May 2000 and published in the November 2000 issue of The Mississippi Rag.

HE'S ONE OF THE GREATEST TRUMPETERS WE'VE HAD in this town." So says veteran reedman and bandleader Jacques Gauthé [who passed away in June 2007] about the 32-year-old trumpet star Duke Heitger. It is quite a tribute in view of the many great trumpet players the city has produced and is continuing to produce.

Gauthé first heard Heitger about ten years ago at the Central City Jazz Festival in Colorado, where Duke was playing with his father's band (clarinetist Ray Heitger's Cakewalkin' Jazz Band from Toledo, Ohio). "I said to myself, that kid has a great future," Gauthé recalls, and almost at once, he made an effort to arrange for the young man to move to the Crescent City and join his band. "I told his dad, if Duke would come to New Orleans, I'd keep an eye on him."

But Gauthé's gratification had to be delayed somewhat, for Heitger made it clear that he wanted to finish college first. When he did so the following spring (1991), the young trumpeter set out immediately for New Orleans and joined Gauthé's Creole Rice Jazz Band on its nightly gig at the Hotel Meridien.

"I came down immediately after graduation—not even a month later," Duke reminisces. "I packed up everything I owned in the car. My mom came with me—sent me off—and flew home. I moved into a little place and had a nice steady gig. Jacques, of course, was great, and his band was nice. We did some traveling. My first opportunities to go to Europe were with Jacques. It was a great experience living the life of a New Orleans musician."

But now we're letting the story get ahead of itself. First things first.

Raymond Albert Heitger III was born in Toledo on May 10, 1968. His nickname, Duke, was conferred virtually at birth by his father after a favorite Pittsburgh beer. (The senior Heitger was raised in nearby Beaver, Pennsylvania.) "It started off as a joke and kinda stuck," Duke explains. "It had nothing to do with any musician or anything like that. It kind of worked out nicely, actually."

While avoiding the somewhat over-used expression "child prodigy," one must acknowledge that Duke Heitger was exposed to—and clearly demonstrated an aptitude for—music from an early age. His home resounded with music. Father Ray, who has been leading his popular band at Tony Packo's club in Toledo since the year Duke was born, was, of course, the prime mover. And there was even a family band for a time—with Duke and his mother and three sisters joining the clarinetist. "When we realized my mom was so bad on the piano, we were going to fire her," the trumpeter laughs, "so eventually the family band disbanded.

"As a kid I started out on a bunch of instruments," Heitger says. "I dabbled with the clarinet and drums and took some lessons early on on the piano. But once I hit the cornet, it was pretty apparent that that's where I was going to end up."

He started playing cornet at the age of eight and eventually began lessons with Hershey Cohen, "a great trumpet teacher back in Toledo. He taught me how to read music, and I still do the exercises he taught me."

While you can't catch him often at the keyboards around New Orleans, Duke is a pretty fair piano player, too. "Piano didn't happen until later, after I got serious about music," he says. "I didn't take any more lessons—just every time I passed a piano I wanted to play a little and did it for enjoyment. Actually, I probably ended up spending a little more time on the piano at home than I would on the horn just because it's a little more musical by itself. I didn't start developing the piano . . ." he says, pausing to laugh. "I'm still working on the piano, obviously. I'm still working on everything! I didn't play gigs on the piano until I was in college. But the cornet came early on, about eight years old."

And he started sitting in with his father's band not long after that. "Probably when I was nine, ten, eleven years old I had a repertoire of 'The Saints,' 'Tin Roof Blues,' and a few others. I remember that it was eight songs. So, I'd sit in with the band and always just play the melody. He'd try to get me to improvise a little bit, but it just wasn't in me yet. Finally, I remember one day his kind of challenging me—it was on 'The Saints'—so I dabbled in a little improvised solo that seemed to go okay. But that was before I was 12 or 13."

Then came a pivotal moment in his incipient musical career. "I was about 12 years old when I heard a young cornetist up in Detroit, Jon Kellso, who has become a very good friend of mine. He's a real special friend because he was kind of a turning point for me. I went up [to Detroit] and heard Jon playing at a place called Roger's Roost, kind of a fun place. He was about 16 at the time. I was about 12. It was an overnight inspiration. I went up there as a young kid who had a repertoire of eight songs and didn't yet have a passion for the music. I heard him and his friend [bassist] Mike Karoub, two young guys 16–17 years old, up on a stage playing Dixieland jazz in a club and I thought, 'Jeez, I can do that. I think I want to do that, too.'

"I came back home," he continues, "and got rid of all my rock-and-roll records and started listening to Louis Armstrong, Sidney Bechet, and classical music and all of that—and that was it! It was an overnight turn-around.

"My repertoire went from eight songs to maybe three or four hundred quickly because I'd been around my dad's music all of my life, and those songs were kind of in the back of my head but I didn't realize it. That's where I was lucky, that exposure—my dad having that music on a cassette player in the car or having it on at the house. I remember him specifically pulling out records and saying, 'Listen to this.'"

That kind of thing might have turned some kids off. It certainly suggests a strong and positive relationship between father and son. "It was a fantastic relationship," Duke says unequivocally. "I think early on he realized there was some musical aptitude. He'll tell stories that, when I was two years old, I was pulling off certain things—musicians were playing and I was picking out a melody on something or playing with the clarinet or whatever. So, I think he had an idea that I might be interested in music and might have purposely exposed me to it.

"In that case, needless to say, I am eternally grateful. . . . I was extremely fortunate."

Once hooked on the music, Heitger gained experience by playing with his dad at Tony Packo's on the weekends. But equally valuable were the Wednesday night jam sessions at Ragtime Rick's Pub in his hometown, run by pianist Rick Grafing (who, incidentally, is now a member of the senior Heitger's band). By his mid-teens he was even leading his father's band on occasion.

Duke also worked frequently in the Detroit area, which is only an hour or so from Toledo. "I would sub for Jon Kellso or he'd sub for me in Toledo. We worked with a lot of the same guys. I worked a few gigs with [pianist and bandleader] Jim Dapogny. I also worked with Bob Milne's band in the Detroit area, Mike Montgomery, Hugh Leal, the list goes on. And then I actually got hired on a few other things."

He remembers in particular a recording session—his first—with New Orleans clarinetist Orange Kellin and members of the (Boston-based) New Black Eagle Jazz Band. "It was a CD under the two piano players, Bob Pilsbury and Bob Pelland," he recalls.

"They used the Black Eagle Band as a core and brought in some guest artists—[clarinetist] Joe Muranyi and myself and Orange Kellin. So, that was my first recording session, with some pretty decent company. It was my first meeting with Orange. I remember a story. Orange and I are good friends now, so we joke around about it. My father always spoke very highly of Orange Kellin, and he spoke about him for years and years, so I was expecting this old guy. We were meeting him at the airport when I was doing that recording session, and off walks Orange looking probably younger than I am. It was quite a surprise," he laughs. "It's really good to continue working with him down here."

When did it first become clear that he wanted to be a professional musician?

"Well, it's strange," he answers. "It never crossed my mind that, 'Okay, this is what I'm going to do for the rest of my life.' Even when I moved to New Orleans I wasn't exactly sure what was going to happen. It's the same now as it was then. The music business is not like you choose it; it's like it chooses you. It was an income for me, number one, when I was a kid. All of a sudden, I was a 15- or 16-year-old kid making pretty decent money—better than a paper route. I put myself through private high school. I paid my own high school and my own college. I put myself through the University of Toledo. So, it was income, and it was easy. It was something that was coming relatively natural, and it was progressing. I don't think I necessarily made a conscious decision: 'This is what I am going to do.' It just kind of happened."

Duke was a geology major in college, not a music major. How did that come about? "It's interesting," he now reflects. "My father taught high school mathematics for years, just until a couple of years ago. He retired from the high school where he was, and he's now teaching at Bowling Green University. My father's very well read, and very well educated and very interested in science and math. So, on our way to gigs, we would often talk either about music or we would talk about physics—Einstein or something to do with astronomy, some science anyway. I found it fascinating and just loved that stuff. I was undecided in college for about a year and a half. I had thought about majoring in astronomy, but my math skills were pretty lame. I didn't inherit my father's mathematics ability. I took a geology course with a very enthusiastic professor, and I realized right then that that was the field I wanted to go into. No regrets, I love it. It's a great science, and I'm finishing up hopefully soon."

Heitger is currently [i.e., in 2000] enrolled at the University of New Orleans, where he's completing a master's degree in geology. "I just finished my [thesis] proposal and basically an introduction to it," he explains. "Most of my research is under remote sensing—using thermal imaging to detect ground contamination, detecting oil contaminants in an abandoned industrial waste site, for example. Things are rolling. I'm done with the coursework basically, so once I finish the thesis, that's just about it.

"When I first moved down here, I wasn't exactly sure what I would do," he goes on. "I was kind of saying that doing this [graduate degree] gives me something to fall back on. But I have to be honest with you now. The longer I have stayed in the music business and it keeps getting a little better and better, it's pretty evident that that's what I should and probably will do as my primary living for the rest of my life. I think eventually you realize that there is something you ought to be doing. I'm an average geologist and—not to say that I've got it together in the music business—but I certainly thrive more in music than in geology."

In any case, it was the job opportunity with Jacques Gauthé—not graduate work in geology—that brought Heitger to New Orleans. "As a matter of fact," he emphasizes, "I didn't even start graduate school until about a year and a half after coming here, but I knew I would do it at some point. I didn't take the job [with Gauthé] until practically a year after I was offered it. I had had another offer to check out Vince Giordano's gig in New York at the time and decided the same thing—to finish up [undergraduate] school. My buddy Jon [Kellso] ended up taking that gig obviously. He went off to New York about a year before I came to New Orleans. I think we both really enjoyed the choices we ended up making. I was very happy that I ended up down here, and he's just doing great up there."

The Kellso-Heitger story is an interesting one. Since first meeting in Detroit twenty years ago, they have maintained a close friendship. And their birthdays are even on successive days: Jon's on May 9 and Duke's on May 10. Kellso was in town this year in early May and stayed with Duke, and the two of them were able to celebrate their birthdays (as well as play a few gigs) together. Kellso is a frequent visitor to New Orleans.

"I tell you, it's really neat," Duke says. "He's one of my favorite players, and we're good pals. Unfortunately, there aren't that many people who you really, really like the way they play. He is certainly one of them that I am knocked out by, and he happens to be a great friend."

Asked what other trumpet players "knock him out," Duke responds, "I'm going to borrow a line from another good friend, [trombonist and cornetist] Dan Barrett. We were talking about one of our favorite subjects one night, that being Louis Armstrong, and he says, 'If you ask me who my favorite trumpet player and the most influential jazz musician on me was, that's easy. It's Louis Armstrong. Now if you ask me who the second on the list is, that's a harder question.'

"I feel the same way. Especially after I moved to New Orleans, Louis Armstrong became a real serious influence—not just on the trumpet, but his musicianship. Just to hear how he treats a melody. Then it becomes difficult. I remember as a kid copying a couple of Bix Beiderbecke solos, of course. Even these days I still get people who come up and say they're hearing a lot of Bix. There are so many favorites that sometimes you catch yourself sounding a bit like—like Red Allen or Bunny Berigan or Muggsy Spanier or Roy Eldridge. Allen and Berigan are major influences on my playing. You never consciously try to imitate, maybe occasionally emulate, but your favorite guys will certainly influence you an awful lot—and those are some of my favorite guys."

And what kind of music does he listen to when he's not studying or preparing for a performance? "First of all," he says, "I do listen to a lot of classical music and some opera. I think that's very important. I think [listening to classical music] helps you to become a musician. It helps your ear, your knowledge of harmonies, and it's just good music. But, of course, I put on a lot of jazz, too, at home, it depends on the mood. Put on a Billie Holiday record with all your favorites, Teddy Wilson and all those guys. How can you beat that? Throw on Jelly Roll Morton when

Duke Heitger leads his New Orleans Wanderers at the French Quarter Festival, April 2008. Bassist Sébastien Girardot is in the background.

you're doing some work around the house, and Jelly's music makes you happy no matter what. But I'm also learning that a lot of other musics can be real influential. I think I'm starting to open up my mind a little more the older I get. I really love ethnic folk musics—Hungarian, Italian, French, Martinique, folk musics that have a real connection with what we're doing. But to be honest with you, I don't listen to music as much as I would like to because I'm playing the horn half the time—work in the mornings, work in the evenings. Maybe someday down the road when musicians get paid more, we won't have to work as hard as we do."

Since moving to New Orleans, Heitger has kept very busy. In fact, he's one of the busiest jazz musicians in town these days. In addition to his regular gig with Jacques Gauthé at the Meridien, he worked with trombonist Steve Yocum and, subsequently, multi-instrumentalist and vocalist John Gill at the Maison Bourbon. Then, in 1993, he joined Banu Gibson's popular band.

"About when Jacques lost the steady gig at the Meridien is when Banu's thing popped up, although it was only road work," he recalls. "Also, it was around then when the Can Can [club in the Royal Sonesta Hotel on Bourbon Street] started happening. Mahogany Hall [a defunct club on Bourbon Street] was still in existence. I actually had a little trio there briefly in the afternoons, one day a week. Good things were happening—1993 was a pretty important year in New Orleans because I had a nice variety of music. That was also the beginning of some of my steady work for the next six or seven years. When I joined Banu's band, she didn't have a steady gig, so most of the work I've done with her has been road work. But it was nice to get out on the road, and, of course, Banu had great gigs—symphony pops concerts, community jazz concerts—there were some really nice gigs."

Heitger has recently left the Gibson organization. "I enjoyed playing with the band," he emphasizes. "The reason I decided to leave was because eventually it's kinda time to do your own thing. You have to make some changes to have change happen sometimes. We love playing with each other, and I still do quite a bit with the band. I'll probably continue to do so."

One of Duke's main reasons for leaving the Gibson band was that he had taken over the leadership of the afternoon jazz cruises on the steamboat *Natchez* from veteran cornetist Eddie Bayard. He had been subbing for Bayard for some time, and when the latter decided to retire in 1998, Duke took over the band.

"When you start leading a band, time flies," he laughs. "Your hair turns gray and you start forgetting one, two, three years of your life. It's a big step. Eddie's been a great person for me here in town. He laid a lot of responsibility on me, thought I was ready for it, and I appreciated the offer.

"It's a seven-day gig, jazz on the cruises everyday," he goes on. "It's a great gig. It's a very important gig, and I don't underestimate its importance. Here's an authentic steamboat, and steamboats have a real long tradition of music on the rivers. It's one of six actual steamers in the country, and fortunately they are dedicated to putting New Orleans jazz on it. It's only a trio, but it's good music. Normally, I have either David Boeddinghaus or Steve Pistorius on piano—obviously two fantastic piano players. I have Tom Fischer, Brian Ogilvie, or Jack Maheu on clarinet. Often, instead of clarinet, I'll have Tom Saunders on tuba, and, of course, Eddie plays my off days. Sometimes I'll have a banjo, either Neil Unterseher or John Parker. That's the core of the guys I use on a pretty regular basis."

The band recently made a recording, *Duke Heitger's Steamboat Stompers*, Heitger's first as a leader. "It's doing pretty well," he says modestly. "It's something that was representative of what we were doing every day on the boat. People seem to enjoy it."

Speaking of recordings, Heitger achieved some recognition a few years ago with his participation in the hit CD *Hot* by the retro-swing band Squirrel Nut Zippers. It seems that the group was looking for a trumpet player to do some of its original material, and the fine local trombonist Mark Mullins (who occasionally plays with Banu Gibson) recommended Duke.

"I took the job," he says, "because the pay was real good, really nice. It was going to be the best one-day paycheck in my life. So, I took it, and the session went real well. They hit upon something that the public wanted because they went through the roof with record sales. You know, they ended up selling over a million records. Unfortunately, jazz records never come close to hitting those numbers. To come home one night and flip through the channels and hear your trumpet solo on MTV was kind of exciting for a while. And I did get a platinum record. It's neat. You just do not know how many other chances you'll get for platinum records. So, it was a great experience to be part of a real pop movement, as brief as it was. Since then I did another record with one of the lead guys in the band—Tom Maxwell is his name—who broke off and started his own band. That just came out recently."

But the recent recording that Heitger is most proud of is his latest CD, *Rhythm Is Our Business*, on the Fantasy label. Featuring a stellar group of sidemen (including Rebecca Kilgore on vocals), it was produced by George Hocutt, who has featured Duke on a number of his recordings for Good Time Jazz.

"I had always wanted to record Duke as a leader in a more swing-era, small-group setting," Hocutt said. "We talked about it for nearly three years before everything came together. We picked many tunes recorded by small groups in the '30s and '40s that featured Roy Eldridge, Gene Krupa, Ellington sidemen, and so on. The principal concept was to create an environment that allowed Duke to explore this glowing facet of his talent. We are very proud of the end product."

"They wanted their answer to the swing craze," Heitger adds, "but didn't want all of the jump-jive swing.

"They wanted what George considered real swing. George knew my playing well enough that he knew I was comfortable with that, and I am. I love that era and make my living often playing that era of jazz. So, I welcomed the project. Conceptually, it wasn't a difficult project. Determining the material was a little rough—there's so much to choose from. The logistics of the project ended up being kind of a hassle, getting people in town and things like that. [The recording] has some great moments—how can it not with those players? The guys played great on it.

"Needless to say, my biggest criticism is of myself. You know, you're trying to pop out a record in three days, and you're under the gun, and it's one of your first major projects. Sometimes you think you're hearing that in your playing. Don't get me wrong, I am very happy with it and I'd like to do another one somewhere down the road probably a little similar, maybe change a couple things. Generally, it's getting very nice reviews from the musicians themselves, which is important." (And one might add that the critics are writing very favorably about it as well.)

Given the success of the new CD and his interest in the Swing Era, one wonders if Heitger has any thoughts about putting a big band together. "Yeah," he says emphatically. "After hearing the CD, several of the guys in the band wanted to take it a little further. I don't think there's a whole lot of people doing this stuff. I think there's a market for it. I am interested in exposing it to a whole other scene that's out there that a lot of us aren't aware of, a very young scene. A thriving scene that will hire jazz bands, western swing bands, the list goes on, in these basically rock clubs all over the country or even all over the world. I don't mean that we would be playing any rock-and-roll music. I mean that we would have access to these 'young hip crowds,' if you will.

"I think there's a few things on [the new CD] that would go over quite well. For instance, I've been doing some things at the Shim Sham Club [formerly the Toulouse Theater, Jimmy Maxwell's] on Toulouse Street lately. The first time I walked into that place, it had a vibe that I knew it was going to be around for a little while. My association with it right now is this 'Shim Sham Burlesque Revue.' It's the hottest thing in town right now. They've brought back burlesque with a live six-piece band and the girls dancing. It's sold out every time they do it. We're packing the place with about two hundred people at about $20 a head, and people are pushing to get in. People get dressed up like the old days. It's a successful club. It's clubs like that that I'm talking about."

By now Duke is really warming to the topic. "But I also have a couple other ideas. I've talked for a few years about putting together a bigger band, maybe even slightly larger than the one on the CD [eight pieces, plus a singer]. If it takes renting a room, then I'll do it—the Blue Room at the Fairmont Hotel, for example, and carry on the tradition. It's a beautiful room that's dark half the time. I would like to put a tuxedoed, hot big band in there, hopefully, in the relatively near future. But something along those lines—the elegant hotel ballroom with a tuxedoed hot dance band. [The Fairmont—formerly the Roosevelt Hotel—was badly damaged by Hurricane Katrina. It (including the legendary Blue Room) was subjected to major renovation and only reopened as the Roosevelt once again in 2009.]

"You know, Vince Giordano has been quite successful up in New York, but my concept would be a little different from Vince's. I think there's room for that kind of band in New Orleans. There's a little of that being done in town, but Luis Russell things and things like that aren't being done, where you have riffing saxophones behind [you]. So, that's been on my mind quite a bit.

"You know," he goes on, "I've only dabbled in the band-leading thing for a couple of years now. It's moving along nicely so far. I'm looking forward to booking some of my own bands somewhere. I'll see how the band-leading thing works. It's nice because it provides you the opportunity to do the kind of music you want to do.

"As for other projects, I have been talking to [clarinetist] Evan Christopher. We haven't done a whole lot together. We had a very successful French Quarter Fest weekend [the well-received "Jazzin' on the River" cruise], just one of those special moments. So, Evan and I have talked since. We're about the same age. Maybe we'll try to do a little work together, maybe do some traveling, on a smaller-band scale. Who knows? So, there's quite a bit on the books for me."

The handsome trumpet player is considered to be one of the most eligible bachelors in the city. Does his busy work schedule leave time for the ladies, or thoughts of marriage? "I've managed to avoid it so far," he laughs.

"Musicians traditionally have strange relationships—maybe it's because of being out a lot of the time. I have a couple special girlfriends, but not too many down here, long-term. It would be nice someday. It's a dilemma. By the time I'm 40, I don't really want to have to be working the hours that I'm working now to be making a decent living. Eventually, I do want more time at home, whether it's with a family or not. I haven't hit the panic button yet—32's not panic-button time. But I need to cut down the hours at some point. I'll figure out a way. I haven't figured it out yet."

In the meantime, Duke Heitger is just happy to be where he is and doing what he's doing. "I'm playing a lot of things I like to play," he says. "In my afternoon set [on the boat], for instance, I'll span a couple of decades or more in a 45-minute time period—play some ragtime, which I love to do, play some '20s Armstrong or whoever, and end up swinging out on some '30s Ellington thing, which I love to do as well. I love all that era: the teens, twenties, and thirties."

As for living in the Big Easy, he says, "I'm liking it more as the years go on. After a while you find out all the really beautiful and enjoyable things to do in New Orleans, and there are plenty of them. It's quite a city. I don't look at New Orleans as a [musical stepping stone] anymore. I look at it as a real serious place where you can make a living. My living may change, but it could certainly be the home base for me for years to come."

11

TOM FISCHER
Versatile Reedman

Tom Fischer is one of the best and most versatile clarinetists in a city with more than its share of first-rate clarinet players. A virtual "first-call" on clarinet, he commands the full panoply of saxophones as well, and is a highly respected player on all of them. Fischer is surely one of the busiest musicians working in New Orleans today.

A Chicago-area native, Fischer was summoned to the Crescent City by popular local bandleader Banu Gibson more than twenty years ago and has been a mainstay of her band and a city resident ever since. During that time he has also worked regularly with a number of other bands, including those of the late Al Hirt, Eddie Bayard, Duke Heitger, and Don Vappie. He has led a tour of New Orleans all-star musicians to Japan for the last three years, and his other activities include adjunct status on the music faculty at the University of New Orleans.

Like so many other Crescent City musicians, Fischer was a victim of Hurricane Katrina in late August 2005. His home on 32nd Street in the flooded Lakeview neighborhood was totally ruined. He immortalized the event with his first CD as a leader, 32nd Street Blues, recorded less than six months after the disaster. After a brief sojourn in nearby Algiers, he and his family are now back in Lakeview, where they have rebuilt their flooded home. "New home, old location," as he put it.

Fischer's latest recorded effort is with fellow clarinetist Tommy Sancton and guitarist John Rankin. Together they call themselves the Classic Jazz Trio. Their excellent CD of that name was released in the spring of 2010.

I caught up with Fischer between sets on the steamboat Natchez *one afternoon in August 2001 for the following interview. It appeared in a slightly different form in* The Mississippi Rag *of March 2002.*

TOM FISCHER WAS BORN IN EVANSTON, ILLINOIS, ON January 20, 1958, but he grew up in nearby Des Plaines. He was raised in a musical family. His mother played piano, his older brother played alto saxophone, and his younger brother played oboe. His maternal uncle was a professor of church music, an organist, and choir director.

"He composed a good deal of sacred music for choirs and organ," Fischer adds. "He has some hymns in the hymnbooks, Lutheran and other churches as well, if you look under the name of Carl Schalk."

"I heard a lot of music at home," he goes on. "I started taking piano lessons when I was in first or second grade, started playing clarinet in the fourth grade, and took up the alto sax in high school so I could play in the jazz band. My older brother was a really good alto sax player, and he played in the jazz band. But I also discovered quite a bit of music on my own. I started listening to the classical [radio] station in Chicago— WFMT—and they played good music all the time. That was, believe it or not, the first music that I really loved. I listened to just about every-thing—Beethoven, Mozart, chamber music. I bought the Schnabel re-cordings of the Beethoven piano sonatas when I was twelve. I just really liked the music."

He went on to play in the Youth Symphony of Chicago, performing on clarinet and bass clarinet. In his senior year in high school he began to take on aspiring young clarinetists as private students.

"So my Saturdays were very busy," he says. "All morning I would be rehearsing with the orchestra and all afternoon till five o'clock I'd be giv-ing clarinet lessons. It was good to have the extra money."

Fischer was first exposed to jazz through his older brother's collec-tion of records by Count Basie, Charlie Parker, and other greats. This inspired him to follow in his sibling's footsteps by joining the high school jazz band, where charts by Stan Kenton, Basie, Sammy Nestico, and the like were the standard fare.

Growing up in such a musical environment left little doubt where Fischer would attend college. He enrolled in Indiana University's presti-gious School of Music in the fall of 1976.

"It was a very natural progression to go to IU and major in music," he says. "Everyone told me to get a degree in music education, which is what I did. They said I could fall back on teaching. But I had the same classes and clarinet teachers as the music majors. I studied with Earl Bates, Henry Gulick, and Bernard Portnoy."

During his first year in Bloomington, he and some others in the university's famous marching band decided to start a Dixieland band. With the help of bookings through the Music School they were soon playing concerts, festivals, and other gigs throughout the state of Indiana and beyond. Their first summer job was at Six Flags theme park in Atlanta, followed by three summers in the New Orleans section of Opryland in Nashville. During that time, he says, "I was buying records because I thought, if I'm going to be playing this stuff, I'd better learn what it sounds like. I tried to hit the used-record stores in Bloomington and, if the price was right, I'd buy it. Once I got this Pee Wee Russell record—it was one of his later ones with Nat Pierce on piano—which I didn't like, so I sold it back. I love Pee Wee now."

It was in those years at Indiana, too, that Fischer met up with another young music student who was to have a significant impact on his musical career. That young man was David Boeddinghaus, a classical piano major who had recently returned to Bloomington after taking a year off to play with Vince Giordano's Nighthawks back home in New York. Boeddinghaus is now Banu Gibson's music director and one of the top jazz piano players in New Orleans.

"I really didn't meet him until my fourth year at IU," Fischer recalls. "We had been playing at Rapp's [an off-campus pizza joint] with various combinations for four years, once a week, but we never used a piano for some reason. We just had tuba, drums, and three horns. Someone else knew him and knew that he played that kind of music, so he came in to hear the band and ended up playing with us every week. We sometimes had a few disagreements, stylistically. I really liked the four-beat Chicago style, and—this is a gross generalization—he was more interested in the [more traditional] two-beat. He knew a lot more about the music than I did and about traditional jazz in general. I'd never heard records of most of these people until my first year in college."

Fischer spent five years in Bloomington and, after completing his student-teaching requirement, graduated in 1981. He returned to Chicago and decided to lay off from music for a year. "IU was pretty intense," he recalls, "and maybe I just needed a break. After about a year I got out my clarinet and started playing along with Benny Goodman records. It felt good, so I started going around town and sitting in. I went down to Andy's Jazz at Noon, and [trombonist] Jim Beebe had a band playing some place. So I sort of went to places, hung out, and sat in. Five years later I was working five nights a week playing with different bands in Chicago.

"That's when I picked up the tenor," he goes on, "because everyone said, 'If you want to get work, you really have to play tenor.' Chicago was really a tenor town. That's when I started buying more records of tenor sax players. I know Lester Young, Coleman Hawkins, and Bud Freeman are three very different approaches, but those are probably my favorites. The alto was still there. In fact, when I played with the Red Rose Ragtime Band, I played clarinet and alto. Some of the '20s stuff sounded good with alto."

He played with a number of different bands in Chicago. "It was a nice mix, a chance to play a lot of different things," he recalls.

One of his main gigs was with the Red Rose Ragtime Band. "John Otto was the reed player," he explains, "and when he decided to leave the band for whatever reason, I joined them. We played rags and early jazz. I played with them for five years. We made a couple of records, went to Holland—it was great.

"On Thursday nights I played in Northbrook at the Cypress Inn with Jim Clark's band. That's where I met Bobby Wright, a great piano player, one of the best piano players I ever worked with—along with David Boeddinghaus. We played Dixieland, straight-ahead Chicago jazz, that sort of thing. Wright also played modern jazz, as well as ragtime. In fact, he's listed and pictured in the *They All Played Ragtime* book. But he could play like ["modernist"] Red Garland. A remarkable musician.

"We had a quartet," he continues, "with Wayne Jones on the drums and a couple of different bass players and Wright on piano. We played Andy's periodically and a place called the Raccoon Club. We did everything from '20s and '30s music—Fats Waller to some Brubeck tunes and Dizzy Gillespie stuff. I played almost entirely clarinet. I played alto on a couple of tunes, an Art Pepper number called 'Straight Life' which was based on 'After You've Gone,' and then we did some Lennie Tristano tunes. There's so much good music and so much good jazz, and I really like playing it all. I don't think any one style suffers from being able to play some of the other styles."

Boeddinghaus was the first of the two Indiana alums to come to New Orleans. In fact, after wrestling with the decision of returning to New York, he accepted Banu Gibson's invitation to join her band in 1983— barely a month after completing his master's degree in classical performance. His admiration for Fischer's playing is quite clear.

"Tom Fischer is a very, very versatile musician," he says. "He has his own style, but if you told him to play specifically like Frank Teschemacher or Pee Wee Russell or Benny Goodman, he could pull it off. He can also play like Charlie Parker or Zoot Sims and some other musicians of that period and later."

In those days Gibson did not have a clarinet in her band, and Boeddinghaus thought Fischer would make a good fit. "I wanted Tom real bad," he recently recalled. He seems to have persuaded Gibson to give Fischer a listen.

"So in '83 I guess he convinced her to get me to play with her band," Fischer says. "I hadn't been back to playing very long, so she hired me to play the ragtime festival in St. Louis, the Sacramento festival, and the L.A. Classic Jazz Festival. I don't think I particularly impressed her. Then I'd see her and the band over the years at different festivals and I'd sit in. And over the years I got better, I think. Eventually she decided to get a reed player. She was working fulltime at the Hilton, and she had permission from them to hire another piece. So, in the fall of '88, she said, 'Do you want to move to New Orleans?' I hemmed and hawed for a long time wondering if I wanted to leave Chicago since I was working five nights a week. Eventually I decided to move and came down here in January 1989."

Fischer is now one of the veteran members of the band, and he still appreciates the musicality of the group. "Every time I play a concert with Banu and her whole band—and it's usually out of town—there's a real high level of musicianship and the musical integrity of what we do is, I think, at a very high level," he says. "Every time I do something like that it reminds me of why I wanted to play music. All those people are great players, and the material we're playing right now is the best of American popular music."

And Gibson clearly values his contributions too. "Tom Fischer brings a lot of riches to his musical treasure chest," she says. "Not only does he play the usual clarinet–tenor saxophone double, but he adds to his expertise the alto, C-melody, soprano, and bass saxophones. He also has the wonderful ability to be a musical time travel machine and play in the styles of early jazz and ragtime through the late swing styles of the '40s. I've always been drawn to the musician who can cover all the styles of the first half of the century. And he's also fun to travel with on the road! Being on the road is hard, and it's nice to have someone who is intelligent, witty, and silly all in one person. It took a lot to get him to move to New Orleans, but I'm glad I finally won him over."

While drawn to New Orleans with the prospect of steady work at home, Fischer admits that most of the Gibson band's gigs are now on the road—a situation that no longer appeals to him much. For one thing, he married a New Orleans woman, Jean, an artist, in 1995, and the couple now has a three-year-old daughter, Analise.

"I think it gets harder the older I get," he says, referring to travel. "I really want to spend time with my family. It gets a little hard when you're leaving the house at seven o'clock at night and saying good-bye to your three-year-old, or when you're going off on a tour for a few days or a few weeks. That's rough. I've been fortunate in that I haven't done these six-month tours or three-month tours, that sort of thing. The most I've been gone in the last few years is three weeks, and that's too long. Analise is at an age where she knows when I'm leaving and when I'm gone, and she was real excited to see me come home when I took this last trip. So it's hard to leave."

And the situation was further complicated with the arrival of a son, Jack Henry, last December. All of which means that Fischer has had to find work around town, which has been no trouble for him. He worked regularly with Al Hirt for a couple of years in the early nineties—two nights a week at the old Jelly Roll's on Bourbon Street.

"He did pretty much the same show—the same tunes, same order, pretty much the same thing—every night," Tom recalls. "He never warmed up. He'd take the horn out of the case and play a couple of notes and say, 'okay.' There were moments there when the old Al Hirt came through. He would just play something, and it would blow you away—with such power and total command. I mean, he had total command of

Tom Fischer performing at the New Orleans Jazz and Heritage Festival, April 2009.

the trumpet. There's no doubt about it—whether or not you liked what he played or thought it was great jazz. I love those LPs he did with Pete Fountain and Abe Lincoln on trombone, back in the late fifties, I think. They're fun, they're great. There's a CD on the Laser Light label which recorded the band live at the club, and I'm on that, and a video as well. He called all those tunes he recorded—'Sugar Lips,' 'Java,' and all that. He knew exactly what those tunes were about. He knew that it was fluff, but it made him a lot of money. It was just a kick to be on the bandstand playing with Al Hirt."

Fischer has been playing regularly with another popular local band since its inception in the mid-nineties, the Creole Jazz Serenaders, led by Don Vappie.

"Tom is a very integral part of CJS," says Vappie. "He was my first choice when [wife] Milly and I put together the band. Tom has a lot to give, and when we work together he knows that I want him to be himself and to strive for the sound that defines who he is. Since playing with the CJS, I think many people around town have come to see what I always knew he had. We are all better for our experiences together."

Vappie and Fischer seem to be on the same wave length. "One of the things that Don said at the very beginning was, 'I want you to play what you feel.' The spirit of what he said was, this is great music from the '20s and I've transcribed it, but if you feel something, I just want you to play it. That's what we've done with that band. It hasn't always been stylistically in keeping with the 1920s and 1930s. It's taken the music in a different direction. I see it as injecting another spark into the music. I see playing that music in the spirit in which those people originally played it—that is the spirit of creating something new. When you consider what happened in jazz from 1920 to 1930—in ten years—it's incredible. Every time they were recording something, they were thinking of new things. 'Hey, let's do this. . . .' That's where I think CJS is coming from, from that spirit."

But perhaps Fischer's steadiest gig since coming to New Orleans has been the daily afternoon cruises on the riverboat *Natchez* with the Steamboat Stompers. First hired in 1990 by Eddie Bayard when he was leading the band, he's been there ever since, except for a couple of years in the mid-nineties when there was no music on the boat. Duke Heitger now leads the trio.

"We have some great days on the *Natchez*," he says, "and we do that with three people. You've got to have the right three people. It was a good day today. It was fun. In the middle of the last set I'm thinking, 'I'm on a paddle-wheel steamboat in the Mississippi River playing traditional jazz and I'm doing this for a living.' You know how many people would dream of doing this? I'm very fortunate. I'm very fortunate to be doing what I'm doing in the place I'm doing it."

Fischer seems quite content in New Orleans. While recognizing the

city's shortcomings—politics, public education, and an uncertain economy based largely on tourism—he can also say, "There's no place like
New Orleans. It's a unique city. I have really all the work that I want,
so I'm actually able to make a living playing music. That's great. People
come to New Orleans looking for this music. A guy came up to me today
and said, 'I have a huge collection of Sidney Bechet records and I really
enjoyed your version of "Petite Fleur."' Yes, it's true that we do get knowledgeable people here. It's an interesting mix, actually. You get people
who say, 'I've finally got to New Orleans. I've wanted to come here all
my life,' and some of those people say, 'We walked up and down Bourbon
Street and we couldn't find any jazz.' That's because, across from the Can
Can at the Famous Door, where they used to have great jazz, it's rock-
and-roll and the place is full of kids drinking and dancing. So you have
an interesting mix of people who are knowledgeable about the music and
people who are totally clueless. And we touch some of the clueless ones.
They say, 'Wow, I really like this. Where can I find more of this music?'
There's very little down-side to playing music here. There are some very
talented musicians here, some very good players. I have a chance to work
with a lot of really good musicians."

As a graduate of a prestigious music school, Tom Fischer has definite
opinions about music and the music he plays. "You know," he says, "college and university jazz programs seem to believe that real jazz didn't
begin until around 1940 or 1945. That was the beginning of jazz as an art
form, as opposed to being popular entertainment. Just because Mozart
came before Beethoven does not mean that Beethoven was better than
Mozart.

"Mozart stands on his own, and music from the fourteenth century
stands on its own as music. It doesn't have a value purely as a predecessor to something that came later. It has a value all its own. So does the
Original Dixieland Jass Band—they are what they are. They played the
music they played at the time they played it. It's good music and, yes, it
led to something else, but it's great music on its own. It stands on its own
as music—as does Jelly Roll Morton, King Oliver, and everybody else. So
that music is just as valid artistically as Charlie Parker was and as Clifford
Brown was, and Miles Davis and John Coltrane. People also forget that
'modern jazz' is sixty years old and all the 'avant garde' jazz is forty years

old. If we're going to talk about how old jazz is, I don't see why music that is seventy years old is any less valid than music that is sixty years old.

"I know there is a lot more to jazz than the blues," he goes on, "though blues is a big part of it. I think you play with a lot of soul, play from the heart, in a form other than the blues. It's funny, if you want to talk about soul, you listen to the second, the slow movement of the Brahms violin concerto and you'll hear as much 'soul'—in the right hands—as you will in a Johnny Dodds playing the blues. I hear it. There's soul there. There's a lot of different kinds of soul. There's a lot of music out there, and a lot of music with 'soul.' Jazz isn't alone in that regard. I would just like to see people open their ears and listen to whatever music they're listening to for what it is—and not for what they want it to be or what they think it should be. Listen to it for what it is. Just stop, put aside what you think is worthy or what it should be, and just listen to it. Either it's good or it's bad."

And what is his approach to playing the music?

"I like to think I play Tom Fischer style and, depending on the situation, with leanings towards more traditional New Orleans players. When we're playing 'Perdido Street Blues' on the boat, it's hard to avoid influences from Johnny Dodds or Sidney Bechet. What I like to think is that I put my personality into what I play, while trying to play what the situation calls for. If it's a modern type of rhythm section, I tend to play a little more modern. I play some notes that maybe wouldn't have been played in the '20s or '30s.

"At this point, I really don't want to just copy the style of somebody else anymore—or play someone else's solo note for note. I can pay homage to somebody, and you're always borrowing from somebody. There's really nothing new under the sun. But I'm really interested in finding my own voice—and that's hard to do, especially with more traditional jazz because there's a lot of emphasis on re-creating a sound and a style. I would like to play my style within that framework. It's like, what would I have played if I'd been in the studio in 1927 maybe? And I didn't have somebody to copy—that's kind of what I'm thinking. The thing is it's not 1927, no matter how much some people would like it to be. A lot of music has gone on since then. A lot of jazz has happened over the last hundred years. You know, I haven't really decided myself about this. I'm still up in the air as to how I really want to play this kind of music."

As Fischer searches for his own voice, he continues to keep busy by playing and recording with a variety of groups in a variety of styles. He has made countless recordings as a sideman or featured soloist, but he has yet to record or perform as the leader of his own group. That is definitely in his plans for the near future.

"A lot of people have told me, 'you've got to do something under your own name,'" he says. "I would like to. I would like to put something out there that illustrates what I do. I've talked to George Buck about it and he said, 'Sure.' So I just need to do it."

As for the kind of group and style of music he would play, he says, "It would depend. In New Orleans, in order to work, you generally have to play New Orleans style. That's probably what it would be. Although— and now I'm just thinking out loud—there's no doubt that I could put a quartet into Snug Harbor and play some modern jazz, play some tunes. Bobby Wright and I one time did a thing where we just played for forty-five minutes or an hour totally free. I don't know what it sounded like.

"There were two people there, and they were our friends," he laughs. "They stayed the whole hour, so it must not have been too bad. But to have a group where I would determine the direction it would go. I think I would like to do that."

Teaching has been part of Tom Fischer's life since he taught clarinet during his high school years. A music education major in college, he has recently returned to teaching, on a part-time basis, in the jazz studies program at the University of New Orleans.

"I was in New Orleans for twelve years before I started teaching again," he says. "There was a stretch of twelve years where I didn't do any teaching. Then I got a call from Ed Peterson [jazz saxophonist and member of the UNO music faculty], who said, 'I need someone to teach a clarinet student every now and then.' Last year I had one student first semester, I had two students second semester, and we'll see what I have this year."

As for the future, Fischer sums it up in the following way. "I don't plan on going anywhere else right now. You never know what the future holds, but I'm not looking to move. If something should appear, I would certainly consider it. You know, Jean's family is here. I'm established here, and I do like it here. I'd like to do some recording under my name, maybe doing more as a single, doing more projects under my supervision. I can see myself teaching more, and I can see myself stretching my musical boundaries a little bit and doing some things that I haven't done before—while still playing Dixieland for people who want to hear 'When the Saints Go Marching In.'"

12

CLIVE WILSON
English Accent, New Orleans Soul

Trumpeter Clive Wilson, now in his sixties, came to New Orleans from England in the 1960s. He eventually became an American citizen, established himself here permanently, and has been recognized internationally for decades through his touring and recordings as a leading exponent of traditional New Orleans jazz.

He continues to tour and record. His most recent recordings are those of a group—the New Orleans Serenaders—that he and pianist Butch Thompson conceived early in this decade: Hot and Sweet: The Music of Louis Armstrong and Kid Ory *(2003) and* Heart Full of Rhythm *(2007). A third volume was in the planning stages as these lines were being written.*

Wilson was in England when Hurricane Katrina struck New Orleans. He returned to the States two weeks later and was escorted through the blockade of the city by a civil sheriff (a friend) to check on his home in the Irish Channel neighborhood—fortunately an unflooded area—and found only minor wind damage. "These types of disasters bring out the best in some people and the worst in others," he observes, stressing that both sides of the story should be made public in the media reports. Wilson stayed with friends in Greensburg, Louisiana, for some seven weeks before returning home to initiate the repair of his property (now fully completed).

The following interview was conducted on June 30, 2001, and was published, essentially in its present form, in the December 2001 issue of The Mississippi Rag.

THE 1960S WERE PARTICULARLY INTERESTING FOR NEW Orleans music because, despite the popularity of rock-and-roll, R&B, and, perhaps to a lesser extent, contemporary jazz, classic jazz experienced a significant revival during that decade. In his excellent book *Jazz in New Orleans: The Postwar Years through 1970*, Charles Suhor writes of the "reimaging" of the city as a national center of traditional jazz and Dixieland at that time and attributes it in no small measure to the opening of Preservation Hall in 1961.

Pioneer jazz musicians were passing on, however, and few of the younger New Orleanians seemed interested in carrying on the tradition. Danny Barker's Fairview Baptist Church youth band was certainly an important exception, but there was another, often overlooked moving force that helped to keep the music alive—the influx of young foreign musicians who arrived in the city in the '60s.

Trumpeter Clive Wilson, from England, was one of these newcomers. He speaks of New Orleans as having been "inundated with an ever-increasing tide of Europeans, Australians, Canadians, and Japanese" in those days.

"At one time," he says, "931 Royal Street sounded like a music school from morning till night, with so many of us living in apartments there. Over a two-year period, the place housed Lars Edegran [from Sweden], 'Orange' Kellin [Sweden], Sammy and Nina Rimington [U.K.], Dick and Sandra Cook [U.K.], Trevor Richards [U.K.], Dan Pawson [U.K.], Spud Spedding [Australia], John 'Legs' Lancaster [U.K.], Dick and John Edser [Australia], Geoff Bull [Australia], Mike Casimir [U.K.], John Simmons [U. K.], Dick Douthwaite [U.K.], and myself."

Still others—such as Les Muscutt (U.K.), Jim Finch (U.K.), and Sven Stahlberg (Sweden)—lived elsewhere, as did "the Japanese contingent" —Yoshio and Keiko Toyama, Yoichi Kimura, and Kioshi Arai.

Many of the newcomers stayed for only a relatively short time before returning to their homelands (though some do return to New Orleans now and then), while others chose to stay and have become major contributors to the local jazz scene over the last thirty years or more. Clive Wilson is one of the latter.

Wilson was born in London on August 19, 1942, the son of a clergyman for the Church of England. His musical education began with piano lessons at age seven and lasted five or six years, but it was not until he reached secondary school that he was first exposed to jazz.

"I was nearly 14," he recalls. "Somebody came to school with a record and played it on the school record player. [It was] Bunk [Johnson] with George Lewis playing 'Tishomingo Blues.' The sounds were so enticing I couldn't quite figure it out because there were three voices going at the same time. I wasn't used to listening to that, but it was very attractive and just drew me in—the combination of tone and rhythm and the three lines going at once. So I started listening to more and more jazz records, almost exclusively traditional jazz."

It was not long before he wanted to start playing jazz himself.

"I had heard a lot of Armstrong and [Brit bandleaders] Humphrey Lyttelton and Chris Barber, Bunk Johnson, George Lewis, Kid Ory," he says, "and I think I found a cornet in a pawn shop for five pounds. So, I bought it. I think I was 16, and I tried to play it—of course, with no lessons. It was pretty rough, but that's how you start. A year later, my father got me a trumpet that cost only ten pounds. It was old and second-hand, but it was a lot better than the cornet. Right around then—I think I was still 16—there was a concert. The George Lewis band was doing a tour in Britain, and a group of us from school went up to London to see them. It was a huge auditorium, and they did two shows that night. Both were sold out. They were a huge hit. That was the first live jazz I ever heard, which is crazy, really, but it was a great experience."

Soon he and school friends started their own band. "We knew about three songs," he laughs. "We played at a concert and played our three songs. So, I became hooked on performing, right at that moment, knowing almost nothing. It was a start."

He continued to play after going off to college at the University of Newcastle in the north of England.

"We had quite a lot of jazz bands in the area," he recalls. "There were a couple of jazz clubs, and there were other places—like pubs—where bands would play. I would sit in with these groups. Then, towards my last year, I actually had a Thursday night at one of the pubs, and I played there for a while on a weekly basis. But the repertoire was limited, and musicianship was limited. I had a few lessons on trumpet by that time, not really legitimate lessons—you know, scales, chords, general structure of songs."

His teacher was jazz cornetist Owen Bryce, who taught, says Wilson, "in sort of an extension of the London school system. He would do night classes, teaching jazz."

Wilson graduated from college in 1964 with an honors degree in physics. "Third class, nothing dramatic," he smiles. "I was good enough to get through a very tough course. I really didn't know what I was going to do with it."

Then came an opportunity he could not pass up.

"There was a student charter flight going to the States. It was a good price, and I decided to sign up for it. I had saved up pennies for a few years, scratching things together. I came to the States at the beginning of July in '64. I think it was $120 round trip to New York, and I got a Greyhound bus ticket for $99 for 99 days. I was going to be here for three months, so that covered my transportation. After a few days in New York, which was colorful in itself, I set off on a Greyhound to visit my sponsor in San Francisco, a friend of the family. To get a green card, you needed a sponsor. So, I went to San Francisco via the Grand Canyon and arrived at the start of the Goldwater/Republican convention."

He heard some jazz in San Francisco, but he wasn't much impressed.

"Turk Murphy was at Earthquake McGoon's [club]. I'd heard him on records. Some of the early records have something to offer, but, hearing them live, they had become so tired, listless, I couldn't believe how bad they were—even compared with their own recordings. I think it was just a bad phase in his career. The whole thing was completely ludicrous compared to what I was later to hear in New Orleans. I had limited funds, so I didn't see any other West Coast jazz.

"I arrived in New Orleans with $50 in my pocket. But no problem," he explains, "I had intended to get a summer job to pay for my vacation. Luckily, with the help of people I met at Preservation Hall who became friends, I was referred to Tulane Medical Center and got a job there for nine weeks as assistant to an electronics wizard. So, that paid for my vacation."

Wilson had no intention of using his green card to get musical gigs.

"At that time I was really a beginner," he stresses. "I was here to listen, and, of course, I heard music every night—at Preservation Hall and Dixieland Hall. Everybody I heard was one of my idols. It was a dream come true. Not only that, but the musicians were very friendly. They'd take us with them to private jobs they had, take us out to neighborhood restaurants, sit down with us and have a beer—I mean, it was unbelievable. We were on a first-name basis with famous musicians like Punch Miller, Slow Drag Pavageau, Louis Nelson, George Lewis, Kid Howard . . . everybody. It was quite extraordinary.

"Going from one culture to another was very, very different. In those days it was almost like going to a Third World country, coming here. It wasn't like the rest of America. In some way, you could call it an oasis from America. In another way, it was a part of America that had somehow been forgotten and stayed old-fashioned. It was exotic to someone like myself. One of the reasons we were so welcomed into the musicians' community, I think, was that most of the black musicians were in a sort of survival situation dealing with segregation. I arrived in New Orleans within weeks of the passing of the Civil Rights Act of 1964, maybe two or three weeks later. Coming from Europe, I hadn't grown up with any color prejudice. It wasn't in my experience. So, black people could be on an equal footing with us, and we with them. I think they took us around because—first of all, it was legal to do so for the first time—they knew we didn't have an attitude. Our situation was different, and one felt it. I mean, I had maybe a hundred black friends and a dozen white friends.

"We were here to listen to black musicians, predominantly, and a few white musicians," he smiles. "But I didn't run into too many white musicians at first because there were only a few of them playing at Preservation Hall. Within a short time I ran into a lot of white musicians as well. But, initially, Harold Dejan would take me around, and I could play with the Olympia Brass Band, not being paid, and play a parade. Everybody was cool about that. All the other musicians knew me from that, and I was also involved in the society in which it thrived and in which it was used on a daily basis. It is a tradition to have music for as many events as possible, which doesn't really exist elsewhere in the States. Here it's part of life and has been for a long time. During the '60s, it was like catching the very end of the old days."

During that brief visit, Wilson attended a couple of recording sessions at San Jacinto Hall and played a few parades with the Olympia Brass Band, "courtesy of Harold Dejan," as he puts it. But then it was time to return home.

"I went back to Newcastle University because I thought I'd better get something I could do as a day job," he remembers. "I took a teacher's training course for one year, and I played in Newcastle in the pubs once or twice a week. And I played in London with a brass band—it was Mike Casimir's Paragon Brass Band—[during] vacations. Then I decided this wasn't what I really wanted to do either. So, I thought, I'll go back to New Orleans. I've still got my green card.

"So, I came back to New Orleans right after Hurricane Betsy. It was late September 1965. By then Lars Edegran had moved here, and he and I found an apartment together on Royal Street. He'd been here a few months. Everybody knew me from the year before, and I just fell right into the life here again. Lars [later] moved out and found his place, and Orange [Kellin] moved into my apartment because it was very cheap with two people sharing it. We were both living on very tight budgets. But I had a day job by this time, working as a computer programmer in a bank. Financially, I was okay. Still the situation with all of us—we weren't getting work as musicians, we weren't looking for work, we were listening, and we were sitting in and playing at parties, things like that. There wasn't a lot of work here anyway. Not only did we not want to take any work away from people, but we didn't have the contacts to get the work. We were beginners.

"Several of us joined the union in '65 through the help of Allan Jaffe [of Preservation Hall]. There was a TV special in Preservation Hall, and they wanted to film some young guys sitting in with the band. [Jaffe] said, 'The gig pays, but you have to join the union.' So, we joined the union, and the initiation fees were paid for by playing this job for the TV company. It was Local 496, which was the black union. So, the black union was able to say that they had integrated, and they sure had. Eventually, they got a lot of white rock-and-roll bands joining them. So, they were quite an integrated union long before the merger [with the white union]. Allan Jaffe was in that same local.

"We were mainly hanging out with the black musicians and sitting in with the black musicians, so that was the natural union to join. It wasn't a big deal. Just one more case of 'welcome!'

"After that," he continues, "Lars [Edegran] and I wanted to hear Louis James play. He was no longer playing at Preservation Hall and was getting to be kind of an old man and not playing as well as he did when he was younger. [James died in 1967 at the age of 77.] But he said he wanted to form a band and asked if we would play with him. Of course, we said yes! The band was called 'The Louis James Footwarmers.' Basically, most of the time we just rehearsed, which was really just an excuse for a party on Sunday afternoons. And it would either be at Andrew Morgan's house or Louis James's house or Lawrence Trotter's house. We'd play in someone's front room, then the lady of the house would serve gumbo or red beans and rice—we'd have a big meal. We'd all bring drinks and have a good time. By Sunday evening, when the sun was going down, we'd all go home.

"As a result of that, Andrew Morgan, when he re-formed the Young Tuxedo Brass Band, asked me to join the band. I was pretty amazed, but I did know most of the hymns and the traditional repertoire by that time. This was in January 1966. He had two funerals coming up at the weekend, and he asked, 'Can you play these funerals?' Thomas Jefferson was Morgan's number-one trumpet player, but he couldn't make it.

"I had never actually seen a funeral at that point, so I played on my first New Orleans 'jazz funeral.' It was me, Reginald Koeller, and Kid Thomas [Valentine], and they expected me to be the leader because I was 'Andrew Morgan's trumpet player' with the Louis James Orchestra. This was so ludicrous, and I said, 'But I've never played one before.' Whatever, I played lead—just played the melody, you know, and everybody fit right in! It was really funny," he chuckles.

Wilson stayed with the band for two more years, playing second trumpet to Thomas Jefferson's lead. He would sit in with other groups as well, playing some private jobs, but there wasn't a lot of work.

"It wasn't our priority. Our priority was listening," he reiterates. "Now today everything is completely different. Not everybody, but a good many people come here and they just want to play somewhere. This is the opposite from what we were doing. In our day there was a tremendous number of really worthwhile musicians to go and hear, from a much earlier period of traditional jazz, players who had learned to play in the '20s or before. Peter Bocage and Willie Humphrey go way before that. I heard Peter Bocage play, and I think he became a professional musician in 1904 or something. So, this was a whole different thing from today."

Who were young Wilson's inspirations on trumpet in those days?

"I always loved Louis Armstrong—his sound was just majestic—but I went through a period when I would not listen to him that much. If we talk about trumpet players, I loved most of them. No two sounded alike. The ones I liked at the time were Kid Howard, Lee Collins, De De Pierce, and Kid Thomas. Later on, I came to really enjoy Alvin Alcorn. That was because my ear got better, and I could see the qualities he had, and that other people didn't have."

In 1968 Wilson returned to England, where he played with the Barry Martyn Jazz Band. They toured Europe with several New Orleans musicians, and they also revisited the States playing the famous "Hello, Louis" concert at the Shrine Auditorium in Los Angeles on July 4, 1970.

"Floyd Levin put it together, and Hoagy Carmichael was the emcee," he recalls. "We played as the warmup band. It was a delightful evening."

During his time away from New Orleans, Wilson also began taking serious trumpet lessons in London. "I was trying to undo my bad habits and learn to play correctly, which was quite difficult," he says. "I realized if I was going to get anywhere, I would have to learn the more correct technique in breathing, blowing, embouchure, etc. When I came back here [in 1970], I continued that study. I enrolled at Loyola to take music theory and trumpet, just part-time. That was for two and a half years, then I continued legit trumpet lessons for another year or so after that. If I had started at, say, 11 instead of 26 it would have made a huge difference. I don't know, my career could have taken off considerably earlier. So, my trumpet playing started late. You learn slower when you get older. Then when you start the wrong way and have to re-learn, that's even harder."

In any case, after his two-year stint in Britain, Wilson was back in New Orleans in 1970, this time for good. He became a regular on Bourbon Street with bands led by drummer Freddie Kohlman and pianist Dave "Fat Man" Williams. He also resumed an activity—record producing—that he had first undertaken in the '60s.

"Yeah, I managed the session—hired the equipment, lined up the place to play, and made sure that it was recorded properly," he recalls, "and that's about all you can do. I helped pick the tunes with the bandleader and just oversaw production. I recorded the Louis James Orchestra and sold it to another company. It came out on La Croix in England and on Center Records. Then it came out on Biograph. Then I recorded Kid Thomas at Kohlman's Tavern for La Croix, and that later came out on my own label [New Orleans Records]. I also recorded Tony Fougerat, the band that played at Munster's Bar in the Irish Channel, for George Buck. Beyond that, I didn't do any more recording in the '60s.

"Later on," he continues, "Paige Van Vorst was visiting from Minneapolis—he now lives in Chicago—and we decided to start a record company. So, we got the Kid Thomas session and issued that right away. A year later we had a session out with Raymond Burke that Raymond had never shown anybody. He produced it out of his files and asked if we would issue it. That was *Raymond Burke's Speakeasy Boys*. It had never come out before. Then I recorded a band I had begun working with on Bourbon Street, which was [that of] Dave Williams. He was like a crossover between rhythm and blues and traditional jazz. He could play both. So, we did a session [on which Wilson also performed], entitled *I Ate Up the Apple Tree* [New Orleans LP NOR 7204]. It's a knockout. It sounds like a New Orleans barroom; it's informal and really swinging. That was in 1974."

Later in the same year, Wilson joined Albert "Papa" French's Original Tuxedo Jazz Band. He played with the band for three years, during which they maintained a busy schedule of recording, club dates, and appearances at festivals such as the Newport/New York Jazz Festival. The circumstances under which he joined (and continued in) the band were fortuitous.

"Jack Willis had been the cornet player," he recalls, "and in the early '70s—I forget the date—his face dropped on one side. I think it was the palsy, or something, and he had to stop playing for a few years. He made a comeback and was able to play again, but without the high notes. In 1974 Papa French was looking for a new trumpet player, and I got the call because I filled in on one job and they liked the way I played. They were looking for someone who knew the repertoire and was available. Others, for example Teddy Riley, knew the repertoire, but he was playing with George French's band at Crazy Shirley's. John Brunious was still on the road. So, I got the job.

"But three years later," he goes on, "Wendell Brunious became old enough and knew the repertoire, so he joined the band. By the end of the '70s, there were four or five available trumpet players who knew the repertoire. There was just a little window there, when there was a shortage. It was lucky for me and a wonderful experience. I was expected to follow the same arrangements they had used for years. So, I was to play stuff like Alvin Alcorn at one point, and stuff like Jack Willis, at another point. Since I was familiar with the band, having listened to them for years, I could fit in.

"We played a lot of society work, Papa French had all the [Papa] Celestin jobs, so I got to play at country clubs and those kinds of places. We had to wear tuxedos on all those jobs, and in the summer we wore white tuxedos. It was like in the old days—today nobody does that. I had to get a white tuxedo and a black tuxedo. We were always in uniform. I still have my white tuxedo. I'm going to bring it out sometime, just for fun."

By the late 1970s, Wilson decided it was time to form his own band, the Original Camellia Jazz Band. That was in 1979, and, apart from some personnel changes, he continues to lead the band today. The band has toured Europe many times and been a regular at major local events such as the French Quarter Festival and Jazzfest.

More recently, Clive Wilson has been deeply involved in a project that he calls "Satchmo Serenade." He formed excellent local bands that appeared at the French Quarter Festival and, with Butch Thompson on piano, at Jazzfest last spring [i.e., 2001]. Then he and Thompson led a fine international group—including native New Orleanian (now living in Paris) Tommy Sancton, clarinet; Swedish trombonist Freddie John; and Brits Alyn Shipton, bass, and Norman Emberson, drums—at the Ascona Jazz Festival in Switzerland in July.

"I've always liked Louis Armstrong," he says, "and it comes through more and more the better I get on trumpet. Many years ago I learned to play 'Cornet Chop Suey' and, over the years, other of his pieces, like 'West End Blues,' 'Dear Old Southland,' 'Potato Head Blues,' and so on. One is, of course, influenced by the way he phrases anytime. It goes into almost everybody's playing. So, the opportunity presented itself this year, with the celebration of his music, to do something with it. It was a challenge to play some Louis Armstrong pieces, and I think it helped my technique to study his playing. So, with this year being Louis's centennial, it seemed like a good idea to put together a program with Butch Thompson for the Jazz Festival.

"I've known Butch for years," he adds, "since at least 1965, and he's become a friend and is such a good piano player. He knows the material very well. I thought it would fit musically, and he was able to help me with some of the arrangements. It was very quick for him to write some stuff down that we needed. 'Satchmo Serenade' doesn't fit into a day-to-day job basis, but it's wonderful for festivals or special events. We will keep the book and from time to time be able to revive it, probably for the rest of our lives. We have no plans for recording, but it would be a good idea. We would have to talk to a record company."

Do he and Thompson have plans for future collaboration?

"Yes," he responds. "I said to Butch, 'What are we going to do next year? Let's come up with a new project.' So, we're trying to think of who was born in 1902.

"I'm only joking. We could always say that the real birthday of Bunk Johnson was 1902 and do a Bunk Johnson memorial, but I think not! Actually, we wanted to focus on somebody with really worthwhile music that's a little different than what we usually do. After talking about it, we decided to call ourselves the 'New Orleans Serenaders' and present the music of Kid Ory. Freddie John would be back on trombone, and would be just great for that. We expect to perform at several festivals next year."

As one who came to New Orleans from abroad and has now lived and worked here for nearly four decades (he became a U.S. citizen in the mid-eighties), Wilson expressed thoughts about our country and its problems that are not inappropriate in today's troubled times.

"I can only speak of my experience and for myself," he stresses. "The 'race issue' doesn't exist for me. There were no barriers for me when I arrived. The barriers that used to be law up until 1964 were terribly destructive to people, relationships, society. And there is no denying we are still living with this lingering legacy. But, if you stop thinking about 'race,' you will notice that there are some people you get along with, and some you don't, and those categories are not divided along racial lines. This country is multi-racial, multi-cultural, multi-religious, and multi-lingual. We have the opportunity to welcome the diversity that our constitution protects.

"When I first came here, it's true I was more interested in the way black musicians like De De Pierce and Kid Howard played New Orleans jazz than the whites, although I also enjoyed the way the whites played—in typically New Orleans style—their tempos and rhythm and focus on the melody. But my initial goal was to play like a black New Orleans trumpet player. Later on, I suppose, I just wanted to play like a New Orleans trumpet player.

"Today, when I hire musicians, I hire them according to who's available, who's going to play in the style I want. So, my bands tend to be a mixture because race is not a consideration. So you might see an African American, and Italian American, along with myself, an Anglo-American. It's all a case of how are we going to get the job done best and enjoy the music we make."

Along the same lines, New Orleans musicians sometimes object to being told by club owners who should be in their bands. "It happens," he says, "because of the way those venues have evolved. You have to remember that, for example, Preservation Hall did experiment in the early '60s with allowing the bandleader to pick his own musicians. With the Sweet Emma [Barrett]/Percy Humphrey band, with George Lewis and Kid Thomas, this worked fine. But as Kid Howard pointed out to me, the other 'bandleaders' had never been leaders before, and they just called up their friends. So, frequently you had the same 'friend' playing every night of the week because he was the friendliest guy in town! Well, the manager wanted to rotate the musicians because everyone was out of work, and he wanted to spread the work around. So, he started to tell the bandleader, 'Can you get so-and-so instead of so-and-so because he's playing tomorrow.' So, in that context, rather than throw blame around, you can understand how the situation evolved.

"But it's true you sometimes get a disaster on the bandstand if the musicians are incompatible. I was lucky at Preservation Hall. When I played there occasionally as a substitute, Jaffe would tell me to bring my regular band members from the Camellia—you know, like Frog Joseph and Jeanette Kimball. But would I get so-and-so on banjo as it was his regular night? Of course, I said yes!

"The way a band works best is when the leader picks the musicians and pays them himself. Then it's natural for the bandleader to tell everyone what he wants to play and how he wants to play it, and natural for the musicians to cooperate and play well together."

A final dimension of Clive Wilson's multifaceted talents is his writing. Over the years he has written numerous informative pieces intended primarily for a British audience, recounting his early musical experiences in New Orleans. Most of these well-written little articles—sometimes called simply "letters"—have appeared in the English magazine *New Orleans Music* (formerly *Footnote*), edited by Mike Hazeldine. A couple of them have been reprinted in George Buck's *Jazzbeat* magazine, and it is Wilson's intention to make more of them available through reprint in various jazz periodicals. They provide an intimate perspective on the local music scene in the 1960s and should therefore be of interest to anyone who enjoys traditional New Orleans jazz. Look for them.

Clive Wilson leads his band at the French Quarter Festival, April 2004. Brian Ogilvie is the clarinetist. This photo was taken just four months before the latter's death.

13

BRIAN OGILVIE
New Orleans Pilgrim

Gifted reedman Brian Ogilvie died in a hospital in Inverness, Scotland, on August 14, 2004, just a few days after performing in two concerts at the Nairn (Scotland) Jazz Festival. He was 50 years old.

Ogilvie had been a resident of New Orleans for more than seven years. He was married there in 2001, and he and his wife Kerstin had every intention of making the city their permanent home. His death was mourned widely in the local music community.

The following interview was conducted some five years before his death and published in the July 2000 issue of The Mississippi Rag.

FIRST-CLASS CLARINET PLAYERS ARE DRAWN TO NEW Orleans like pilgrims to Mecca. The city has justly gained a reputation as a "great clarinet town" since the earliest days of jazz, and that venerable tradition has been kept alive by a long line of home-grown talent right down to the present day. At the same time, this heritage has also attracted a host of skilled practitioners from all over the country and around the world—many of whom have chosen to settle down in the city and further enhance the tradition.

One of the most recent of these "pilgrims" is Brian Ogilvie, a 46-year-old Canadian who has been in town for about three years and has quickly secured a position for himself as one of the top reedmen in these parts.

Ogilvie arrived in the Crescent City as an established player, having first achieved an award-winning reputation while playing in Toronto, then becoming known in this country through his work with the New Black Eagle Jazz Band in Boston and Jim Cullum's Jazz Band in San Antonio. His first gig in New Orleans was with Banu Gibson's fine band (with whom he still frequently performs), and shortly thereafter he was invited by veteran cornetist and bandleader Connie Jones to join his band on the riverboat *Delta Queen*. He continues to be a member of that band, which clearly suits its leader just fine.

"I was familiar with Brian from hearing him on the Jim Cullum radio shows from the River Walk [in San Antonio] and was very impressed with his playing," recalls Jones when asked how he came to hire Ogilvie. "When he consented to come on the band with me aboard the *Delta Queen*, I can't tell you how happy I was. I learned quickly just how well rounded a musician he really is. His fire and enthusiasm are contagious, and it is a real treat having a chance to work beside him." High praise indeed from one who has played with some of the best and is himself one of the most highly respected horn players in this part of the world.

Brian Ogilvie was born in Ottawa in 1954 but grew up in Vancouver, where, after the premature death of his father, he and his six siblings were heroically raised by his mother. His is a very musical family.

"Music was everywhere in my house and in our neighborhood when I was a kid," he says. His older brothers—John (cello), Don (viola and guitar), and Kenny (bass)—all played musical instruments. His younger sister, Elaine, started out on flute. It is almost incredible that all four, along with Brian, have since become professional musicians. Only his younger brother and sister have chosen other careers.

"They're the smart ones," he laughs.

It all began as something of a neighborhood phenomenon. "Our little neighborhood in the district of Kitsilano in Vancouver was jammed with kids, all baby boomers," explains Ogilvie. "Just by coincidence there were three blind kids within four houses on our block—Mary Brunner next door, Shelly Hanna two doors the other way, and my brother John, who has only 5 percent vision and is considered legally blind. Ira McKeever, an Irish fiddler across the lane, thought it would be good for these blind kids to learn music. Of course, they took to it so fast that they were soon playing complicated pieces—Mary on violin, John on cello, and Shelly on piano. My brother Don went with viola and guitar soon after."

Young Brian got started in music later because he was heavily into sports, but a football injury at age 15 caused him to say "enough of this." He returned to the clarinet (his grandfather's instrument) that he had started playing a couple of years earlier but had given up out of lack of interest after about a year. Brother John directed him to a good teacher who worked him very hard on the basics and introduced him to the classical repertoire. He was soon taking part in neighborhood "concerts" with the rest of the kids. But he found himself unmoved by the music, whether classical, pop, or rock.

Then he found jazz. "My brother's girlfriend's dad had a part-time jazz band rehearsing once a week at their house," he remembers. "I was there one night and I heard the music and this clarinet player bending notes, growling, using vibrato, and swinging—which was what I was looking for in music. The whole improvising thing fascinated me. The clarinet player in the band, a Swedish lumberjack named Eric Nilsson, was my first inspiration, and I would turn up at rehearsals to listen to him. He would go out of town for months doing his lumberjack thing, and I got the courage up to ask the leader, Dave Todd, if I could sit in on a rehearsal. He agreed since it was only practice. I think the guys in the band felt that I had potential because they helped me out a lot, giving me Louis Armstrong, Jelly Roll Morton, and Benny Goodman records to listen to. I was 16. Once I got into jazz I stopped listening to pop music and totally immersed myself in jazz."

Todd's Lion's Gate Jazz Band, as it was called, began getting more and more gigs, and eventually Brian was asked to sit in on a regular basis. Much to his surprise, he even got paid for having fun! He played with the band for a couple of years while in high school, and their success was such that Todd formed the non-profit Hot Jazz Society. That, in turn, led to the opening of the Hot Jazz Club, which eventually presented jazz programs six nights a week. The club proved to be a wonderfully fortuitous springboard for Ogilvie's budding jazz career.

Ogilvie picked up the saxophones, favoring especially the tenor, in the high school band. After graduation, he spent a summer in Toronto during which his jazz education continued. He had an opportunity to sit in with a number of the local bands, like the Climax Jazz Band, Kid Bastien's Magnolia Jazz Band, and Dr. McJazz. Back home in the fall of 1973, he enrolled at Vancouver City College, where he did a diploma course in the jazz program for two years. There he worked with tenor saxophonist Fraser MacPherson and did big band and studied arranging with Dave Robbins, the head of the program.

"Robbins was fantastic," he says. "He got me listening, thinking more analytically—he really opened me up to a lot of new things. MacPherson was a really good swing player and taught me a lot about saxophone, especially because up to that time I was taking just clarinet lessons. So, I really started playing more tenor, and I played in the big band at school and basically stretched out quite a bit. I tried a lot of different things, including playing more modern stuff—Coltrane and the like—but I just didn't feel it."

At about that time, he also started his own band, the West Side Feet-warmers, which played a variety of things—from Bechet to bossa nova, as he puts it. Then his brothers and a couple other guys formed a band called Hot Club, which featured Django Reinhardt music.

"It really snowballed," he remembers, "because we had this venue to play at. The Hot Jazz Club provided to many of us musicians the possibility to play in public, and it gave us the chance to try different things.

"During those Hot Jazz Club years we brought in many guests. We brought in [New Orleans clarinetist] Joe Darensbourg a few times, and it was very inspiring for me as a young player to be sitting beside Louis [Armstrong]'s clarinet player. He played one New Year's gig with us and also stayed at my house. Joe loved to cook, and New Year's Day he made red beans and rice, black-eyed peas, and ham hocks. That was the first time I ever had New Orleans cuisine. We had a hard time finding the ingredients, actually. But he was just a real nice guy. I learned so much from him."

Ogilvie laughed as he added, "He tried to teach me slap-tonguing, and to this day I still can't do it. I also got to play with Wingy Manone, Jim Goodwin, Bert Noah, the Great Excelsior Jazz Band, and Dan Barrett. I first met Dan at the Sacramento Jubilee at a jam session. I had never heard anybody swing like that before. We began a friendship, and to this day Dan has been one of the most important people in my musical life."

Ogilvie gigged around Vancouver (with a few out-of-town dates mixed in) for a few more years, but then he was overcome with wanderlust.

He explains, "I guess it was about 1978—I had finished school and was married at the time—Patti and I decided to pack our bags and leave Vancouver. Why, I don't know, we just wanted a change. We didn't know where we were going. So, we sold everything and took a bus across Canada, and even went down to New Orleans. That was the first time I was here and the first time I saw Willie Humphrey play—and I saw Sweet Emma [Barrett] one night. We were only here two nights, and we went to Preservation Hall both nights. We went on to New York and saw some great players there—there's always great players in New York. Then we decided to go over to Spain. So, we flew to Madrid and went to Malaga and the Canary Islands and Tangiers, Morocco. Then we ran out of money.

"We went back to Canada in April 1979 and stayed with my sister in Montreal," he continues. "There wasn't much traditional jazz going on, so I ended up playing on the street with my brother-in-law, who played guitar. He was also in my band, the West Side Feetwarmers, out in Vancouver. After a couple of months, we went on to Toronto. I got work right away with trombonist Pete Savory [who now lives in New Orleans], and I got a few other gigs, so I decided this was a good place to be. I joined the Climax Jazz Band late in 1979 after Jim Buchmann left, and played full-time with the band for over a year. It was great because they were a seasoned band and had lots of work. We did some nice festivals in the U.S. and did a number of gigs in Boston with the New Black Eagle Jazz Band.

"After I left the Climax in 1981, the Black Eagles asked me to join their band to replace Stan McDonald. I did that for about six months while still living in Toronto, commuting back and forth for gigs. I was still pretty new in Toronto, and we just rented a nice little house, so I decided to stay in Toronto. I also enjoyed the variety of gigs I was starting to get there. The Black Eagles got Hugh Blackwell as a full-time clarinet player, but over the years I have subbed in the band on tours and guested with them. I really enjoyed working with those guys and learned a lot from the experience."

Ogilvie lived and worked in Toronto for thirteen years, during which time he established himself as one of Canada's top clarinet players. In fact, in 1993, the Canadian jazz periodical the *Jazz Report* named him "Clarinetist of the Year." The great Oscar Peterson was the acoustic piano award winner that same year, which elicited the following reaction from the soft-spoken and modest clarinet player: "To have my name next to his was like a dream. Someone you've listened to all your life. It's my own personal joy."

The Toronto years were a busy time and one of great variety in his musical activities.

"My brothers, Don and Kenny, moved to Toronto in the early '80s, and we started working a lot together in jazz clubs as well as convention work. As 'The Ogilvie Brothers,' we have worked together on and off our whole musical lives, most recently at a private party New Year's Eve 1999 when I was back in Vancouver for the holidays."

But much of Ogilvie's work in Toronto was freelance, playing with big bands and small groups doing commercials, shows, and even a feature film. He did a ten-month run with the New Orleans show *One Mo' Time* after it finished running in New York. And he did a great deal of traveling in North America and abroad on tours, cruises, and festivals with bands such as the Black Eagles, the Climax Jazz Band, and Grand Dominion Jazz Band from the West Coast.

One of the big bands he played with was Jim Galloway's Wee Big Band, in which he doubled on clarinet and tenor sax.

"Jim Galloway has always been really kind to me," he notes. "He would often get me to fill in for him on his live radio shows when he was out of town. The show usually featured a guest star from the U.S. who was playing at one of the local clubs. I got to play with people like Dick Wellstood, Johnny Guarnieri, Art Hodes, and some other of these great players who were passing through town. That was a real nice experience. But I didn't have a lot of steady work until I got this call from San Antonio. It was from Jim Cullum."

Cullum's call came in the fall of 1991, when Allan Vaché announced that he was leaving the band. While Ogilvie admits that his knowledge of San Antonio's geographical location was rather fuzzy, he went down for an audition the following spring and was hired to start with the band in September 1992.

"The band had great arrangements by John Sheridan," he says, "and all the guys played so well. It was great for my clarinet chops to play six nights a week. I also played saxophone four days a week with Sheridan on the club's patio. Most afternoons I would bring in new tunes I had learned and try to stump John, but he knew them all, plus the verses! I learned a lot of tunes while doing those afternoon duos with John. And the band's weekly radio show had some great guests while I was there, like Joe Williams, Harry 'Sweets' Edison, Clark Terry, Ken Peplowski, and Dick Hyman. It was a real thrill doing those shows.

"I played exclusively with the Jim Cullum Jazz Band for three and a half years," he goes on. "I really enjoyed working with the band and learned a lot. But it was the longest steady gig I ever did, and it was time to try some other things. I got a call in 1996 to work on the *Mississippi Queen* riverboat. The gig called for me to live and work on the boat six weeks, with two weeks off. I was going through some personal problems at the time [he and his wife separated in San Antonio], and I thought floating up and down the Mississippi, Ohio, and Tennessee rivers might be good therapy."

Ogilvie stayed with the riverboat gig for a year and a half, during which time he also did some festivals and tours. One tour took him to Germany with trumpeter Randy Sandke and the New York Allstars and resulted in a fine double CD, *Count Basie Remembered*, on the German Nagel Heyer label. Ogilvie played alto and tenor saxes as well as clarinet on the recording.

The *Mississippi Queen*'s home port was New Orleans, and that gave him an opportunity to get to know the local music scene and some of the local musicians. He was told that there was plenty of work in the city, so he decided to settle down there in January 1997.

Ogilvie's first job in New Orleans was with Banu Gibson's band at Swing Town, the short-lived club on Bourbon Street. There was no trombone in the band that night, and he played tenor saxophone.

"I think that was the first time Banu experimented with a different sound, using a trumpet and two reeds," he recalls. "It was kind of a nice sound, but I think trombonist Dave Sager is her main choice, of course. If he can't make it, she likes to go with the two-reed thing [clarinet and tenor]. They have two books, a trombone book and a tenor sax book. The tenor and trombone are the exact same range, so it works out perfect."

He clearly enjoys playing with that band. "Tom Fischer is so great to work with, he's fabulous. And, of course, working with Duke Heitger or Charlie Fardella, the two trumpet players she uses, is just great. I've done gigs where I've subbed for Tom—I play the clarinet chair as well—so I move around a bit. Again, that's one of the reasons I left Cullum's band. I like the variety of doing different things."

And he clearly enjoys working with Connie Jones. "I didn't really know his playing very well, except everybody talked about him a lot. Then when I heard him play I just went, 'This is fantastic.' Playing with him is like going to school. His way of playing is so melodic, and he's got such an understanding of the whole spectrum of improvising from chords, melody, lyrics—when he improvises, he's thinking of all those things. It's just a beautiful way of playing. Every year in January, February, and March we have special 'Dixie Fest' cruises which feature Connie's band playing exclusively New Orleans jazz." The band's latest CD, *Sweet, Hot and Blue*, appeared earlier this year on the Jazzology label.

Working with Jones is two weeks on and six weeks off, the opposite of Ogilvie's old *Mississippi Queen* gig, and that gives him a chance to work with other bands around town. He frequently sits in, for example, with Chris Tyle's Silver Leaf Jazz Band at the Can-Can Café in the Royal Sonesta Hotel on Bourbon Street. Ogilvie clearly enjoys working with a variety of groups and in a variety of jazz styles—anything, as he often says, "from Jelly Roll Morton to Stan Getz."

When asked how he's adjusting to his new home, he says firmly, "I love New Orleans. I live right on the edge of the French Quarter, which is great for me not owning a car. I can walk or ride my bike to all my gigs. There is a great feeling among the musicians in town, and they have been very kind to me. There's always plenty of work here, and it's a good place to be based out of. There's a lot of road gigs—jazz parties, festivals, and that kind of thing. I've been doing more and more touring and jazz festivals. Last October I went to Germany with Ralph Sutton, Marty Grosz, Jon-Erik Kellso, Dave Green, and Frank Capp. It was a wonderful tour and a thrill to play with those guys, especially Ralph Sutton, whom I first listened to on records when I was 16. We recorded a two-CD set for the Nagel Heyer label while there."

Ogilvie has spent a good deal of time in recording studios since moving to the States. Indeed, he's appeared on a couple of dozen recordings in the last few years, all as a sideman. Yet it was not until February 2000 that his first album as a leader was released.

"It's called *For You*, and it's on the Arbors record label," he says proudly. "John Sheridan is on piano, Phil Flanigan on bass, and Jeff Hamilton drums, basically a quartet album. Then I've added Dan Barrett on six tracks, who is my old buddy for twenty-five years, on trombone and cornet. I really wanted him to be on there because he's been such an influential person in my life. He wrote an original tune and did a couple of arrangements as well. The music is kind of a mixture of styles because I tried to make the album who I am. I play clarinet and tenor, and there's one alto number. John Sheridan wrote a real nice tune called 'Evening Shadows.' It's kind of a Johnny Hodges–sounding thing. The album turned out pretty well. I'm quite happy with it."

Needless to say, this is characteristic Ogilvie modest understatement. The recording is wonderful documentation of the reedman's instrumental versatility and the diversity of his musical tastes. Those who think of him as exclusively a clarinet player will, upon hearing this, clearly have to do some serious rethinking.

Ogilvie used to play soprano saxophone too, "but I could never get a decent sound on it," he quickly adds. "So I sold it to my sister, Elaine. She plays it much better than I ever played it. She's a great player. The sweetest tenor saxophone player you'll ever hear. She actually plays in the same sort of style that Connie Jones plays, that real melodic style—that real sweet Lester Young, Eddie Miller kind of sound. Unfortunately, she lives up in Ottawa, and she doesn't get much work. She recently joined a band that's playing sort of bossa nova style. They wanted someone to play sort of like Stan Getz, and she's perfect for that."

Ogilvie's primary instruments are clarinet and tenor saxophone, in that order. And who are his favorite players?

"On clarinet," he says, "I can't pick a favorite. When I first started playing, I listened to all the early traditional players—they're all my heroes, Omer Simeon especially, Barney Bigard, Johnny Dodds, George Lewis, Darnell Howard—all those players. Then I started getting into Benny [Goodman] a lot. Then I got into some other clarinet players, like Buddy DeFranco, Eddie Daniels [with whom he studied for a time], and some of the more modern players. I sort of missed out on Artie Shaw for some reason. I don't know why. Then I got this three-CD set of Shaw's air checks, and I can't stop listening to it.

"I go through phases like that, where I get totally immersed with a certain player. I went through a real Barney Bigard phase about a year ago, and in the last couple of years I got more interested in Irving Fazola. Recently, I got immersed with Lucky Thompson on tenor, just couldn't stop listening to him and trying to learn from that."

There is, however, no question about his preferred tenor sax player. "Lester Young is my favorite," he says without hesitation. "I just love the way he plays. There's so much emotion in his playing. He can play one note and make you cry. Another player who I've gotten into recently—a player who I never got into before—is Eddie Miller. So, I've been listening to him as much as I could, but it's hard to get his stuff. There's so much music out there," he smiles.

As for the future, Ogilvie seems more than satisfied with his base in New Orleans. But he is also looking to explore further his varied musical interests with his own small group, perhaps a quartet much like that on his current recording.

"I get a lot of work playing in Dixieland bands and that kind of thing," he says, "so I'd like to get a little quartet doing the swing thing, straight ahead, just like the CD—anything from Jelly Roll Morton to Stan Getz— and just keep on doing the variety that I enjoy doing.

"For the year 2000 I will be pursuing more jazz parties and festivals as well as trying to get more quartet gigs. Dan Barrett's new band, Blue Swing, is a swinging band stacked with the best players around playing this kind of music. We just did a recording for Arbors and have several festivals and tours lined up for this year. As far as my future goes, that's another thing that's really starting to click. I'm looking forward to tons of music in this new millennium."

And there may even be time for a gig or two with The Ogilvie Brothers as well. Or should it be The Ogilvie Siblings?

After his death, memorials for Ogilvie were held in his hometown of Vancouver, British Columbia, as well as in his adopted home of New Orleans. The latter took place at the Palm Court Jazz Café on October 18, 2004. I read the following remarks on that occasion.

"If [the music] swings, I like it."

Those were Brian's words, words that he clearly lived by musically.

I really had only one extensive conversation with Brian, and that's when we got together at my house back in December 1999, when I interviewed him for a cover story that appeared in *The Mississippi Rag* the following July [see above].

We talked for several hours—well, of course, Brian did most of the talking—and after it was over I said to myself, "Man, I really like that guy." I already admired him very much as a musician, but I also got a good impression of him as a human being that afternoon. Despite his musical talent and accomplishments, he was an extremely modest—almost self-effacing—man. A warm person with a good sense of humor. A truly sweet man.

And I liked his thoughts about music too, maybe because our tastes and preferences were so similar. In fact, after those three hours or so together, I felt that he and I were on the same musical wave length. I sort of felt like a soul brother. That might in part be because our March birthdays were just two days apart—in spite of the nearly twenty years that separated us in age. We have talked many times since, and I have always felt very comfortable in his presence.

Brian considered the clarinet as his first instrument. He was hard pressed to name a particular favorite, though Goodman, Shaw (in recent years, at least), Barney Bigard, and Omer Simeon would certainly rank among them. But right there with the clarinet was the tenor saxophone, which he played gorgeously. There, his favorite was *definitely* Lester Young.

At the time of the interview he was heavily into Eddie Miller. (He told me he would go into "kicks" listening to the recordings of other musicians, and was on a Miller kick at that time.) But he was having trouble finding certain of Miller's recordings. "I went down to the Louisiana Music Factory," he said. "They've got a whole section of traditional jazz, but there's no card for Eddie Miller. Nothing. Here he is from New Orleans, probably one of the best traditional jazz saxophone players ever, and there's no card for him."

When I mentioned the old recordings that Miller made with the Gordon Jenkins Orchestra in the 1950s, he exclaimed, "Yes!" I happened to have some of them on 78 rpm, and we played and listened to a few.

"That's what I've been looking for," he said. As we listened to "In a Sentimental Mood," he said, "Beautiful. This is what I want. He's got such a pretty sound."

Eddie Miller was of course a clarinet player too, as was Lester Young. I have an impression Brian would have liked their kind of clarinet playing as well—and who wouldn't?

Which brings to mind another occasion a few years later—in February 2002, to be exact. Banu Gibson was in the studio with Bucky Pizzarelli recording their wonderful CD, *Steppin' Out*. Brian was on that recording too, and he invited me to come down for the recording session. So, I showed up at Ultrasonic Studio that afternoon. (I'm not sure that Banu was so thrilled with my barging in, but she let me stay.) One of the tunes they laid down in that session was Hoagy's beautiful "Winter Moon." Banu sang it, and Brian provided some very lovely and sensitive clarinet work.

The musicians took a break soon after recording that tune, and I complimented Brian on his playing. I went on to ask him, "You know who you reminded me of?" He said, "Who?" And I said, "Jimmy Giuffre." Now Giuffre was primarily known as a saxophone player (tenor and baritone) who made some nice recordings on clarinet in the 1950s. Brian responded to my question by saying that's exactly who he wanted to sound like! He went on to say that Giuffre, who rarely ventured into the upper register (of the clarinet), played an Albert system horn (which I hadn't known). And then he added quickly, "I don't like the upper register either."

Incidentally, you can hear that same sound on Brian's lovely treatment of "Nature Boy" on his own CD, *For You*, on the Arbors label, where you'll also hear some nice upper-register clarinet work. But it is interesting: Lester Young, Eddie Miller, Jimmy Giuffre, and Brian—fine tenor saxophonists and clarinetists. Clearly they were more than just "doublers." And there are, of course, other saxophonists who played nice clarinet, too. I would have liked to explore that subject in more detail with him.

There are many other musical topics relating to Brian Ogilvie that would be fun to share with you tonight, but I want to conclude with a theme that recurred throughout our interview that day: his family, especially his brothers and sisters.

It was clear to me that Brian had genuine love and affection for his six siblings. They all grew up in a very musical home. "Basically, our house was chaos," he said with a laugh. "Everyone was playing music. Even my mother, after my dad died, would turn on radios and TVs, and there was sound everywhere." But it was obvious that he had fond memories of that environment.

There was a family band—they called it "Herman" after the family cat—and eventually "The Ogilvie Brothers" trio. Five of the seven kids have performed as professional musicians. He stressed that he learned so much from his older brothers John, a cellist whom he called "a phenomenal musician," and Kenny, a bass player. Then there was Don, who played guitar. Brian, Kenny, and Don were the trio.

Sister Elaine also plays professionally. "She's a great player," Brian said. "She plays soprano and tenor saxophones. The sweetest tenor saxophone player you'll ever hear. That real sweet Lester Young, Eddie Miller kind of sound. It's beautiful." Elaine played one of Brian's favorites, "I Can't Get Started," at the memorial for him in Vancouver last month.

What about the other two siblings who are not musicians, Bobby and Joanne? "They're the smart ones," he laughed. "He's a mechanic—he just loves cars—but he plays a little guitar and drums. She's really artistic. She's a good artist."

So, that's the family. Quite a talented bunch. Brian cared for them very much, and, I know, they for him as well. I had a wonderful telephone conversation with Elaine a few weeks ago, and it was Joanne who wrote the touching program notes for this memorial.

Finally, Brian referred several times to his "girlfriend in St. Louis" during the interview. I didn't know who that was until dear Kerstin later appeared in New Orleans. They were married in November 2001. I remember well the wedding reception, so much splendid music by Brian's many musical friends. His best man, Duke Heitger, played a warm "My Buddy" for his good friend.

I'm just sorry, Kerstin, that the two of you didn't have more time together. But I know how much you loved him and his music, especially those ballads he played so gorgeously. Brian left behind some wonderful memories for you and the rest of us as well as some excellent music on record. We all can be thankful for that. Lastly, to Brian: We miss you, dear friend. Keep swinging.

14

TREVOR RICHARDS
Rhythm Is His Business

Drummer Trevor Richards was devastated—like so many other New Orleans musicians—by the flooding associated with Hurricane Katrina, as he explains in detail at the end of this chapter. Like so many others, he was forced to face his future head-on.

Richards's decision was to leave New Orleans and establish his permanent residence in a village near Frankfurt, Germany. He still returns to the Crescent City at least once a year to see (and play with) old friends. And he continues to do in Germany what he has been doing for decades: play and record music. His latest CD is The Trevor Richards New Orleans Trio and Denise Gordon: Body and Soul *(2010).*

The following was adapted from an article in The Mississippi Rag *(April 2006), which was based on interviews begun in 2003 and completed in 2006.*

TREVOR RICHARDS WAS PART OF THE INVASION OF YOUNG musicians from abroad—multi-instrumentalist Lars Edegran and clarinetist Orjan "Orange" Kellin from Sweden, trumpeters Clive Wilson and John Simmons from England, trumpeter Yoshio Toyama and his wife, Keiko, from Japan, and a host of others—that so characterized the New Orleans jazz scene in the 1960s. Inspired by the trad revival of the 1940s and '50s, they were welcomed in the city because of their talent and commitment to the music—in addition to the fact that so few of their local peer group had similar interests. Like several of the others, Richards chose to remain in the city and has made it his home—on and off—ever since. All of those who have stayed continue to be major figures on the music scene.

Born August 29, 1945, in Bexhill-on-Sea, Sussex, in the south of England, Richards was inspired by percussion instruments at a very tender age and was first turned on to jazz as an adolescent by listening to what was then a popular music on the radio in the U.K. He soon found that some school friends also had a keen interest in traditional jazz. Thus his musical journey got underway.

He began taking lessons from local drummers and took it all very seriously. "I practiced for hours and hours every day," he recalls. "Then I met up with a band in the next town [Hastings], and the drummer [Alan Whitmore] kind of took me under his wing."

Whitmore introduced young Trevor to the recordings of "all those seminal figures"—Zutty Singleton, Baby Dodds, Minor Hall, and the like—which proved to be "an important introduction to music" for the budding drummer.

Richards was playing in bands in England by the time he was a teenager. When he was 17 he spent a year in Hamburg, Germany, as an exchange student and, as he puts it, "made contact with the local jazz scene and local musicians, a lot of whom I still know to this day."

The following year, he began college in England with the intention of studying German and linguistics. "It was a lot of fun. Actually, it was too much fun," he laughs, "because I never got around to studying. I was working with [trombonist and bandleader] Mike Casimir in those days. My days at the university were getting shorter and shorter until I was going down to London on Thursdays and coming back on Tuesdays. That was the time that I made my first record for George Buck, in 1965. It was a brass band in the New Orleans tradition."

Deciding to put his higher education on hold, Richards headed back to Germany, where he had been invited to join a band in Frankfurt. Later that year (1966), he moved back to Hamburg to join another band, but he was already making plans to visit New Orleans. His former band mate in the Casimir band, Clive Wilson, had moved to New Orleans by this time, and Richards had other contacts there, too.

So, Richards decided to make the move, and instead of flying (since money was scarce), he worked his way across the Atlantic on a Norwegian freighter. He spent his days aboard ship scratching off paint and then repainting. His position was, as he puts it, that of a "workaway, as opposed to a stowaway." His first day upon arriving in New York was memorable.

"I got to New York very early one morning. We docked at 6 a.m. or something like that. I had written to Zutty Singleton. In those days, you remember, in *The Encyclopedia of Jazz* [Leonard Feather's first edition, 1960], all the musicians had their contact address listed. So, Zutty was listed as Hotel Alvin in Midtown, and I said I would be coming over and was looking forward to meeting him. By the time I got into town it still was only about eight in the morning and, without thinking, I called his apartment—not realizing that he had been working from 9 p.m. to 3 a.m. [at Jimmy Ryan's]. It was long hours in those days. I woke him, and it was not the best way to start a friendship! Anyway, I met him that night at the club. I spent, on that first trip, a couple of months in New York."

During that time, he began taking lessons from Singleton. "I would often spend the afternoon in his apartment, and he would be talking and showing me things. In the evening it became a sort of parallel demonstration while [he was] working with the band at that time [Max Kaminsky, Tony Parenti, et al.]. He would demonstrate how you have to keep your eye on everything so you can adapt immediately to whatever might happen. Looking back on it, I used to spend much more time in Jimmy Ryan's than I otherwise should have done."

Yet he did get an opportunity to hear some other good drummers in town, like George Wettling. "This was the last few months of Wettling's life, and he was kind of worn out. He was still playing well most of the time. He died the following year" [June 1968].

Richards was not only Singleton's student, but they became good friends during that period. "I was spending most nights [at Ryan's] and trying to stay there six hours a night, or at least a good many hours. I was hearing and watching all this stuff and trying to internalize it, and I thought I'd never forget. Without notes, it's just not true, of course. So, unfortunately, one is left after many years with an impression rather than any detailed information. I'd just go home at night with my head full of all these things that I'd heard. Whereas I'm sure it shaped my development, I can't say now specifically, or demonstrate specifically, everything that I saw although I was convinced at the time that I could never forget a note."

During their time together, Singleton told Richards that there was a lot of music he should be hearing in New Orleans. "So, he urged me to go down to New Orleans, which is what I had intended to do in the first place, of course. I had met Dick Allen [of the Hogan Jazz Archive at Tulane] at Ryan's by then. He was up on a visit to New York, and Zutty introduced me to him. So, I made my plans. Zutty actually gave me some money, I remember, to help me on my way. It was sweet of him considering what he was earning at Ryan's, as I found out later going through his effects with Marge [Zutty's wife]."

Richards got to New Orleans by driving someone else's car for an agency, a procedure that was common in those days. Unfortunately, the trip was truncated by an auto accident in Mississippi.

"I was okay, just a bit shaken up," he recalls. "I got from Mississippi to New Orleans by Greyhound [bus] and arrived early evening on a Sunday. My first experience was at a backyard party with the Eureka Brass Band, so I walked right into live music! There was a band playing, lots of good food, beer, and meeting everyone. Later I went down to Preservation Hall. 'Punch' Miller was playing with 'Slow Drag' Pavageau, Sammy Penn, Charlie Hamilton, and, I think, George Lewis. Clive Wilson took me around and introduced me to everyone and all the places where there was live music and all the places in the Quarter where musicians could get a free beer. I got into the habit of going up to the Tulane Archive regularly, small as it was then. Clive was established here and knew his way around."

Richards's early stay in the city was closely intertwined with that of Wilson and the other Europeans who had taken up residency there. They all became members of the black music union, for example. "The reason why we all—that is, all the Europeans who stayed in New Orleans for various lengths of time—joined the black union was, on the one hand, a matter of principle in as much as we were predominantly interested in black musical culture and, on the other hand, the only musicians that we knew really well were members and officials of the black union—for example, Alvin Alcorn and Louis Cottrell. And we remained members until the [black and white] unions amalgamated [1969].

"Just as an aside, another reason for joining the black union was that the annual fees were slightly lower. To match our budgets. On the other hand, so was the union scale for performances—not that we always managed to get union scale. A lot of brass band street parades were just for change. When the newly amalgamated union clamped down on the black parades—the church parades with all those brass bands that still existed in those days—they died out virtually overnight, thus ending a whole chapter of black cultural history.

"We were adopted, so to speak, by many of the local black musicians. I think that they realized that their next generation was the one that had disappeared, the ones that had gone off to play other music, and we were there as a sort of substitute. We showed this passionate interest in the music, and we came at a time when they couldn't see anyone else around who showed any interest in continuing the style of music they represented. It meant for us that we were accepted wholeheartedly, and we played and got lessons from the older musicians. All of us did that—Clive and Lars, everyone.

"I think Danny Barker had noticed how many Europeans were coming over and getting involved in the music scene. And he wondered why the young people in New Orleans—specifically the young black musicians—were ignoring their own cultural heritage right here on their own doorstep. That's why he went into the schools to find people interested. That was a stroke of genius because otherwise we would most likely not have had people like Leroy Jones, who had no musical background in his family, but through Danny's efforts got into the Fairview Baptist Church band, which eventually became the Hurricane Brass Band. Leroy was on the Louisiana Repertory Orchestra's first LP with Freddie Lonzo. Freddie had, of course, worked a lot with the brass bands, which was inevitable. That's what one does in New Orleans, and that's what we were doing. We had a wonderful grounding in that style of music, thanks to the help of Harold Dejan. And Percy Humphrey hired me to play with the Eureka sometimes. That was a wonderful experience, to play with that band, which was the best organized brass band I ever heard live—or even on record, I suppose. The fact is that New Orleans does offer the most [work] opportunities of any city that I know in the United States, and the fact that there is now less work here is just an indication of how little there is available elsewhere.

"In the summer of '68 we were hired as members of the Olympia Brass Band to go to the Folk Fest in Berlin to play for a couple of weeks, and I was giving [trombonist] Paul Crawford German lessons. That was the end of my first stay here. I was moving back to Europe because I had decided it was a good idea—a sort of safety move—to finish my university education, or rather to start it again."

Richards attended the University of Surrey, graduating in 1972 with a bachelor's degree in linguistics and a subsidiary specialty in music theory. He lived and worked in London for those four years (1968–1972), including a year studying and working in Germany because of his major language and six months in Sweden for his secondary language. He had also studied Russian. With this impressive linguistic background, Richards now considers himself fluent in German, with a "survival" command of French, and "the rest are long gone."

"When I graduated from university in 1972, I moved to Germany with the intention of earning as much money as quickly as possible, to return to New Orleans, by playing music, teaching English, doing technical translations which I was now qualified to do. As it happened, I had a chance to work with [New Orleans clarinetist] Paul Barnes on a tour in a trio with [pianist] Jon Marks."

That seems to have inspired him to revive an old interest of working in the trio format. "[That format] has always been a love of mine," Richards says. "It goes back to the '60s in England when I first started playing and was introduced to this form by [Alan Whitmore]—simply to demonstrate how the drums should sound in an environment where they are best heard, with the fewest instruments surrounding it. It was easy to isolate the sound of the drums in one's mind and to hear how the drums should relate to other instruments and show how the various parts of the drums should sound in relation to each other."

So, after his tour with Barnes, he formed his own trio in Frankfurt, where he was living. He persuaded his old English friends, clarinetist John Defferary and pianist Bob Barton, to join him. Barton "brought his Morris Mini Minor—one of those little 750 cc. cars—over with him, and the trio actually toured for the first six months of its existence in it! Barton, who was 6'4"—Defferary was maybe an inch shorter—would be driving this thing with both knees above the steering wheel, and I'd be sitting next to him with all manner of baggage stuffed around me. John was in the back with the trap case and clothes, and on the roof was the bass drum with saxophones tied on the side. We traveled all around Europe in this thing. I remember one trip from Vienna to Frankfurt—it was awful. People used to come out of the club after a concert just to watch us packing the car and driving off. It was almost more entertainment than the music," he says with a laugh.

"We traveled for ten years, from 1973 to 1983, ten years solid working around Europe, with tours of the United States and regular return trips to New Orleans—mostly in the one month we didn't have much work. At that time it was August. So, for the worst weather month of the year, I would be in New Orleans, sleeping very often in apartments without air conditioning . . . all a part of life's rich tapestry, no doubt.

"We'd get back here regularly, and I continued my interaction with the local music scene, taking lessons from Freddie Kohlman. Eventually, I hired Freddie to come over and guest with my trio. We alternated sets. We did that every Christmas for many years in Berlin, where we had moved to. He would come over at the beginning of December, stay until the middle of January, and stay in my apartment. Like so many New Orleans musicians, he was a master cook. So, he took over the kitchen, and I was allowed to wash dishes—that was it. I learned so much about drumming, and, of course, his personal history, and about tuning drums, repairing drums, everything—not to mention washing dishes. That may have lasted about seven years, I'm not sure, but it was a lot of time to spend with one drummer. I learned an enormous amount from him."

Richards returned to New Orleans in the early 1980s to reestablish residency, but he continued to do a great deal of traveling. "In the mid-eighties, when I was established here in New Orleans and co-leading the Camellia Jazz Band with Clive Wilson, a man from the Holiday Inn chain came to town looking for a maitre d' and a band to open a proposed New Orleans restaurant in a new hotel in Singapore. Through a few recommendations we got the job, and we decided to split the band responsibilities. Clive would look after the home front here, and I would take a number-two band over to Singapore."

That Singapore gig turned out to last more than a year, until June 1986. "We had created such an uproar, with this concept of New Orleans music with New Orleans cuisine, we'd do a little parade through the restaurant every night. The acoustics were perfect. Leroy [Jones, trumpeter and band member] even trained a couple of waiters to second-line with the band. It was a fun job. Towards the end of our stay, I started looking around for jobs elsewhere in Asia."

As it turned out, between 1985 and 1989, Richards's quartet played in every country in eastern Asia except Japan, appearing at a variety of hotels: the Philippines, South Korea, Hong Kong, Thailand, Indonesia, Malaysia, and Borneo, with a number of repeat bookings.

"It was such an incredible lifestyle. I had so much time. We worked six nights a week, with days free. I did a university course in photography while we were there. That was one of the highlights of my career, although being away from the mainstream of musical activity didn't do our careers much good, I suppose. That lasted until '89. I returned to New Orleans, and then I got into this routine of commuting between here and Europe—which is basically what I'm still doing. These days I tend to stay over in Europe for the summer. It's so expensive to get to and fro on a regular basis, so I try to organize it so that I spend the summer in Europe and the winter in New Orleans—which seems to be a perfect arrangement."

When in Europe, Richards regularly works with the Trevor Richards New Orleans Trio, which usually consists of piano, clarinet/saxophone, and drums. "I think it was the clarinet, the minimalism of reducing the melody, harmony, and rhythm just down to the three basic instruments that intrigued me [about this format]—like classic jazz chamber music. As soon as you get into piano, bass, and drums you get a different dynamic. The trumpet doesn't have the versatility or dynamics, normally, as a clarinet or saxophone."

The composition of his trios has varied over the years, but he has worked with some outstanding musicians during that time. He toured with pianist Art Hodes for ten years, starting in 1981, until Hodes had a stroke. Hodes then put him in touch with Ralph Sutton to continue the annual spring tours for another ten years until Sutton's death. For Trevor, it was an education working with those distinguished veterans for three weeks "non-stop" every year, and he has countless stories to tell about each of them. They also made several recordings together, usually

Trevor Richards performing with his trio at a club in Seligenstadt, Germany, 2006. *Photograph courtesy Trevor Richards.*

under the name of "The International Trio." The tours continue to this day, with veteran Parisian pianist Christian Azzi and talented young German pianist Bernd Lhotzky among Sutton's successors. Reedmen have included John Defferary, Charlie Gabriel, Reimer von Essen, Matthias Seuffert, Frank Roberscheuten, and Evan Christopher, to name just a few.

Trevor Richards is a keen student of jazz history, and a project with which he has been involved for more than a decade—he calls it "The Legends of the Swing Era"—stems in large part from that interest. The project had its roots in the late 1980s when he was still working with Art Hodes. The trio was hired by a German advertising tycoon, Heinz Schmied, who also had an interest in jazz, to play for an office party at his ad agency near Frankfurt. One thing led to another, to the extent that Schmied wanted to make a production in the United States featuring older (preferably black) jazz musicians.

"By this time [ca. 1997] it was hardly possible to put together a band of older musicians in New Orleans for the simple reason that most of them had passed. Percy and Willie Humphrey had died. So, I was looking for a concept that would fulfill [Schmied's] expectations and still make it of musical interest and value. I came up with the idea of documenting the surviving active veterans of the Swing Era, which would change the focus from New Orleans to New York but obviously incorporate musicians from all over the United States. This seemed to work out fine because there were enough musicians still active.

"The first band included [trumpeter] Doc Cheatham and [saxophonist] Benny Waters, whom I'd worked a lot with in Europe on tours in the '70s. By this time, when we recorded [Waters] in New Orleans, he was 95 and, if you listen to the recordings, he would do credit to a musician a third of his age. I used Dan Barrett as musical director and, of course, trombonist. And [bassist] Truck Parham, who I had met in the '60s in Chicago, played with all the top bands, Jimmie Lunceford, Earl Hines, and so on. And Red Richards on piano. Then we added Don Vappie because I felt a guitar was an important feature in the rhythm section for music of this kind. The production was in New Orleans. We played a concert at the Palm Court Café and spent two and one-half days in the studio. We needed that long because we wanted to be sure we had enough material.

"To give it more of a feeling of documentation I wanted to incorporate oral history. So, on the second half of the third day we got the musicians around a microphone at the table. I put out a theme in the form of a question, and mostly it then just took off—largely due to the amazing contribution from Red Richards. This was just the older musicians who were doing this: Benny, Truck, Doc, and Red. It was incredible, the stories that came out. We covered a variety of topics, like remembering Louie [Armstrong], Bechet, Billie Holiday. I have no idea how many hundreds or thousands of hours I spent transcribing all the [material], then ordering it, eventually ending up with almost an hour of solid gold in terms of oral history and a revealing insight into the life of a jazz musician in those days.

"Then I repeated the exercise a couple of years later with [pianist] Jay McShann, also in New Orleans—the same process of a live concert at the Palm Court and then the recording session. That was with Laurel Watson as vocalist, McShann and [violinist] Claude Williams from Kansas City, [saxophonist] Franz Jackson from Chicago, and Truck Parham again. We had actually hired Bob Haggart on bass, but when I talked to him the last time—that was after he had been operated on for cancer—he said that the doctor had advised him not to come back playing yet. So, he had to back out and died shortly thereafter.

"The session was good, and the interviews worked out fine although I didn't get the same amount of group discussion as I did in the first one. From that session there is a special edition CD with a booklet including photographs by Herman Leonard [then living in New Orleans], who was hired to document the session. Again, Heinz Schmied was the executive producer. I also interviewed Herman on his life in connection with jazz, which will come out on the CD and in a monograph on his philosophy of photography in the booklet. [Leonard died on August 14, 2010.]

"Then there's a third volume, *Legends of the Swing Era, Volume 3*, that we produced in New York in January 2000. Anita O'Day was the vocalist and, once again, Dan Barrett was musical director. And Tom Baker, who was also on the second session. We had hoped to hire Sweets Edison for that session, but, again, ill health and subsequent death thwarted us. That happened on a number of occasions, unfortunately. Norris Turney had also been hired for that session. We hired Bubba Brooks on tenor. He's a musician who isn't—I should now say, wasn't—that well known, but a wonderful tenor player. We also had Jack Lesberg on bass, Lawrence Lucie on guitar. Tom Baker died in October 2001, and the interview in the second session was especially good." [At the time of this interview, March 2003, the production was short of completion, and it remains so in 2010.]

"All three 'Legends' productions are in the same format. It's an ongoing project. I can't imagine it being completed anytime soon, and, of course, time is running out. It's getting slim pickings, as [jazz historian] Dan Morgenstern told me recently. I was picking his brains for some more ideas and came up with a whole list of people—significantly, the widows of many of the people concerned. So, these productions have formed a significant part of my recorded work in the last ten years."

Oral history has been an important part of Trevor Richards's musical career. "I've always had the interest," he says. "The first interview I did was when I went up to Chicago in the '60s. I hitchhiked from New Orleans to Chicago in the fall of '67. I'd been in communication with Johnny Dodds's son, John Dodds Jr. At that time, as far as I know, he was not in communication with the jazz world. He was still a businessman. He was a retired major from the U.S. Air Force and had started a new career in insurance. I had made contact with him, and he was expecting a visit. The first thing I did when I got into town, which was early in the morning, I went to his office. We talked and got to know each other.

"John Dodds said that he should take me over to visit [trumpeter] Natty Dominique, who knew his uncle—Baby Dodds, who was one of my mentors—since he knew [Baby] as well as anyone. He said he would take his office Dictaphone along to record the interview. So, we went over and met Natty, who was very lucid. We talked the whole afternoon. Unfortunately, Dodds had forgotten to check the batteries in his machine before we went over there and at some point in the interview—it was an interview, but he was just talking and running over his life, particularly talking about Baby and how musical he was—the playback gets faster and faster. In other words, the recording was getting slower and slower. I didn't realize until afterwards. So, that was my first interview and I gave a copy to Tulane [the Hogan Jazz Archive]."

After a hiatus due in large part to a busy work schedule, Richards put his interviewing on hold for a few years. "It wasn't until Zutty [Singleton] died in 1975 that I decided to get started again," he recalls. "I spent a lot of time with his widow Marge, working on interviews with her. She was the sister of Charlie Creath, the St. Louis bandleader, and a piano player herself. In fact, she took lessons from Jelly Roll Morton in 1916, when he was on his way out to California. She gave me all of Zutty's—or their—archival material, in the form of photo albums, newspaper cuttings, autographed photographs, and tapes of interviews and things. I set about getting the material together for a book. I also wanted to incorporate interviews with his contemporaries who had worked with him.

"I started out by interviewing Marge herself because she had total recall and was able to tell me everything she had heard from Zutty and any of his friends. I taped all that, and I went around New York interviewing all the people who, to my knowledge, had dealings with Zutty: Al Hall, the bass player; Milt Gabler, Herman Autrey, Dick Wellstood, Roy Eldridge. I did this for a couple of years as time and finances allowed, which was limited in those days because I was on tour almost the whole time with my trio. After that it was sporadic.

"I've been starting again recently, again under the auspices of Heinz Schmied in Germany, who said he would like to produce another collection of CDs. It won't be just two this time, the way it's going. The concept was not quite anchored. He just knew he wanted to get some oral histories together. I thought up this idea of looking at not just the Swing Era but the years when jazz could be reckoned with as a popular music with relevance. That takes us from the '20s, I suppose, through the '50s. [I want to look] at that musical activity from all the different creative viewpoints of not only the musicians, singers, and dancers, but the writers—journalists, promoters, and authors—the photographers, the record producers, the graphic artists, the agents, the club owners. Anyone that is involved in this whole process of creating, presenting, and describing the music that we think of as jazz. In edited form, I think that would present a good work of reference for that era and possibly eventually be adaptable to a book format. At any rate, it is certainly something to keep me busy!"

Despite this ambitious agenda, Richards continues his travels, like a nomadic pastoralist, from his winter home base in New Orleans to his summer base in Europe, all the while playing, writing, interviewing, and reflecting on the music he loves.

"As opposed to my arrangements in the '70s, when I spent the winters in Europe and the worst summer month in New Orleans," he smiles, "It's about time I got it right. Practice makes perfect."

As a student of percussion, Trevor Richards has spent a lifetime observing, working with, and studying with drummers. He has collected a veritable museum of instruments played by legendary percussionists, and during the course of our conversations, he had interesting things to say about many of his idols.

ON ZUTTY SINGLETON

As both student and friend of Singleton, Richards inherited Singleton's drum set. "I was working in Berlin when I heard he had died," he explains. "It wasn't too long before I managed to get over to New York. It was just prior to a tour of the States with my trio, in the same year, 1975. Marge had told me that Zutty wanted me to have the drums. I got there early enough to go round and spend some time at the apartment and also to pick up the drums, and I played the drums on that tour. I remember the first gig was in or just outside Washington, D.C., and we went from there down the East Coast to New Orleans, across to Texas, and then over to California. I certainly wouldn't want to go on a tour like that with a whole drum set again.

"In fact, the next time I went on tour to the States I took my folding bass drum, which was a curiosity from the '30s. Now I keep one set of drums in Europe, at least, and a lot of drums over here, so I don't normally have to ever fly with drums. So, I leave Zutty's in Europe.

"Over the years, I've sort of developed a drum museum almost. I got Zutty's drums. I got Alex Bigard's drums, Chauncey Morehouse's, Freddie Kohlman's, Ray Bauduc's.

"Zutty would vary [his playing] a lot," he continues. "He would often start a number very light. I think that was the distinctive element of Zutty's playing, at least at that time—the breadth of dynamics. He could play so quietly that, even in a small club like [Jimmy Ryan's], you could barely hear him. Then up to a volume that would just about drown everybody out! But only for a short time and was acceptable as a dynamic effect. Paul Barnes once said to me, 'On the last chorus you can't play loud enough!' So he would change from solo to solo, to accompany the soloist in a way he felt was supporting him and giving a variety in feel for the listener. I used to sit there listening and by spending so much time concentrating on it, it gave me a full impression of the variety of his musical vocabulary. I notice that a lot of drummers stick very exactly to a format, a repetitive format. By listening to him so much I noticed that that was not the case with him."

ON ALEX BIGARD

"I took lessons from Alex Bigard in his kitchen. He was not a particularly efficient teacher. He didn't even have a pair of drumsticks. He had one broken drumstick and a ruler, a 12-inch ruler! He used to demonstrate on the kitchen table what he was trying to explain. It was funny. Mike Casimir told me a story which is a little anecdote that gives a little insight on Alex Bigard. He bought an awful new modern Japanese drum set, you know, red glitter or red pearl 20-inch bass drum. He didn't want to use his 28-inch Ludwig & Ludwig any longer, a beautiful old drum from the '20s. So, he got this brand-new Japanese red drum set that really didn't sound very good at all. When Casimir came over in the '60s he wanted to acquire Alex's slapstick as a memento. So, he asked Alex if he could write something on the slapstick for him, sort of like a little dedication. So, Alex got this marker and wrote, 'Paid in full. Alex Bigard' [*uproarious laughter*].

"He was a great drummer. I love his recordings from the early fifties, a very dynamic drummer, but he was losing his hearing by the mid-to-late sixties. When Sammy Penn died and Kid Thomas was looking for a replacement drummer, Alex Bigard was the first one that came to mind. They tried him out at Preservation Hall, but his hearing was so bad by that time that it was not practical. I remember hearing him in '68 at Dixieland Hall on Bourbon Street, where his hearing was already bad and maybe he hadn't switched his hearing aid on. It was with Alvin [Alcorn], and I think it was 'High Society' and he came in one beat late, and he played the whole tune just that much behind everyone else. He played it correctly but finished exactly the same amount of time behind the others."

ON LOUIS BARBARIN

"And that's the reason that Louis Barbarin gave up playing. It just happened once or twice that he misheard the introduction to the tune, and he just made the decision that he was not going to allow himself to be represented in any way that made him appear to be a lesser musician than he was. So, he retired. He was an immaculate musician, maybe the best drummer I heard in the city. He had taste and technique and all-around ability. From a technical point of view, he was far superior to Paul [Barbarin]. But what does it mean, having limitless technique? It doesn't mean that someone is a better musician. It means that they are a better technician. I often think in a lot of modern music that technique has taken on a role that is somewhat exaggerated. Content is often neglected. It's the anatomization of the music, a music that had grown naturally."

ON COZY COLE

Trevor Richards toured Europe with many fine musicians, not the least of whom was drummer Cozy Cole. "Cozy was a wonderful guy," he recalls. "I had met him earlier in Chicago when we were touring in the States and he was working with Jonah Jones and his quartet. This would have been in the mid-seventies. I got to be good friends with him and Evelyn, his wife. We met up whenever possible, and then we did these trips together.

"The last time I saw Cozy he said, 'When this trip is over, why don't you come up to my place in Columbus [Ohio] and stay for a while and we'll work out together every day.' Which amounted to endless lessons offered by one of the greatest drummers. The problem was we were booked for festivals in Europe directly following our U.S. tour, so there was no way we could change our plans. So, I said that we'd do it next time I come back to the States. He died some months after that [January 1981], and I never had a chance to see him again. That was really sad.

"We used to sit down on stage every day before the concert, and he'd go through little routines and show me things. One of his favorite exercises was improvising the last two bars of a tune, the way to close up a number. He'd just sit there and show me endless variations of the last two bars of a tune. It was an interesting exercise. That lasted the whole tour, going through this routine. I just wish I had managed to make it to Columbus, Ohio."

ON SIDNEY CATLETT

"There is a rhythmical barrier between traditional jazz and swing and bebop. I am not able—or not willing—to cross that barrier. Very few drummers have been able to cross that line. The drummer that immediately comes to mind, of course, is Sidney Catlett. The music he plays with Dizzy and Charlie Parker isn't that modern. When you listen to it now, he was able to change from a swing setting to bebop. He just wasn't putting in those bass drum accentuations that Max Roach was doing, and he wasn't fully adapting to the bebop vocabulary. What happened was the drummers, as exemplified by Elvin Jones, completely liberated themselves from the function of drums—which is laying down a rhythmic foundation of some kind. It has to be a rarefied form of art music to be able to take that basic function away from the instrument. Music and dance belong together.

"I find most of [Catlett's] playing the most tasteful you can imagine. There are some live recordings with the [Armstrong] Allstars where he was a little overenthusiastic, but I love his playing. He was just a wonderful musician. I've got nothing but admiration for his playing. He was the one drummer that all the older musicians like Benny Carter, for instance, cited as their all-time favorite. The great drummers of that era played melodically.

"In essence, music is either melodic or it isn't. So, in my most recent recording [*Reeds Write: Compositions by Clarinetists and Saxophonists of the Melodic Era, Volume 1,* NOJP CD 7] I have opted for the concept of a 'melodic era.' That is, jazz from the beginnings up to the '50s with the introduction of modal improvisation. For that CD production, I viewed this era—maybe a half century—from the perspective of compositions by reed players because I usually play with reed players. From [Alphonse] Picou in the 1870s to [John] Coltrane in the 1950s, which still can be interpreted melodically, you've got a history of jazz."

ON CHAUNCEY MOREHOUSE

"I was staying with Bob Wilber in New York—he used to have an apartment in the Village—and he pointed out that Chauncey's widow was still in New Jersey and was planning to move down to Florida and had all these drums in the house and didn't really want them. He said, 'If you're looking for anything, I know there's a lot of cymbals.' So, I went down and looked. There was a beautiful old—it was not a matching—drum set. An old Leedy bass drum, and a Ludwig snare drum that was still made in the era when Ludwig drums were quality, pre-1960s. The only thing I didn't take was this enormous collection of tuned tom-toms that he had. I didn't have room for them. I don't know what happened to them. There are photographs of them—it was like a couple of octaves. There may have been a couple dozen of them. Yes, and a box full of cymbals—cymbals I have never used. Some of them are good, very old, heavy cymbals that have a certain use. I used one on the bass drum for marching band. He had a lot of sound effects because he worked in the radio studio orchestra for many years, NBC, I think. So, he had all imaginable sound effects. You know, Christmas jingle bells, bird calls, everything. It was incredible."

The interviews on which this account is based were conducted mostly in 2003, before Hurricanes Katrina and Rita hit the New Orleans area in late August and early September 2005. Richards's home is in the Broadmoor neighborhood of mid-city New Orleans. He was in Europe at the time of Katrina and the subsequent flooding. He spoke about his reactions to the catastrophe in February 2006.

"That happened, incidentally, on my 60th birthday," he says. "I was out celebrating my birthday when someone called and said maybe I should turn on the television. I was in Germany. I had read the newspaper on Saturday, the 27th, and there was absolutely no mention of a dangerous storm in the Gulf, so I knew nothing until mid-morning on Monday, central European time. By that time, it was just off the coast."

That was not the first time that Richards's home had been ravaged by flooding. "Exactly ten years prior to that I had had over a foot of water in the house, which meant that 800 LPs and a large number of books got under water. But since then they had built a new pump system in Broadmoor, and they'd promised that that would never happen again—which might well have been the case under other circumstances.

"So, this time I had five feet in the house," he goes on. "I'm not saying that I was anticipating this flood, but I had been trying to prioritize my collection and put them on CD. I had not got far enough obviously. I got the rarest 78s and LPs on CD, but those that I had not gotten to were standing propped up against chair legs and tables and the wall in piles ready to be recorded. Unfortunately, after the flood, they had formed sort of an inch-thick carpet across the house.

"The instruments were under water. A lot of the wooden instruments, the plywood of the shells of the drums, had broken open. The metal drums, of course, had rusted considerably. There is a certain kind of metal drum that Leedy and Ludwig brought out in the '20s—Ludwig called it Black Beauty—with a special patinated surface. A brass shell, hand engraved, with a gun-metal, sort of black, finish on it. That finish was eaten off by the floodwater. . . . I am not sure to what extent they will be able to be brought back to their original condition, probably not. Some drums will be playable, some not. And cymbals are an equal problem. They've taken on all the colors of the rainbow; some have just gone green from oxidation. With dozens of them, it's an enormous job to try to clean these things off. I'm just going to have to, again, prioritize and work out what I'm going to do with it all.

"I'm thinking, there's only so many years that one has and whether you want to spend them all renovating instruments and washing records and prying pages of dried books apart. But I'm thinking that historical instruments that are no longer playable—ones that belonged to people like Chauncey Morehouse, Ray Bauduc, Freddie Kohlman, etc., etc.—then the best thing I could do is what I've always said: good instruments are really for playing and not putting in glass cases. So, if they are no longer playable, then their place would be in a museum, and that's what I'm thinking of doing."

When asked about the future of his New Orleans residence and his own future, he said, "To be honest, I have to say that I'm thinking of this flood as being the end, possibly, of a chapter in my life or career. I'm really commuting [between here and Germany], and it's very difficult to rebuild a house when you're not there all the time. You need to be there to supervise, particularly in the present circumstances, with the scarcity of skilled labor. For me as a musician with a lot of professional obligations in Europe, it's going to be more than I can handle. So, I'll probably sell the house and have the remains of my archive, or whatever you want to call them—the books, the records, the instruments, etc.—shipped to Europe.

"I do think the city will be going through a lot of permanent changes as the reconstruction continues. I'll continue moving to and fro and obviously will never break my contact with the city because I've been associated with New Orleans for two-thirds of my life, apart from my philosophical or musical connections beforehand. I guess it's really trying to simplify my life rather than moving from one place to the other all the time.

"As regards to the changes I see, apart from the obvious political polemic that is unavoidable in the aftermath of the flood, the biggest risk that the city as a base for active music in the U.S.—in the world really—is that it was the only city with a deep-seated tradition in this music. Parallel to that there was, of course, the commercial aspect where you had musicians, some local and some emigrated from elsewhere, who were playing the music as entertainment for the tourist industry. But what is at risk at the moment, with the mass evacuation and lack of attempts to repatriate the evacuees, is that you're going to lose that section of the community that really lived this music—not just the jazz that I play, but all other forms of jazz and all other forms of popular music that have evolved from it and have become a part of this city's musical tradition. If you take away that whole lowest strata, you end up with only the superficial levels that are providing the tourist industry with their entertainment. It then becomes essentially the same as any other large convention city in the United States, or anywhere—even in Europe. It does not have that depth anymore that this city has always had since it started.

"There's some hope and talk, and there are some admirable institutions being formed to help bring musicians back to the city. And I've been doing what I can in Europe to instigate benefit performances, anything that will generate funds for these institutions that are trying to help. I think that's the important thing. It's not will there be music on Bourbon Street; the question has to go a lot deeper than that. It's the lower, more important levels that determine whether the city remains what it's always been."

Richards is, at the moment, involved in producing a CD, the proceeds of which will go to the New Orleans Musicians' Clinic, which has been doing such wonderful work post-Katrina. The recording is the product of a live concert held in Hamburg, Germany, on January 12, 2006. It's called *The Trevor Richards British New Orleans All Stars—Live.* Joining him for the occasion were trumpeter Colin Dawson; reedman John Crocker; John Service, trombone and vocal; Simon Holliday, piano and vocal; and Bob Culverhouse, bass and vocal.

AFTERWORD

TRINIDADIAN HISTORIAN OF CALYPSO MUSIC RUDOLPH Ottley, when asked why his books focused only on contemporary calypso musicians, asserted firmly, "Most of them, those calypsonian [*sic*] from the old times, they have passed away, and I don't give belief to much that I read in the papers when the reporters write about them. It's the *living interview* [my italics] that's interesting to me" (Samuel Charters, *A Language of Song: Journeys in the Musical World of the African Diaspora* [2009], 180). That is pretty much the way I see it as well. I believe that the lives of important musicians need to be recorded and documented while they are still alive and in possession of their faculties, and that is what this collection of interviews is all about. The aim was to let the interviewees tell their story in their own words, with a minimum of interference from the interviewer.

I hope that it has become clear to the reader from this relatively small sample that jazz musicians are individuals, with their own personalities musically and otherwise. While all have their idols, models, and/or mentors, each of them strives to achieve his own personal instrumental voice, his own sound. Their intention normally is not to sound like anyone else (though oftentimes they can do so if the situation calls for it). They want to sound only like *themselves*. As Tom Fischer, who is particularly adept at reproducing the stylistic characteristics of many earlier clarinet players, put it, "I like to think that I play Tom Fischer style. . ."

Yet, despite their genuine desire for unique individual expression, jazz musicians are always members of a musical *team*—whether a duo, trio, or much larger combination. The success of that team depends on the ability of each member to cooperate with—and, perhaps most important, listen to—his fellow team members as they are playing. The importance of group collaboration in jazz cannot, I believe, be overstressed. In many ways, this spirit reminds me of what goes on with top athletic teams. Maybe that's why, as I have often observed, so many jazz musicians also seem to be avid followers of professional sports teams. Teamwork is clearly fundamental to success in both activities.

As we draw to a conclusion, a word or two about the many recordings made by those interviewed may be in order. It was never my intention, within the relatively narrow scope of this book, to provide complete or definitive discographies for each of the interviewees. That would result in another book in and of itself. I have tried, however, to make reference to the recordings—especially the most recent ones—by each musician whenever possible. There are, of course, several comprehensive discographies for the reader to consult for all the details, the most complete and up-to-date of which is *The Jazz Discography,* by Tom Lord, now in 26 volumes. It is also available on CD-ROM. The Lord Web site is www .lordisco.com.

For identifying recordings of New Orleans jazz bands or musicians, I would heartily recommend the Louisiana Music Factory at 210 Decatur Street in the French Quarter. Owner Barry Smith and his staff can locate whatever is available by the musicians mentioned in this book, and much more. The LMF can be accessed on the Web at www.louisianamusicfactory.com.

Mention must also be made of the William Ransom Hogan Archive of New Orleans Jazz at Tulane University. It is an unparalleled treasurehouse of all manner of information about New Orleans jazz. Dr. Bruce Raeburn, the curator, and his staff are happy to answer questions about individual musicians or their recordings—or one can do one's own hunting in their rich resource base. The archive, which is a part of Howard-Tilton Memorial Library, can also be found on the Web via Tulane's Web site: www.tulane.edu.

Another important local resource for early jazz is the Historic New Orleans Collection, 533 Royal Street, and the associated Williams Research Center, 410 Chartres Street, in the French Quarter. Of particular interest for information about traditional New Orleans jazz is its William Russell Jazz Collection, which was acquired by the HNOC after the death (in 1992) of the great New Orleans author, composer, and musician. Russell was one of the pioneers in researching and recording the early practitioners of New Orleans jazz. For more about the holdings of the HNOC, see their Web site, www.hnoc.org.

Still another major assemblage of fundamental importance to early New Orleans jazz is the New Orleans Jazz Club Collection, housed in the Louisiana State Museum (Old U.S. Mint) at 400 Esplanade Avenue on the northern margin of the French Quarter. Oftentimes referred to simply as "the Jazz Museum," the building suffered significant damage from Hurricane Katrina. The exhibition has been closed to the public since that time as repairs have been ongoing. The LSM was recently joined by the New Orleans Jazz National Historical Park in arriving at, as one museum official put it, "a complete re-visioning of the Mint as a musical destination." The next phase of the joint project is the design and planning of an entirely new exhibition, and beyond that will come major improvements to the grounds of the Mint to make it "more festival or performance friendly." For more about this excellent resource and its history, visit the Web at www.lsm.crt.state.la.us/collections/jazz.

The New Orleans Jazz National Historical Park, under the aegis of the National Park Service, was established by the U.S. Congress in 1994. Its stated mission includes the preservation "of resources and information that are associated with the origins and early development of jazz in New Orleans" as well as interpreting "the origins, history and progression of jazz." After considerable local deliberation, the decision was made to locate it in what is now called Louis Armstrong Park on Rampart Street along the western periphery of the French Quarter. Work on preparing the site was interrupted and suspended by damage wrought by Katrina. In the meantime, a temporary visitors' center (including a performance venue) has been constructed at 916 North Peters Street in the French Quarter. For more about the Jazz Park, see www.nps.gov/jazz.

Finally, my most sincere apologies go out to those many fine New Orleans musicians who deserved to be included in this collection but were not because of space limitations. Several of them will be recognizable to the reader from reference to them by other musicians in these interviews. Perhaps there will be an opportunity to share some of their stories on a future occasion.

INDEX